CLEP-14   COLLEGE-LEVEL EXAMINATION
PROGRAM SERIES

This is your
PASSBOOK for...

Introductory/ General Psychology

Test Preparation Study Guide
Questions & Answers

COPYRIGHT NOTICE

This book is SOLELY intended for, is sold ONLY to, and its use is RESTRICTED to individual, bona fide applicants or candidates who qualify by virtue of having seriously filed applications for appropriate license, certificate, professional and/or promotional advancement, higher school matriculation, scholarship, or other legitimate requirements of education and/or governmental authorities.

This book is NOT intended for use, class instruction, tutoring, training, duplication, copying, reprinting, excerption, or adaptation, etc., by:

1) Other publishers
2) Proprietors and/or Instructors of "Coaching" and/or Preparatory Courses
3) Personnel and/or Training Divisions of commercial, industrial, and governmental organizations
4) Schools, colleges, or universities and/or their departments and staffs, including teachers and other personnel
5) Testing Agencies or Bureaus
6) Study groups which seek by the purchase of a single volume to copy and/or duplicate and/or adapt this material for use by the group as a whole without having purchased individual volumes for each of the members of the group
7) Et al.

Such persons would be in violation of appropriate Federal and State statutes.

PROVISION OF LICENSING AGREEMENTS – Recognized educational, commercial, industrial, and governmental institutions and organizations, and others legitimately engaged in educational pursuits, including training, testing, and measurement activities, may address request for a licensing agreement to the copyright owners, who will determine whether, and under what conditions, including fees and charges, the materials in this book may be used them. In other words, a licensing facility exists for the legitimate use of the material in this book on other than an individual basis. However, it is asseverated and affirmed here that the material in this book CANNOT be used without the receipt of the express permission of such a licensing agreement from the Publishers. Inquiries re licensing should be addressed to the company, attention rights and permissions department.

All rights reserved, including the right of reproduction in whole or in part, in any form or by any means, electronic or mechanical, including photocopying, recording, or by any information storage and retrieval system, without permission in writing from the Publisher.

Copyright © 2025 by
National Learning Corporation

212 Michael Drive, Syosset, NY 11791
(516) 921-8888 • www.passbooks.com
E-mail: info@passbooks.com

PASSBOOK® SERIES

THE *PASSBOOK® SERIES* has been created to prepare applicants and candidates for the ultimate academic battlefield – the examination room.

At some time in our lives, each and every one of us may be required to take an examination – for validation, matriculation, admission, qualification, registration, certification, or licensure.

Based on the assumption that every applicant or candidate has met the basic formal educational standards, has taken the required number of courses, and read the necessary texts, the *PASSBOOK® SERIES* furnishes the one special preparation which may assure passing with confidence, instead of failing with insecurity. Examination questions – together with answers – are furnished as the basic vehicle for study so that the mysteries of the examination and its compounding difficulties may be eliminated or diminished by a sure method.

This book is meant to help you pass your examination provided that you qualify and are serious in your objective.

The entire field is reviewed through the huge store of content information which is succinctly presented through a provocative and challenging approach – the question-and-answer method.

A climate of success is established by furnishing the correct answers at the end of each test.

You soon learn to recognize types of questions, forms of questions, and patterns of questioning. You may even begin to anticipate expected outcomes.

You perceive that many questions are repeated or adapted so that you can gain acute insights, which may enable you to score many sure points.

You learn how to confront new questions, or types of questions, and to attack them confidently and work out the correct answers.

You note objectives and emphases, and recognize pitfalls and dangers, so that you may make positive educational adjustments.

Moreover, you are kept fully informed in relation to new concepts, methods, practices, and directions in the field.

You discover that you are actually taking the examination all the time: you are preparing for the examination by "taking" an examination, not by reading extraneous and/or supererogatory textbooks.

In short, this PASSBOOK®, used directedly, should be an important factor in helping you to pass your test.

NONTRADITIONAL EDUCATION

Students returning to school as adults bring more varied experience to their studies than do the teenagers who begin college shortly after graduating from high school. As a result, there are numerous programs for students with nontraditional learning curves. Hundreds of colleges and universities grant degrees to people who cannot attend classes at a regular campus or have already learned what the college is supposed to teach.

You can earn nontraditional education credits in many ways:
- Passing standardized exams
- Demonstrating knowledge gained through experience
- Completing campus-based coursework, and
- Taking courses off campus

Some methods of assessing learning for credit are objective, such as standardized tests. Others are more subjective, such as a review of life experiences.

With some help from four hypothetical characters – Alice, Vin, Lynette, and Jorge – this article describes nontraditional ways of earning educational credit. It begins by describing programs in which you can earn a high school diploma without spending 4 years in a classroom. The college picture is more complicated, so it is presented in two parts: one on gaining credit for what you know through course work or experience, and a second on college degree programs. The final section lists resources for locating more information.

Earning High School Credit

People who were prevented from finishing high school as teenagers have several options if they want to do so as adults. Some major cities have back-to-school programs that allow adults to attend high school classes with current students. But the more practical alternatives for most adults are to take the General Educational Development (GED) tests or to earn a high school diploma by demonstrating their skills or taking correspondence classes.

Of course, these options do not match the experience of staying in high school and graduating with one's friends. But they are viable alternatives for adult learners committed to meeting and, often, continuing their educational goals.

GED Program

Alice quit high school her sophomore year and took a job to help support herself, her younger brother, and their newly widowed mother. Now an adult, she wants to earn her high school diploma – and then go on to college. Because her job as head cook and her family responsibilities keep her busy during the day, she plans to get a high school equivalency diploma. She will study for, and take, the GED tests. Every year, about half a million adults earn their high school credentials this way. A GED diploma is accepted in lieu of a high school one by more than 90 percent of employers, colleges, and universities, so it is a good choice for someone like Alice.

The GED testing program is sponsored by the American Council on Education and State and local education departments. It consists of examinations in five subject areas: Writing, science, mathematics, social studies, and literature and the arts. The tests also measure skills such as analytical ability, problem solving, reading comprehension, and ability to understand and apply information. Most of the questions are multiple choice; the writing test includes an essay section on a topic of general interest.

Eligibility rules for taking the exams vary, but some states require that you must be at least 18. Tests are given in English, Spanish, and French. In addition to standard print, versions in large print, Braille, and audiocassette are also available. Total time allotted for the tests is 7 1/2 hours.

The GED tests are not easy. About one-fourth of those who complete the exams every year do not pass. Passing scores are established by administering the tests to a sample of graduating high school seniors. The minimum standard score is set so that about one-third of graduating seniors would not pass the tests if they took them.

Because of the difficulty of the tests, people need to prepare themselves to take them. Often, they start by taking the Official GED Practice Tests, usually available through a local adult education center. Centers are listed in your phone book's blue pages under "Adult Education," "Continuing Education," or "GED." Adult education centers also have information about GED preparation classes and self-study materials. Classes are generally arranged to accommodate adults' work schedules. National Learning Corporation publishes several study guides that aim to thoroughly prepare test-takers for the GED.

School districts, colleges, adult education centers, and community organizations have information about GED testing schedules and practice tests. For more information, contact them, your nearest GED testing center, or:

GED Testing Service
One Dupont Circle, NW, Suite 250
Washington, DC 20036-1163
1(800) 62-MY GED (626-9433)
(202) 939-9490

Skills Demonstration

Adults who have acquired high school level skills through experience might be eligible for the National External Diploma Program. This alternative to the GED does not involve any direct instruction. Instead, adults seeking a high school diploma must demonstrate mastery of 65 competencies in 8 general areas: Communication; computation; occupational preparedness; and self, social, consumer, scientific, and technological awareness.

Mastery is shown through the completion of the tasks. For example, a participant could prove competency in computation by measuring a room for carpeting, figuring out the amount of carpet needed, and computing the cost.

Before being accepted for the program, adults undergo an evaluation. Tests taken at one of the program's offices measure reading, writing, and mathematics abilities. A take-home segment includes a self-assessment of current skills, an individual skill evaluation, and an occupational interest and aptitude test.

Adults accepted for the program have weekly meetings with an assessor. At the meeting, the assessor reviews the participant's work from the previous week. If the task has not been completed properly, the assessor explains the mistake. Participants continue to correct their errors until they master each competency. A high school diploma is awarded upon proven mastery of all 65 competencies.

Fourteen States and the District of Columbia now offer the External Diploma Program. For more information, contact:

External Diploma Program
One Dupont Circle, NW, Suite 250
Washington, DC 20036-1193
(202) 939-9475

Correspondence and Distance Study

Vin dropped out of high school during his junior year because his family's frequent moves made it difficult for him to continue his studies. He promised himself at the time he dropped out that he would someday finish the courses needed for his diploma. For people like Vin, who prefer to earn a traditional diploma in a nontraditional way, there are about a dozen accredited courses of study for earning a high school diploma by correspondence, or distance study. The programs are either privately run, affiliated with a university, or administered by a State education department.

Distance study diploma programs have no residency requirements, allowing students to continue their studies from almost any location. Depending on the course of study, students need not be enrolled full time and usually have more flexible schedules for finishing their work. Selection of courses ranges from vo-tech to college prep, and some programs place different emphasis on the types of diplomas offered. University affiliated schools, for example, allow qualified students to take college courses along with their high school ones. Students can then apply the college credits toward a degree at that university or transfer them to another institution.

Taking courses by distance study is often more challenging and time consuming than attending classes, especially for adults who have other obligations. Success depends on each student's motivation. Students usually do reading assignments on their own. Written exercises, which they complete and send to an instructor for grading, supplement their reading material.

A list of some accredited high schools that offer diplomas by distance study is available free from the Distance Education and Training Council, formerly known as the National Home Study Council. Request the "DETC Directory of Accredited Institutions" from:

The Distance Education and Training Council
1601 18th Street, NW.
Washington, DC 20009-2529
(202) 234-5100

Some publications profiling nontraditional college programs include addresses and descriptions of several high school correspondence ones. See the Resources section at the end of this article for more information.

Getting College Credit For What You Know

Adults can receive college credit for prior coursework, by passing examinations, and documenting experiential learning. With help from a college advisor, nontraditional students should assess their skills, establish their educational goals, and determine the number of college credits they might be eligible for.

Even before you meet with a college advisor, you should collect all your school and training records. Then, make a list of all knowledge and abilities acquired through experience, no matter how irrelevant they seem to your chosen field. Next, determine your educational goals: What specific field do you wish to study? What kind of a degree do you want? Finally, determine how your past work fits into the field of study. Later on, you will evaluate educational programs to find one that's right for you.

People who have complex educational or experiential learning histories might want to have their learning evaluated by the Regents Credit Bank. The Credit Bank, operated by Regents College of the University of the State of New York, allows people to consolidate credits earned through college, experience, or other methods. Special assessments are available for Regents College enrollees whose knowledge in a specific field cannot be adequately evaluated by standardized exams. For more information, contact the Regents Credit Bank at:

Regents College
7 Columbia Circle
Albany, NY 12203-5159
(518) 464-8500

Credit For Prior College Coursework

When Lynette was in college during the 1970s, she attended several different schools and took a variety of courses. She did well in some classes and poorly in others. Now that she is a successful business owner and has more focus, Lynette thinks she should forget about her previous coursework and start from scratch. Instead, she should start from where she is.

Lynette should have all her transcripts sent to the colleges or universities of her choice and let an admissions officer determine which classes are applicable toward a degree. A few credits here and there may not seem like much, but they add up. Even if the subjects do not seem relevant to any major, they might be counted as elective credits toward a degree. And comparing the cost of transcripts with the cost of college courses, it makes sense to spend a few dollars per transcript for a chance to save hundreds, and perhaps thousands, of dollars in books and tuition.

Rules for transferring credits apply to all prior coursework at accredited colleges and universities, whether done on campus or off. Courses completed off campus, often called extended learning, include those available to students through independent study and correspondence. Many schools have extended learning programs; Brigham Young University, for example, offers more than 300 courses through its Department of Independent Study. One type of extended learning is distance learning, a form of correspondence study by technological means such as television, video and audio, CD-ROM, electronic mail, and computer tutorials. See the Resources section at the end of this article for more information about publications available from the National University Continuing Education Association.

Any previously earned college credits should be considered for transfer, no matter what the subject or the grade received. Many schools do not accept the transfer of courses graded below a C or ones taken more than a designated number of years ago. Some colleges and universities also have limits on the number of credits that can be transferred and applied toward a degree. But not all do. For example, Thomas Edison State College, New Jersey's State college for adults, accepts the transfer of all 120 hours of credit required for a baccalaureate degree – provided all the credits are transferred from regionally accredited schools, no more than 80 are at the junior college level, and the student's grades overall and in the field of study average out to C.

To assign credit for prior coursework, most schools require original transcripts. This means you must complete a form or send a written, signed request to have your transcripts released directly to a college or university. Once you have chosen the schools you want to apply to, contact the schools you attended before. Find out how much each transcript costs, and ask them to send your transcripts to the ones you are applying to. Write a letter that includes your name (and names used during attendance, if different) and dates of attendance, along with the names and addresses of the schools to which your transcripts should be sent. Include payment and mail to the registrar at the schools you have attended. The registrar's office will process your request and send an official transcript of your coursework to the colleges or universities you have designated.

Credit For Noncollege Courses

Colleges and universities are not the only ones that offer classes. Volunteer organizations and employers often provide formal training worth college credit. The American Council on Education has two programs that assess thousands of specific courses and make recommendations on the amount of college credit they are worth. Colleges and universities accept the recommendations or use them as guidelines.

One program evaluates educational courses sponsored by government agencies, business and industry, labor unions, and professional and voluntary organizations. It is the Program on Noncollegiate Sponsored Instruction (PONSI). Some of the training seminars Alice has participated in covered topics such as food preparation, kitchen safety, and nutrition. Although she has not yet earned her GED, Alice can earn college credit because of her completion of these formal job-training seminars. The number of credits each seminar is worth does not hinge on Alice's current eligibility for college enrollment.

The other program evaluates courses offered by the Army, Navy, Air Force, Marines, Coast Guard, and Department of Defense. It is the Military Evaluations Program. Jorge has never attended college, but the engineering technology classes he completed as part of his military training are worth college credit. And as an Army veteran, Jorge is eligible for a service that takes the evaluations one step further. The Army/American Council on Education Registry Transcript System (AARTS) will provide Jorge with an individualized transcript of American Council on Education credit recommendations for all courses he completed, the military occupational specialties (MOS's) he held, and examinations he passed while in the Army. All Army and National Guard enlisted personnel and veterans who enlisted after October 1981 are eligible for the transcript. Similar services are being considered by the Navy and Marine Corps.

To obtain a free transcript, see your Army Education Center for a 5454R transcript request form. Include your name, Social Security number, basic active service date, and complete address where you want the transcript sent. Mail your request to:

AARTS Operations Center
415 McPherson Ave.
Fort Leavenworth, KS 66027-1373

Recommendations for PONSI are published in *The National Guide to Educational Credit for Training Programs;* military program recommendations are in *The Guide to the Evaluation of Educational Experiences in the Armed Forces.* See the Resources section at the end of this article for more information about these publications.

Former military personnel who took a foreign language course through the Defense Language Institute may request course transcripts by sending their name, Social Security number, course title, duration of the course, and graduation date to:

Commandant, Defense Language Institute
Attn: ATFL-DAA-AR
Transcripts
Presidio of Monterey
Monterey, CA 93944-5006

Not all of Jorge's and Alice's courses have been assessed by the American Council on Education. Training courses that have no Council credit recommendation should still be assessed by an advisor at the schools they want to attend. Course descriptions, class notes, test scores, and other documentation may be helpful for comparing training courses to their college equivalents. An oral examination or other demonstration of competency might also be required.

There is no guarantee you will receive all the credits you are seeking – but you certainly won't if you make no attempt.

Credit By Examination

Standardized tests are the best-known method of receiving college credit without taking courses. These exams are often taken by high school students seeking advanced placement for college, but they are also available to adult learners. Testing programs and colleges and universities offer exams in a number of subjects. Two U.S. Government institutes have foreign language exams for employees that also may be worth college credit.

It is important to understand that receiving a passing score on these exams does not mean you get college credit automatically. Each school determines which test results it will accept, minimum scores required, how scores are converted for credit, and the amount of credit, if any, to be assigned. Most colleges and universities accept the American Council on Education credit recommendations, published every other year in the 250-page *Guide to Educational Credit by Examination*. For more information, contact:

The American Council on Education
Credit by Examination Program
One Dupont Circle, Suite 250
Washington, DC 20036-1193
(202) 939-9434

Testing programs:

You might know some of the five national testing programs by their acronyms or initials: CLEP, ACT PEP: RCE, DANTES, AP, and NOCTI. (The meanings of these initialisms are explained below.) There is some overlap among programs; for example, four of them have introductory accounting exams. Since you will not be awarded credit more than once for a specific subject, you should carefully evaluate each program for the subject exams you wish to take. And before taking an exam, make sure you will be awarded credit by the college or university you plan to attend.

CLEP (College-Level Examination Program), administered by the College Board, is the most widely accepted of the national testing programs; more than 2,800 accredited schools award credit for passing exam scores. Each test covers material taught in basic undergraduate courses. There are five general exams – English composition, humanities, college mathematics, natural sciences, and social sciences and history – and many subject exams. Most exams are entirely multiple-choice, but English composition exams may include an essay section. For more information, contact:

    CLEP
    P.O. Box 6600
    Princeton, NJ 08541-6600
    (609) 771-7865

ACT PEP: RCE (American College Testing Proficiency Exam Program: Regents College Examinations) tests are given in 38 subjects within arts and sciences, business, education, and nursing. Each exam is recommended for either lower- or upper-level credit. Exams contain either objective or extended response questions, and are graded according to a standard score, letter grade, or pass/fail. Fees vary, depending on the subject and type of exam. For more information or to request free study guides, contact:

    ACT PEP: Regents College Examinations
    P.O. Box 4014
    Iowa City, IA 52243
    (319) 337-1387
    (New York State residents must contact Regents College directly.)

DANTES (Defense Activity for Nontraditional Education Support) standardized tests are developed by the Educational Testing Service for the Department of Defense. Originally administered only to military personnel, the exams have been available to the public since 1983. About 50 subject tests cover business, mathematics, social science, physical science, humanities, foreign languages, and applied technology. Most of the tests consist entirely of multiple-choice questions. Schools determine their own administering fees and testing schedules. For more information or to request free study sheets, contact:

    DANTES Program Office
    Mail Stop 31-X
    Educational Testing Service
    Princeton, NJ 08541
    1(800) 257-9484

The AP (Advanced Placement) Program is a cooperative effort between secondary schools and colleges and universities. AP exams are developed each year by committees of college and high school faculty appointed by the College Board and assisted by consultants from the Educational Testing Service. Subjects include arts and languages, natural sciences, computer science, social sciences, history, and mathematics. Most tests are 2 or 3 hours long and include both multiple-choice and essay questions. AP courses are available to help students prepare for exams, which are offered in the spring. For more information about the Advanced Placement Program, contact:

    Advanced Placement Services
    P.O. Box 6671
    Princeton, NJ 08541-6671
    (609) 771-7300

NOCTI (National Occupational Competency Testing Institute) assessments are designed for people like Alice, who have vocational-technical skills that cannot be evaluated by other tests. NOCTI assesses competency at two levels: Student/job ready and teacher/experienced worker. Standardized evaluations are available for occupations such as auto-body repair, electronics, mechanical drafting, quantity food preparation, and upholstering. The tests consist of multiple-choice questions and a performance component. Other services include workshops, customized assessments, and pre-testing. For more information, contact:

NOCTI
500 N. Bronson Ave.
Ferris State University
Big Rapids, MI 49307
(616) 796-4699

Colleges and universities:

Many colleges and universities have credit-by-exam programs, through which students earn credit by passing a comprehensive exam for a course offered by the institution. Among the most widely recognized are the programs at Ohio University, the University of North Carolina, Thomas Edison State College, and New York University.

Ohio University offers about 150 examinations for credit. In addition, you may sometimes arrange to take special examinations in non-laboratory courses offered at Ohio University. To take a test for credit, you must enroll in the course. If you plan to transfer the credit earned, you also need written permission from an official at your school. Books and study materials are available, for a cost, through the university. Exams must be taken within 6 months of the enrollment date; most last 3 hours. You may arrange to take the exam off campus if you do not live near the university.

Ohio University is on the quarter-hour system; most courses are worth 4 quarter hours, the equivalent of 3 semester hours. For more information, contact:

Independent Study
Tupper Hall 302
Ohio University
Athens, OH 45701-2979
1(800) 444-2910
(614) 593-2910

The University of North Carolina offers a credit-by-examination option for 140 independent study (correspondence) courses in foreign languages, humanities, social sciences, mathematics, business administration, education, electrical and computer engineering, health administration, and natural sciences. To take an exam, you must request and receive approval from both the course instructor and the independent studies department. Exams must be taken within six months of enrollment, and you may register for no more than two at a time. If you are not near the University's Chapel Hill campus, you may take your exam under supervision at an accredited college, university, community college, or technical institute. For more information, contact:

Independent Studies
CB #1020, The Friday Center
UNC-Chapel Hill
Chapel Hill, NC 27599-1020
1(800) 862-5669 / (919) 962-1134

The Thomas Edison College Examination Program offers more than 50 exams in liberal arts, business, and professional areas. Thomas Edison State College administers tests twice a month in Trenton, New Jersey; however, students may arrange to take their tests with a proctor at any accredited American college or university or U.S. military base. Most of the tests are multiple choice; some also include short answer or essay questions. Time limits range from 90 minutes to 4 hours, depending on the exam. For more information, contact:

Thomas Edison State College
TECEP, Office of Testing and Assessment
101 W. State Street
Trenton, NJ 08608-1176
(609) 633-2844

New York University's Foreign Language Program offers proficiency exams in more than 40 languages, from Albanian to Yiddish. Two exams are available in each language: The 12-point test is equivalent to 4 undergraduate semesters, and the 16-point exam may lead to upper level credit. The tests are given at the university's Foreign Language Department throughout the year.

Proof of foreign language proficiency does not guarantee college credit. Some colleges and universities accept transcripts only for languages commonly taught, such as French and Spanish. Nontraditional programs are more likely than traditional ones to grant credit for proficiency in other languages.

For an informational brochure and registration form for NYU's foreign language proficiency exams, contact:

New York University
Foreign Language Department
48 Cooper Square, Room 107
New York, NY 10003
(212) 998-7030

Government institutes:

The Defense Language Institute and Foreign Service Institute administer foreign language proficiency exams for personnel stationed abroad. Usually, the tests are given at the end of intensive language courses or upon completion of service overseas. But some people – like Jorge, who knows Spanish – speak another language fluently and may be allowed to take a proficiency exam in that language before completing their tour of duty. Contact one of the offices listed below to obtain transcripts of those scores. Proof of proficiency does not guarantee college credit, however, as discussed above.

To request score reports from the Defense Language Institute for Defense Language Proficiency Tests, send your name, Social Security number, language for which you were tested, and, most importantly, when and where you took the exam to:

Commandant, Defense Language Institute
Attn: ATFL-ES-T
DLPT Score Report Request
Presidio of Monterey
Monterey, CA 93944-5006

To request transcripts of scores for Foreign Service Institute exams, send your name, Social Security number, language for which you were tested, and dates or year of exams to:

Foreign Service Institute
Arlington Hall
4020 Arlington Boulevard
Rosslyn, VA 22204-1500
Attn: Testing Office (Send your request to the attention of the testing office of the foreign language in which you were tested)

Credit For Experience

Experiential learning credit may be given for knowledge gained through job responsibilities, personal hobbies, volunteer opportunities, homemaking, and other experiences. Colleges and universities base credit awards on the knowledge you have attained, not for the experience alone. In addition, the knowledge must be college level; not just any learning will do. Throwing horseshoes as a hobby is not likely to be worth college credit. But if you've done research on how and where the sport originated, visited blacksmiths, organized tournaments, and written a column for a trade journal – well, that's a horseshoe of a different color.

Adults attempting to get credit for their experience should be forewarned: Having your experience evaluated for college credit is time-consuming, tedious work – not an easy shortcut for people who want quick-fix college credits. And not all experience, no matter how valuable, is the equivalent of college courses.

Requesting college credit for your experiential learning can be tricky. You should get assistance from a credit evaluations officer at the school you plan to attend, but you should also have a general idea of what your knowledge is worth. A common method for converting knowledge into credit is to use a college catalog. Find course titles and descriptions that match what you have learned through experience, and request the number of credits offered for those courses.

Once you know what credit to ask for, you must usually present your case in writing to officials at the college you plan to attend. The most common form of presenting experiential learning for credit is the portfolio. A portfolio is a written record of your knowledge along with a request for equivalent college credit. It includes an identification and description of the knowledge for which you are requesting credit, an explanatory essay of how the knowledge was gained and how it fits into your educational plans, documentation that you have acquired such knowledge, and a request for college credit. Required elements of a portfolio vary by schools but generally follow those guidelines.

In identifying knowledge you have gained, be specific about exactly what you have learned. For example, it is not enough for Lynette to say she runs a business. She must identify the knowledge she has gained from running it, such as personnel management, tax law, marketing strategy, and inventory review. She must also include brief descriptions about her knowledge of each to support her claims of having those skills.

The essay gives you a chance to relay something about who you are. It should address your educational goals, include relevant autobiographical details, and be well organized, neat, and convey confidence. In his essay, Jorge might first state his goal of becoming an engineer. Then he would explain why he joined the Army, where he got hands-on training and experience in developing and servicing electronic equipment.

This, he would say, led to his hobby of creating remote-controlled model cars, of which he has built 20. His conclusion would highlight his accomplishments and tie them to his desire to become an electronic engineer.

Documentation is evidence that you've learned what you claim to have learned. You can show proof of knowledge in a variety of ways, including audio or video recordings, letters from current or former employers describing your specific duties and job performance, blueprints, photographs or artwork, and transcripts of certifying exams for professional licenses and certification – such as Alice's certification from the American Culinary Federation. Although documentation can take many forms, written proof alone is not always enough. If it is impossible to document your knowledge in writing, find out if your experiential learning can be assessed through supplemental oral exams by a faculty expert.

Earning a College Degree

Nontraditional students often have work, family, and financial obligations that prevent them from quitting their jobs to attend school full time. Can they still meet their educational goals? Yes.

More than 150 accredited colleges and universities have nontraditional bachelor's degree programs that require students to spend little or no time on campus; over 300 others have nontraditional campus-based degree programs. Some of those schools, as well as most junior and community colleges, offer associate's degrees nontraditionally. Each school with a nontraditional course of study determines its own rules for awarding credit for prior coursework, exams, or experience, as discussed previously. Most have charges on top of tuition for providing these special services.

Several publications profile nontraditional degree programs; see the Resources section at the end of this article for more information. To determine which school best fits your academic profile and educational goals, first list your criteria. Then, evaluate nontraditional programs based on their accreditation, features, residency requirements, and expenses. Once you have chosen several schools to explore further, write to them for more information. Detailed explanations of school policies should help you decide which ones you want to apply to.

Get beyond the printed word – especially the glowing words each school writes about itself. Check out the schools you are considering with higher education authorities, alumni, employers, family members, and friends. If possible, visit the campus to talk to students and instructors and sit in on a few classes, even if you will be completing most or all of your work off campus. Ask school officials questions about such things as enrollment numbers, graduation rate, faculty qualifications, and confusing details about the application process or academic policies. After you have thoroughly investigated each prospective college or university, you can make an informed decision about which is right for you.

Accreditation

Accreditation is a process colleges and universities submit to voluntarily for getting their credentials. An accredited school has been investigated and visited by teams of observers and has periodic inspections by a private accrediting agency. The initial review can take two years or more.

Regional agencies accredit entire schools, and professional agencies accredit either specialized schools or departments within schools. Although there are no national accrediting standards, not just any accreditation will do. Countless "accreditation associations" have been invented by schools, many of which have no academic programs and sell phony degrees, to accredit themselves. But 6 regional and about 80 professional accrediting associations in the United States are recognized by the U.S. Department of Education or the Commission on Recognition of Postsecondary Accreditation. When checking accreditation, these are the names to look for. For more information about accreditation and accrediting agencies, contact:

>Institutional Participation Oversight Service Accreditation and State Liaison Division
>U.S. Department of Education
>ROB 3, Room 3915
>600 Independence Ave., SW
>Washington, DC 20202-5244
>(202) 708-7417

Because accreditation is not mandatory, lack of accreditation does not necessarily mean a school or program is bad. Some schools choose not to apply for accreditation, are in the process of applying, or have educational methods too unconventional for an accrediting association's standards. For the nontraditional student, however, earning a degree from a college or university with recognized accreditation is an especially important consideration. Although nontraditional education is becoming more widely accepted, it is not yet mainstream. Employers skeptical of a degree earned in a nontraditional manner are likely to be even less accepting of one from an unaccredited school.

Program Features

Because nontraditional students have diverse educational objectives, nontraditional schools are diverse in what they offer. Some programs are geared toward helping students organize their scattered educational credits to get a degree as quickly as possible. Others cater to those who may have specific credits or experience but need assistance in completing requirements. Whatever your educational profile, you should look for a program that works with you in obtaining your educational goals.

A few nontraditional programs have special admissions policies for adult learners like Alice, who plan to earn their GEDs but want to enroll in college in the meantime. Other features of nontraditional programs include individualized learning agreements, intensive academic counseling, cooperative learning and internship placement, and waiver of some prerequisites or other requirements – as well as college credit for prior coursework, examinations, and experiential learning, all discussed previously.

Lynette, whose primary goal is to finish her degree, wants to earn maximum credits for her business experience. She will look for programs that do not limit the number of credits awarded for equivalency exams and experiential learning. And since well-documented proof of knowledge is essential for earning experiential learning credits, Lynette should make sure the program she chooses provides assistance to students submitting a portfolio.

Jorge, on the other hand, has more credits than he needs in certain areas and is willing to forego some. To become an engineer, he must have a bachelor's degree; but because he is accustomed to hands-on learning, Jorge is interested in getting experience as he gains more technical skills. He will concentrate on finding schools with strong cooperative education, supervised fieldwork, or internship programs.

Residency Requirements

Programs are sometimes deemed nontraditional because of their residency requirements. Many people think of residency for colleges and universities in terms of tuition, with in-state students paying less than out-of-state ones. Residency also may refer to where a student lives, either on or off campus, while attending school.

But in nontraditional education, residency usually refers to how much time students must spend on campus, regardless of whether they attend classes there. In some nontraditional programs, students need not ever step foot on campus. Others require only a very short residency, such as one day or a few weeks. Many schools have standard residency requirements of several semesters but schedule classes for evenings or weekends to accommodate working adults.

Lynette, who previously took courses by independent study, prefers to earn credits by distance study. She will focus on schools that have no residency requirement. Several colleges and universities have nonresident degree completion programs for adults with some college credit. Under the direction of a faculty advisor, students devise a plan for earning their remaining credits. Methods for earning credits include independent study, distance learning, seminars, supervised fieldwork, and group study at arranged sites. Students may have to earn a certain number of credits through the degree-granting institution. But many programs allow students to take courses at accredited schools of their choice for transfer toward their degree.

Alice wants to attend lectures but has an unpredictable schedule. Her best course of action will be to seek out short residency programs that require students to attend seminars once or twice a semester. She can take courses that are televised and videotape them to watch when her schedule permits, with the seminars helping to ensure that she properly completes her coursework. Many colleges and universities with short residency requirements also permit students to earn some credits elsewhere, by whatever means the student chooses.

Some fields of study require classroom instruction. As Jorge will discover, few colleges and universities allow students to earn a bachelor's degree in engineering entirely through independent study. Nontraditional residency programs are designed to accommodate adults' daytime work schedules. Jorge should look for programs offering evening, weekend, summer, and accelerated courses.

Tuition and Other Expenses

The final decisions about which schools Alice, Jorge, and Lynette attend may hinge in large part on a single issue: Cost. And rising tuition is only part of the equation. Beginning with application fees and continuing through graduation fees, college expenses add up.

Traditional and nontraditional students have some expenses in common, such as the cost of books and other materials. Tuition might even be the same for some courses, especially for colleges and universities offering standard ones at unusual times. But for nontraditional programs, students may also pay fees for services such as credit or transcript review, evaluation, advisement, and portfolio assessment.

Students are also responsible for postage and handling or setup expenses for independent study courses, as well as for all examination and transcript fees for transferring credits. Usually, the more nontraditional the program, the more detailed the fees. Some schools charge a yearly enrollment fee rather than tuition for degree completion candidates who want their files to remain active.

Although tuition and fees might seem expensive, most educators tell you not to let money come between you and your educational goals. Talk to someone in the financial aid department of the school you plan to attend or check your library for publications about financial aid sources. The U.S. Department of Education publishes a guide to Federal aid programs such as Pell Grants, student loans, and work-study. To order the free 74-page booklet, *The Student Guide: Financial Aid from the U.S. Department of Education,* contact:

Federal Student Aid Information Center
P.O. Box 84
Washington, DC 20044
1 (800) 4FED-AID (433-3243)

Resources

Information on how to earn a high school diploma or college degree without following the usual routes is available from several organizations and in numerous publications. Information on nontraditional graduate degree programs, available for master's through doctoral level, though not discussed in this article, can usually be obtained from the same resources that detail bachelor's degree programs.

National Learning Corporation publishes study guides for all of these exams, for both general examinations and tests in specific subject areas. To order study guides, or to browse their catalog featuring more than 5,000 titles, visit NLC online at www.passbooks.com, or contact them by phone at (800) 632-8888.

Organizations

Adult learners should always contact their local school system, community college, or university to learn about programs that are readily available. The following national organizations can also supply information:

American Council on Education
One Dupont Circle
Washington, DC 20036-1193
(202) 939-9300

Within the American Council on Education, the Center for Adult Learning and Educational Credentials administers the National External Diploma Program, the GED Program, the Program on Noncollegiate Sponsored Instruction, the Credit by Examination Program, and the Military Evaluations Program.

College-Level Examination Program (CLEP)

1. WHAT IS CLEP?

CLEP stands for the College-Level Examination Program, sponsored by the College Board. It is a national program of credit-by-examination that offers you the opportunity to obtain recognition for college-level achievement. No matter when, where, or how you have learned – by means of formal or informal study – you can take CLEP tests. If the results are acceptable to your college, you can receive credit.

You may not realize it, but you probably know more than your academic record reveals. Each day you, like most people, have an opportunity to learn. In private industry and business, as well as at all levels of government, learning opportunities continually occur. If you read widely or intensively in a particular field, think about what you read, discuss it with your family and friends, you are learning. Or you may be learning on a more formal basis by taking a correspondence course, a television or radio course, a course recorded on tape or cassettes, a course assembled into programmed tests, or a course taught in your community adult school or high school.

No matter how, where, or when you gained your knowledge, you may have the opportunity to receive academic credit for your achievement that can be counted toward an undergraduate degree. The College-Level Examination Program (CLEP) enables colleges to evaluate your achievement and give you credit. A wide range of college-level examinations are offered by CLEP to anyone who wishes to take them. Scores on the tests are reported to you and, if you wish, to a college, employer, or individual.

2. WHAT ARE THE PURPOSES OF THE COLLEGE-LEVEL EXAMINATION PROGRAM?

The basic purpose of the College-Level Examination Program is to enable individuals who have acquired their education in nontraditional ways to demonstrate their academic achievement. It is also intended for use by those in higher education, business, industry, government, and other fields who need a reliable method of assessing a person's educational level.

Recognizing that the real issue is not how a person has acquired his education but what education he has, the College Level Examination Program has been designed to serve a variety of purposes. The basic purpose, as listed above, is to enable those who have reached the college level of education in nontraditional ways to assess the level of their achievement and to use the test results in seeking college credit or placement.

In addition, scores on the tests can be used to validate educational experience obtained at a nonaccredited institution or through noncredit college courses.

Some colleges and universities may use the tests to measure the level of educational achievement of their students, and for various institutional research purposes.

Other colleges and universities may wish to use the tests in the admission, placement, and guidance of students who wish to transfer from one institution to another.

Businesses, industries, governmental agencies, and professional groups now accept the results of these tests as a basis for advancement, eligibility for further training, or professional or semi-professional certification.

Many people are interested in the examination simply to assess their own educational progress and attainment.

The college, university, business, industry, or government agency that adopts the tests in the College-Level Examination Program makes its own decision about how it will use and interpret the test scores. The College Board will provide the tests, score them, and report the results either to the individuals who took the tests or the college or agency that administered them. It does NOT, and cannot, award college credit, certify college equivalency, or make recommendations regarding the standards these institutions should establish for the use of the test results.

Therefore, if you are taking the tests to secure credit from an institution, you should FIRST ascertain whether the college or agency involved will accept the scores. Each institution determines which CLEP tests it will accept for credit and the amount of credit it will award. If you want to take tests for college credit, first call, write, or visit the college you wish to attend to inquire about its policy on CLEP scores, as well as its other admission requirements.

The services of the program are also available to people who have been requested to take the tests by an employer, a professional licensing agency, a certifying agency, or by other groups that recognize college equivalency on the basis of satisfactory CLEP scores. You may, of course, take the tests SOLELY for your own information. If you do, your scores will be reported only to you.

While neither CLEP nor the College Board can evaluate previous credentials or award college credit, you will receive, with your scores, basic information to help you interpret your performance on the tests you have taken.

3. WHAT ARE THE COLLEGE-LEVEL EXAMINATIONS?

In order to meet different kinds of curricular organization and testing needs at colleges and universities, the College-Level Examination Program offers 35 different subject tests falling under five separate general categories: Composition and Literature, Foreign Languages, History and Social Sciences, Science and Mathematics, and Business.

4. WHAT ARE THE SUBJECT EXAMINATIONS?

The 35 CLEP tests offered by the College Board are listed below:

COMPOSITION AND LITERATURE:
- American Literature
- Analyzing and Interpreting Literature
- English Composition
- English Composition with Essay
- English Literature
- Freshman College Composition
- Humanities

FOREIGN LANGUAGES
- French
- German
- Spanish

HISTORY AND SOCIAL SCIENCES
- American Government
- Introduction to Educational Psychology
- History of the United States I: Early Colonization to 1877
- History of the United States II: 1865 to the Present
- Human Growth and Development
- Principles of Macroeconomics
- Principles of Microeconomics
- Introductory Psychology
- Social Sciences and History
- Introductory Sociology
- Western Civilization I: Ancient Near East to 1648
- Western Civilization II: 1648 to the Present

SCIENCE AND MATHEMATICS
- College Algebra
- College Algebra-Trigonometry
- Biology
- Calculus
- Chemistry
- College Mathematics
- Natural Sciences
- Trigonometry
- Precalculus

BUSINESS
- Financial Accounting
- Introductory Business Law
- Information Systems and Computer Applications
- Principles of Management
- Principles of Marketing

CLEP Examinations cover material taught in courses that most students take as requirements in the first two years of college. A college usually grants the same amount of credit to students earning satisfactory scores on the CLEP examination as it grants to students successfully completing the equivalent course.

Many examinations are designed to correspond to one-semester courses; some, however, correspond to full-year or two-year courses.

Each exam is 90 minutes long and, except for English Composition with Essay, is made up primarily of multiple-choice questions. Some tests have several other types of questions besides multiple choice. To see a more detailed description of a particular CLEP exam, visit www.collegeboard.com/clep.

The English Composition with Essay exam is the only exam that includes a required essay. This essay is scored by college English faculty designated by CLEP and does not require an additional fee. However, other Composition and Literature tests offer optional essays, which some college and universities require and some do not. These essays are graded by faculty at the individual institutions that require them and require an additional $10 fee. Contact the particular institution to ask about essay requirements, and check with your test center for further details.

All 35 CLEP examinations are administered on computer. If you are unfamiliar with taking a test on a computer, consult the CLEP Sampler online at www.collegeboard.com/clep. The Sampler contains the same tutorials as the actual exams and helps familiarize you with navigation and how to answer different types of questions.

Points are not deducted for wrong or skipped answers – you receive one point for every correct answer. Therefore it is best that an answer is supplied for each exam question, whether it is a guess or not. The number of correct answers is then converted to a formula score. This formula, or "scaled," score is determined by a statistical process called *equating*, which adjusts for slight differences in difficulty between test forms and ensures that your score does not depend on the specific test form you took or how well others did on the same form. The scaled scores range from 20 to 80 – this is the number that will appear on your score report.

To ensure that you complete all questions in the time allotted, you would probably be wise to skip the more difficult or perplexing questions and return to them later. Although the multiple-choice items in these tests are carefully designed so as not to be tricky, misleading, or ambiguous, on the other hand, they are not all direct questions of factual information. They attempt, in their way, to elicit a response that indicates your knowledge or lack of knowledge of the material in question or your ability or inability to use or interpret a fact or idea. Thus, you should concentrate on answering the questions as they appear to be without attempting to out-guess the testmakers.

5. WHAT ARE THE FEES?

The fee for all CLEP examinations is $55. Optional essays required by some institutions are an additional $10.

6. WHEN ARE THE TESTS GIVEN?

CLEP tests are administered year-round. Consult the CLEP website (www.collegeboard.com/clep) and individual test centers for specific information.

7. WHERE ARE THE TESTS GIVEN?

More than 1,300 test centers are located on college and university campuses throughout the country, and additional centers are being established to meet increased needs. Any accredited collegiate institution with an explicit and publicly available policy of credit by examination can become a CLEP test center. To obtain a list of these centers, visit the CLEP website at www.collegeboard.com/clep.

8. HOW DO I REGISTER FOR THE COLLEGE-LEVEL EXAMINATION PROGRAM?

Contact an individual test center for information regarding registration, scheduling and fees. Registration/admission forms can also be obtained on the CLEP website.

9. MAY I REPEAT THE COLLEGE-LEVEL EXAMINATIONS?

You may repeat any examination providing at least six months have passed since you were last administered this test. If you repeat a test within a period of time less than six months, your scores will be cancelled and your fees forfeited. To repeat a test, check the appropriate space on the registration form.

10. WHEN MAY I EXPECT MY SCORE REPORTS?

With the exception of the English Composition with Essay exam, you should receive your score report instantly once the test is complete.

11. HOW SHOULD I PREPARE FOR THE COLLEGE-LEVEL EXAMINATIONS?

This book has been specifically designed to prepare candidates for these examinations. It will help you to consider, study, and review important content, principles, practices, procedures, problems, and techniques in the form of varied and concrete applications.

12. QUESTIONS AND ANSWERS APPEARING IN THIS PUBLICATION

The College-Level Examinations are offered by the College Board. Since copies of past examinations have not been made available, we have used equivalent materials, including questions and answers, which are highly recommended by us as an appropriate means of preparing for these examinations.

If you need additional information about CLEP Examinations, visit www.collegeboard.com/clep.

THE COLLEGE-LEVEL EXAMINATION PROGRAM

How The Program Works

CLEP examinations are administered at many colleges and universities across the country, and most institutions award college credit to those who do well on them. The examinations provide people who have acquired knowledge outside the usual educational settings the opportunity to show that they have learned college-level material without taking certain college courses.

The CLEP examinations cover material that is taught in introductory-level courses at many colleges and universities. Faculties at individual colleges review the tests to ensure that they cover the important material taught in their courses. Colleges differ in the examinations they accept; some colleges accept only two or three of the examinations while others accept nearly all of them.

Although CLEP is sponsored by the College Board and the examinations are scored by Educational Testing Service (ETS), neither of these organizations can award college credit. Only accredited colleges may grant credit toward a degree. When you take a CLEP examination, you may request that a copy of your score report be sent to the college you are attending or plan to attend. After evaluating your scores, the college will decide whether or not to award you credit for a certain course or courses, or to exempt you from them. If the college gives you credit, it will record the number of credits on your permanent record, thereby indicating that you have completed work equivalent to a course in that subject. If the college decides to grant exemption without giving you credit for a course, you will be permitted to omit a course that would normally be required of you and to take a course of your choice instead.

What the Examinations Are Like

The examinations consist mostly of multiple-choice questions to be answered within a 90-minute time limit. Additional information about each CLEP examination is given in the examination guide and on the CLEP website.

Where To Take the Examinations

CLEP examinations are administered throughout the year at the test centers of approximately 1,300 colleges and universities. On the CLEP website, you will find a list of institutions that award credit for satisfactory scores on CLEP examinations. Some colleges administer CLEP examinations to their own students only. Other institutions administer the tests to anyone who registers to take them. If your college does not administer the tests, contact the test centers in your area for information about its testing schedule.

Once you have been tested, your score report will be available instantly. CLEP scores are kept on file at ETS for 20 years; and during this period, for a small fee, you may have your transcript sent to another college or to anyone else you specify. (Your scores will never be sent to anyone without your approval.)

APPROACHING A COLLEGE ABOUT CLEP

The following sections provide a step-by-step approach to learning about the CLEP policy at a particular college or university. The person or office that can best assist students desiring CLEP credit may have a different title at each institution, but the following guidelines will lead you to information about CLEP at any institution.

Adults returning to college often benefit from special assistance when they approach a college. Opportunities for adults to return to formal learning in the classroom are now widespread, and colleges and universities have worked hard to make this a smooth process for older students. Many colleges have established special service offices that are staffed with trained professionals who understand the kinds of problems facing adults returning to college. If you think you might benefit from such assistance, be sure to find out whether these services are available at your college.

How to Apply for College Credit

STEP 1. Obtain the General Information Catalog and a copy of the CLEP policy from the colleges you are considering. If you have not yet applied for admission, ask for an admissions application form too.

Information about admissions and CLEP policies can be obtained by contacting college admissions offices or finding admissions information on the school websites. Tell the admissions officer that you are a prospective student and that you are interested in applying for admission and CLEP credit. Ask for a copy of the publication in which the college's complete CLEP policy is explained. Also get the name and the telephone number of the person to contact in case you have further questions about CLEP.

At this step, you may wish to obtain information from external degree colleges. Many adults find that such colleges suit their needs exceptionally well.

STEP 2. If you have not already been admitted to the college you are considering, look at its admission requirements for undergraduate students to see if you can qualify.

This is an important step because if you can't get into college, you can't get college credit for CLEP. Nearly all colleges require students to be admitted and to enroll in one or more courses before granting the students CLEP credit.

Virtually all public community colleges and a number of four-year state colleges have open admission policies for in-state students. This usually means that they admit anyone who has graduated from high school or has earned a high school equivalency diploma.

If you think you do not meet the admission requirements, contact the admissions office for an interview with a counselor. Colleges do sometimes make exceptions, particularly for adult applicants. State why you want the interview and ask what documents you should bring with you or send in advance. (These materials may include a high school transcript, transcript of previous college work, completed application for admission, etc.) Make an extra effort to have all the information requested in time for the interview.

During the interview, relax and be yourself. Be prepared to state honestly why you think you are ready and able to do college work. If you have already taken CLEP examinations and scored high enough to earn credit, you have shown that you are able to do college work. Mention this achievement to the admissions counselor because it may increase your chances of being accepted. If you have not taken a CLEP examination, you can still improve your chances of being accepted by describing how your job training or independent study has helped prepare you for college-level work. Tell the counselor what you have learned from your work and personal experiences.

STEP 3. Evaluate the college's CLEP policy.

Typically, a college lists all its academic policies, including CLEP policies, in its general catalog. You will probably find the CLEP policy statement under a heading such as Credit-by-Examination, Advanced Standing, Advanced Placement, or External Degree Program. These sections can usually be found in the front of the catalog.

Many colleges publish their credit-by-examination policies in a separate brochure, which is distributed through the campus testing office, counseling center, admissions office, or registrar's office. If you find a very general policy statement in the college catalog, seek clarification from one of these offices.

Review the material in the section of this guide entitled Questions to Ask About a College's CLEP Policy. Use these guidelines to evaluate the college's CLEP policy. If you have not yet taken a CLEP examination, this evaluation will help you decide which examinations to take and whether or not to take the free-response or essay portion. Because individual colleges have different CLEP policies, a review of several policies may help you decide which college to attend.

STEP 4. If you have not yet applied for admission, do so early.

Most colleges expect you to apply for admission several months before you enroll, and it is essential that you meet the published application deadlines. It takes time to process your application for admission; and if you have yet to take a CLEP examination, it will be some time before the college receives and reviews your score report. You will probably want to take some, if not all, of the CLEP examinations you are interested in before you enroll so you know which courses you need not register for. In fact, some colleges require that all CLEP scores be submitted before a student registers.

Complete all forms and include all documents requested with your application(s) for admission. Normally, an admissions decision cannot be reached until all documents have been submitted and evaluated. Unless told to do so, do not send your CLEP scores until you have been officially admitted.

STEP 5. Arrange to take CLEP examination(s) or to submit your CLEP score(s).

You may want to wait to take your CLEP examinations until you know definitely which college you will be attending. Then you can make sure you are taking tests your college will accept for credit. You will also be able to request that your scores be sent to the college, free of charge, when you take the tests.

If you have already taken CLEP examinations, but did not have a copy of your score report sent to your college, you may request the College Board to send an official transcript at any time for a small fee. Use the Transcript Request Form that was sent to you with your score report. If you do not have the form, you may find it online at www.collegeboard.com/clep.

Your CLEP scores will be evaluated, probably by someone in the admissions office, and sent to the registrar's office to be posted on your permanent record once you are enrolled. Procedures vary from college to college, but the process usually begins in the admissions office.

STEP 6. Ask to receive a written notice of the credit you receive for your CLEP score(s).

A written notice may save you problems later, when you submit your degree plan or file for graduation. In the event that there is a question about whether or not you earned CLEP credit, you will have an official record of what credit was awarded. You may also need this verification of course credit if you go for academic counseling before the credit is posted on your permanent record.

STEP 7. Before you register for courses, seek academic counseling.

A discussion with your academic advisor can prevent you from taking unnecessary courses and can tell you specifically what your CLEP credit will mean to you. This step may be accomplished at the time you enroll. Most colleges have orientation sessions for new students prior to each enrollment period. During orientation, students are usually assigned an academic advisor who then gives them individual help in developing long-range plans and a course schedule for the next semester. In conjunction with this counseling, you may be asked to take some additional tests so that you can be placed at the proper course level.

External Degree Programs

If you have acquired a considerable amount of college-level knowledge through job experience, reading, or noncredit courses, if you have accumulated college credits at a variety of colleges over a period of years, or if you prefer studying on your own rather than in a classroom setting, you may want to investigate the possibility of enrolling in an external degree program. Many colleges offer external degree programs that allow you to earn a degree by passing examinations (including CLEP), transferring credit from other colleges, and demonstrating in other ways that you have satisfied the educational requirements. No classroom attendance is required, and the programs are open to out-of-state candidates as well as residents. Thomas A. Edison State College in New Jersey and Charter Oaks College in Connecticut are fully accredited independent state colleges; the New York program is part of the state university system and is also fully accredited. If you are interested in exploring an external degree, you can write for more information to:

Charter Oak College
The Exchange, Suite 171
270 Farmington Avenue
Farmington, CT 06032-1909

Regents External Degree Program
Cultural Education Center
Empire State Plaza
Albany, New York 12230

Thomas A. Edison State College
101 West State Street
Trenton, New Jersey 08608

Many other colleges also have external degree or weekend programs. While they often require that a number of courses be taken on campus, the external degree programs tend to be more flexible in transferring credit, granting credit-by-examination, and allowing independent study than other traditional programs. When applying to a college, you may wish to ask whether it has an external degree or weekend program.

Questions to Ask About a College's CLEP Policy

Before taking CLEP examinations for the purpose of earning college credit, try to find the answers to these questions:

1. Which CLEP examinations are accepted by this college?

A college may accept some CLEP examinations for credit and not others - possibly not the one you are considering. The English faculty may decide to grant college English credit based on the CLEP English Composition examination, but not on the Freshman College Composition examination. Or, the mathematics faculty may decide to grant credit based on the College Mathematics to non-mathematics majors only, requiring majors to take an examination in algebra, trigonometry, or calculus to earn credit. For these reasons, it is important that you know the specific CLEP tests for which you can receive credit.

2. Does the college require the optional free-response (essay) section as well as the objective portion of the CLEP examination you are considering?

Knowing the answer to this question ahead of time will permit you to schedule the optional essay examination when you register to take your CLEP examination.

3. Is credit granted for specific courses? If so, which ones?

You are likely to find that credit will be granted for specific courses and the course titles will be designated in the college's CLEP policy. It is not necessary, however, that credit be granted for a specific course in order for you to benefit from your CLEP credit. For instance, at many liberal arts colleges, all students must take certain types of courses; these courses may be labeled the core curriculum, general education requirements, distribution requirements, or liberal arts requirements. The requirements are often expressed in terms of credit hours. For example, all students may be required to take at least six hours of humanities, six hours of English, three hours of mathematics, six hours of natural science, and six hours of social science, with no particular courses in these disciplines specified. In these instances, CLEP credit may be given as 6 hrs. English credit or 3 hrs. Math credit without specifying for which English or mathematics courses credit has been awarded. In order to avoid possible disappointment, you should know before taking a CLEP examination what type of credit you can receive and whether you will only be exempted from a required course but receive no credit.

4. How much credit is granted for each examination you are considering, and does the college place a limit on the total amount of CLEP credit you can earn toward your degree?

Not all colleges that grant CLEP credit award the same amount for individual tests. Furthermore, some colleges place a limit on the total amount of credit you can earn through CLEP or other examinations. Other colleges may grant you exemption but no credit toward your degree. Knowing several colleges' policies concerning these issues may help you decide which college you will attend. If you think you are capable of passing a number of CLEP examinations, you may want to attend a college that will allow you to earn credit for all or most of them. For example, the state external degree programs grant credit for most CLEP examinations (and other tests as well).

5. What is the required score for earning CLEP credit for each test you are considering?

Most colleges publish the required scores or percentile ranks for earning CLEP credit in their general catalog or in a brochure. The required score may vary from test to test, so find out the required score for each test you are considering.

6. What is the college's policy regarding prior course work in the subject in which you are considering taking a CLEP test?

Some colleges will not grant credit for a CLEP test if the student has already attempted a college-level course closely aligned with that test. For example, if you successfully completed English 101 or a comparable course on another campus, you will probably not be permitted to receive CLEP credit in that subject, too. Some colleges will not permit you to earn CLEP credit for a course that you failed.

7. Does the college make additional stipulations before credit will be granted?

It is common practice for colleges to award CLEP credit only to their enrolled students. There are other stipulations, however, that vary from college to college. For example, does the college require you to formally apply for or accept CLEP credit by completing and signing a form? Or does the college require you to validate your CLEP score by successfully completing a more advanced course in the subject? Answers to these and other questions will help to smooth the process of earning college credit through CLEP.

The above questions and the discussions that follow them indicate some of the ways in which colleges' CLEP policies can vary. Find out as much as possible about the CLEP policies at the colleges you are interested in so you can choose a college with a policy that is compatible with your educational goals. Once you have selected the college you will attend, you can find out which CLEP examinations your college recognizes and the requirements for earning CLEP credit.

DECIDING WHICH EXAMINATIONS TO TAKE

If You're Taking the Examinations for College Credit or Career Advancement:

Most people who take CLEP examinations do so in order to earn credit for college courses. Others take the examinations in order to qualify for job promotions or for professional certification or licensing. It is vital to most candidates who are taking the tests for any of these reasons that they be well prepared for the tests they are taking so that they can advance as rapidly as possible toward their educational or career goals.

It is usually advisable that those who have limited knowledge in the subjects covered by the tests they are considering enroll in the college courses in which that material is taught. Those who are uncertain about whether or not they know enough about a subject to do well on a particular CLEP test will find the following guidelines helpful.

There is no way to predict if you will pass a particular CLEP examination, but answers to the questions under the seven headings below should give you an indication of whether or not you are likely to succeed.

1. Test Descriptions

Read the description of the test provided. Are you familiar with most of the topics and terminology in the outline?

2. Textbooks

Examine the suggested textbooks and other resource materials following the test descriptions in this guide. Have you recently read one or more of these books, or have you read similar college-level books on this subject? If you have not, read through one or more of the textbooks listed, or through the textbook used for this course at your college. Are you familiar with most of the topics and terminology in the book?

3. Sample Questions

The sample questions provided are intended to be typical of the content and difficulty of the questions on the test. Although they are not an exact miniature of the test, the proportion of the sample questions you can answer correctly should be a rough estimate of the proportion of questions you will be able to answer correctly on the test.

Answer as many of the sample questions for this test as you can. Check your answers against the correct answers. Did you answer more than half the questions correctly?

Because of variations in course content at different institutions, and because questions on CLEP tests vary from easy to difficult - with most being of moderate difficulty - the average student who passes a course in a subject can usually answer correctly about half the questions on the corresponding CLEP examination. Most colleges set their passing scores near this level, but some set them higher. If your college has set its required score above the level required by most colleges, you may need to answer a larger proportion of questions on the test correctly.

4. Previous Study

Have you taken noncredit courses in this subject offered by an adult school or a private school, through correspondence, or in connection with your job? Did you do exceptionally well in this subject in high school, or did you take an honors course in this subject?

5. Experience

Have you learned or used the knowledge or skills included in this test in your job or life experience? For example, if you lived in a Spanish-speaking country and spoke the language for a year or more, you might consider taking the Spanish examination. Or, if you have worked at a job in which you used accounting and finance skills, Principles of Accounting would be a likely test for you to take. Or, if you have read a considerable amount of literature and attended many art exhibits, concerts, and plays, you might expect to do well on the Humanities exam.

6. Other Examinations

Have you done well on other standardized tests in subjects related to the one you want to take? For example, did you score well above average on a portion of a college entrance examination covering similar skills, or did you obtain an exceptionally high score on a high school equivalency test or a licensing examination in this subject? Although such tests do not cover exactly the same material as the CLEP examinations and may be easier, persons who do well on these tests often do well on CLEP examinations, too.

7. Advice

Has a college counselor, professor, or some other professional person familiar with your ability advised you to take a CLEP examination?

If your answer was yes to questions under several of the above headings, you probably have a good chance of passing the CLEP examination you are considering. It is unlikely that you would have acquired sufficient background from experience alone. Learning gained through reading and study is essential, and you will probably find some additional study helpful before taking a CLEP examination.

If You're Taking the Examinations to Prepare for College

Many people entering college, particularly adults returning to college after several years away from formal education, are uncertain about their ability to compete with other college students. They wonder whether they have sufficient background for college study, and those who have been away from formal study for some time wonder whether they have forgotten how to study, how to take tests, and how to write papers. Such people may wish to improve their test-taking and study skills prior to enrolling in courses.

One way to assess your ability to perform at the college level and to improve your test-taking and study skills at the same time is to prepare for and take one or more CLEP examinations. You need not be enrolled in a college to take a CLEP examination, and you may have your scores sent only to yourself and later request that a transcript be sent to a college if you then decide to apply for credit. By reviewing the test descriptions and sample questions, you may find one or several subject areas in which you think you have substantial knowledge. Select one examination, or more if you like, and carefully read at least one of the textbooks listed in the bibliography for the test. By doing this, you will get a better idea of how much you know of what is usually taught in a college-level course in that subject. Study as much material as you can, until you think you have a good grasp of the subject matter. Then take the test at a college in your area. It will be several weeks before you receive your results, and you may wish to begin reviewing for another test in the meantime.

To find out if you are eligible for credit for your CLEP score, you must compare your score with the score required by the college you plan to attend. If you are not yet sure which college you will attend, or whether you will enroll in college at all, you should begin to follow the steps outlined. It is best that you do this before taking a CLEP test, but if you are taking the test only for the experience and to familiarize yourself with college-level material and requirements, you might take the test before you approach a college. Even if the college you decide to attend does not accept the test you took, the experience of taking such a test will enable you to meet with greater confidence the requirements of courses you will take.

You will find information about how to interpret your scores in WHAT YOUR SCORES MEAN, which you will receive with your score report, and which can also be found online at the CLEP website. Many colleges follow the recommendations of the American Council on Education (ACE) for setting their required scores, so you can use this information as a guide in determining how well you did. The ACE recommendations are included in the booklet.

If you do not do well enough on the test to earn college credit, don't be discouraged. Usually, it is the best college students who are exempted from courses or receive credit-by-examination. The fact that you cannot get credit for your score means that you should probably enroll in a college course to learn the material. However, if your score was close to the required score, or if you feel you could do better on a second try or after some additional study, you may retake the test after six months. Do not take it sooner or your score will not be reported and your fee will be forfeited.

If you do earn the score required to earn credit, you will have demonstrated that you already have some college-level knowledge. You will also have a better idea whether you should take additional CLEP examinations. And, what is most important, you can enroll in college with confidence, knowing that you do have the ability to succeed.

PREPARING TO TAKE CLEP EXAMINATIONS

Having made the decision to take one or more CLEP examinations, most people then want to know if it is worthwhile to prepare for them - how much, how long, when, and how should they go about it? The precise answers to these questions vary greatly from individual to individual. However, most candidates find that some type of test preparation is helpful.

Most people who take CLEP examinations do so to show that they have already learned the important material that is taught in a college course. Many of them need only a quick review to assure themselves that they have not forgotten some of what they once studied, and to fill in some of the gaps in their knowledge of the subject. Others feel that they need a thorough review and spend several weeks studying for a test. A few wish to take a CLEP examination as a kind of final examination for independent study of a subject instead of the college course. This last group requires significantly more study than those who only need to review, and they may need some guidance from professors of the subjects they are studying.

The key to how you prepare for CLEP examinations often lies in locating those skills and areas of prior learning in which you are strong and deciding where to focus your energies. Some people may know a great deal about a certain subject area, but may not test well. These individuals would probably be just as concerned about strengthening their test-taking skills as they are about studying for a specific test. Many mental and physical skills are used in preparing for a test. It is important not only to review or study for the examinations, but to make certain that you are alert, relatively free of anxiety, and aware of how to approach standardized tests. Suggestions on developing test-taking skills and preparing psychologically and physically for a test are given. The following section suggests ways of assessing your knowledge of the content of a test and then reviewing and studying the material.

Using This Study Guide

Begin by carefully reading the test description and outline of knowledge and skills required for the examination, if given. As you read through the topics listed there, ask yourself how much you know about each one. Also note the terms, names, and symbols that are mentioned, and ask yourself whether you are familiar with them. This will give you a quick overview of how much you know about the subject. If you are familiar with nearly all the material, you will probably need a minimum of review; however, if less than half of it is familiar, you will probably require substantial study to do well on the test.

If, after reviewing the test description, you find that you need extensive review, delay answering the sample question until you have done some reading in the subject. If you complete them before reviewing the material, you will probably look for the answers as you study, and then they will not be a good assessment of your ability at a later date.

If you think you are familiar with most of the test material, try to answer the sample questions.

Apply the test-taking strategies given. Keeping within the time limit suggested will give you a rough idea of how quickly you should work in order to complete the actual test.

Check your answers against the answer key. If you answered nearly all the questions correctly, you probably do not need to study the subject extensively. If you got about half the questions correct, you ought o review at least one textbook or other suggested materials on the subject. If you answered less than half the questions correctly, you will probably benefit from more extensive reading in the subject and thorough study of one or more textbooks. The textbooks listed are used at many colleges but they are not the only good texts. You will find helpful almost any standard text available to you., such as the textbook used at your college, or earlier editions of texts listed. For some examinations, topic outlines and textbooks may not be available. Take the sample tests in this book and check your answers at the end of each test. Check wrong answers.

Suggestions for Studying

The following suggestions have been gathered from people who have prepared for CLEP examinations or other college-level tests.

1. Define your goals and locate study materials

First, determine your study goals. Set aside a block of time to review the material provided in this book, and then decide which test(s) you will take. Using the suggestions, locate suitable resource materials. If a preparation course is offered by an adult school or college in your area, you might find it helpful to enroll.

2. Find a good place to study

To determine what kind of place you need for studying, ask yourself questions such as: Do I need a quiet place? Does the telephone distract me? Do objects I see in this place remind me of things I should do? Is it too warm? Is it well lit? Am I too comfortable here? Do I have space to spread out my materials? You may find the library more conducive to studying than your home. If you decide to study at home, you might prevent interruptions by other household members by putting a sign on the door of your study room to indicate when you will be available.

3. Schedule time to study

To help you determine where studying best fits into your schedule, try this exercise: Make a list of your daily activities (for example, sleeping, working, and eating) and estimate how many hours per day you spend on each activity. Now, rate all the activities on your list in order of their importance and evaluate your use of time. Often people are astonished at how an average day appears from this perspective. They may discover that they were unaware how large portions of time are spent, or they learn their time can be scheduled in alternative ways. For example, they can remove the least important activities from their day and devote that time to studying or another important activity.

4. Establish a study routine and a set of goals

In order to study effectively, you should establish specific goals and a schedule for accomplishing them. Some people find it helpful to write out a weekly schedule and cross out each study period when it is completed. Others maintain their concentration better by writing down the time when they expect to complete a study task. Most people find short periods of intense study more productive than long stretches of time. For example, they may follow a regular schedule of several 20- or 30-minute study periods with short breaks between them. Some people like to allow themselves rewards as they complete each study goal. It is not essential that you accomplish every goal exactly within your schedule; the point is to be committed to your task.

5. Learn how to take an active role in studying.

If you have not done much studying for some time, you may find it difficult to concentrate at first. Try a method of studying, such as the one outlined below, that will help you concentrate on and remember what you read.

    a. First, read the chapter summary and the introduction. Then you will know what to look for in your reading.

    b. Next, convert the section or paragraph headlines into questions. For example, if you are reading a section entitled, The Causes of the American Revolution, ask yourself: *What were the causes of the American Revolution?* Compose the answer as you read the paragraph. Reading and answering questions aloud will help you understand and remember the material.

c. Take notes on key ideas or concepts as you read. Writing will also help you fix concepts more firmly in your mind. Underlining key ideas or writing notes in your book can be helpful and will be useful for review. Underline only important points. If you underline more than a third of each paragraph, you are probably underlining too much.

d. If there are questions or problems at the end of a chapter, answer or solve them on paper as if you were asked to do them for homework. Mathematics textbooks (and some other books) sometimes include answers to some or all of the exercises. If you have such a book, write your answers before looking at the ones given. When problem-solving is involved, work enough problems to master the required methods and concepts. If you have difficulty with problems, review any sample problems or explanations in the chapter.

e. To retain knowledge, most people have to review the material periodically. If you are preparing for a test over an extended period of time, review key concepts and notes each week or so. Do not wait for weeks to review the material or you will need to relearn much of it.

Psychological and Physical Preparation

Most people feel at least some nervousness before taking a test. Adults who are returning to college may not have taken a test in many years or they may have had little experience with standardized tests. Some younger students, as well, are uncomfortable with testing situations. People who received their education in countries outside the United States may find that many tests given in this country are quite different from the ones they are accustomed to taking.

Not only might candidates find the types of tests and the kinds of questions on them unfamiliar, but other aspects of the testing environment may be strange as well. The physical and mental stress that results from meeting this new experience can hinder a candidate's ability to demonstrate his or her true degree of knowledge in the subject area being tested. For this reason, it is important to go to the test center well prepared, both mentally and physically, for taking the test. You may find the following suggestions helpful.

1. Familiarize yourself, as much as possible, with the test and the test situation before the day of the examination. It will be helpful for you to know ahead of time:

a. How much time will be allowed for the test and whether there are timed subsections.

b. What types of questions and directions appear on the examination.

c. How your test score will be computed.

d. How to properly answer the questions on the computer (See the CLEP Sample on the CLEP website)

e. In which building and room the examination will be administered. If you don't know where the building is, locate it or get directions ahead of time.

f. The time of the test administration. You might wish to confirm this information a day or two before the examination and find out what time the building and room will be open so that you can plan to arrive early.

g. Where to park your car or, if you wish to take public transportation, which bus or train to take and the location of the nearest stop.

h. Whether smoking will be permitted during the test.

i. Whether there will be a break between examinations (if you will be taking more than one on the same day), and whether there is a place nearby where you can get something to eat or drink.

2. Go to the test situation relaxed and alert. In order to prepare for the test:

a. Get a good night's sleep. Last minute cramming, particularly late the night before, is usually counterproductive.

b. Eat normally. It is usually not wise to skip breakfast or lunch on the day of the test or to eat a big meal just before the test.

c. Avoid tranquilizers and stimulants. If you follow the other directions in this book, you won't need artificial aids. It's better to be a little tense than to be drowsy, but stimulants such as coffee and cola can make you nervous and interfere with your concentration.

d. Don't drink a lot of liquids before the test. Having to leave the room during the test will disturb your concentration and take valuable time away from the test.

e. If you are inclined to be nervous or tense, learn some relaxation exercises and use them before and perhaps during the test.

3. Arrive for the test early and prepared. Be sure to:

a. Arrive early enough so that you can find a parking place, locate the test center, and get settled comfortably before testing begins. Allow some extra time in case you are delayed unexpectedly.

b. Take the following with you:

- Your completed Registration/Admission Form
- Two forms of identification – one being a government-issued photo ID with signature, such as a driver's license or passport
- Non-mechanical pencil
- A watch so that you can time your progress (digital watches are prohibited)
- Your glasses if you need them for reading or seeing the chalkboard or wall clock

      c. Leave all books, papers, and notes outside the test center. You will not be permitted to use your own scratch paper; it will be provided. Also prohibited are calculators, cell phones, beepers, pagers, photo/copy devices, radios, headphones, food, beverages, and several other items.

      d. Be prepared for any temperature in the testing room. Wear layers of clothing that can be removed if the room is too hot but will keep you warm if it is too cold.

4. When you enter the test room:

      a. Sit in a seat that provides a maximum of comfort and freedom from distraction.

      b. Read directions carefully, and listen to all instructions given by the test administrator. If you don't understand the directions, ask for help before test timing begins. If you must ask a question after the test has begun, raise your hand and a proctor will assist you. The proctor can answer certain kinds of questions but cannot help you with the test.

      c. Know your rights as a test taker. You can expect to be given the full working time allowed for the test(s) and a reasonably quiet and comfortable place in which to work. If a poor test situation is preventing you from doing your best, ask if the situation can be remedied. If bad test conditions cannot be remedied, ask the person in charge to report the problem in the Irregularity Report that will be sent to ETS with the answer sheets. You may also wish to contact CLEP. Describe the exact circumstances as completely as you can. Be sure to include the test date and name(s) of the test(s) you took. ETS will investigate the problem to make sure it does not happen again, and, if the problem is serious enough, may arrange for you to retake the test without charge.

TAKING THE EXAMINATIONS

A person may know a great deal about the subject being tested, but not do as well as he or she is capable of on the test. Knowing how to approach a test is an important part of the testing process. While a command of test-taking skills cannot substitute for knowledge of the subject matter, it can be a significant factor in successful testing.

Test-taking skills enable a person to use all available information to earn a score that truly reflects his or her ability. There are different strategies for approaching different kinds of test questions. For example, free-response questions require a very different tack than do multiple-choice questions. Other factors, such as how the test will be graded, may also influence your approach to the test and your use of test time. Thus, your preparation for a test should include finding out all you can about the test so that you can use the most effective test-taking strategies.

Before taking a test, you should know approximately how many questions are on the test, how much time you will be allowed, how the test will be scored or graded, what types of questions and directions are on the test, and how you will be required to record your answers.

Taking Multiple-Choice Tests

1. Listen carefully to the instructions given by the test administrator and read carefully all directions before you begin to answer the questions.

2. Note the time that the test administrator starts timing the test. As you proceed, make sure that you are not working too slowly. You should have answered at least half the questions in a section when half the time for that section has passed. If you have not reached that point in the section, speed up your pace on the remaining questions.

3. Before answering a question, read the entire question, including all the answer choices. Don't think that because the first or second answer choice looks good to you, it isn't necessary to read the remaining options. Instructions usually tell you to select the best answer. Sometimes one answer choice is partially correct, but another option is better; therefore, it is usually a good idea to read all the answers before you choose one.

4. Read and consider every question. Questions that look complicated at first glance may not actually be so difficult once you have read them carefully.

5. Do not puzzle too long over any one question. If you don't know the answer after you've considered it briefly, go on to the next question. Make sure you return to the question later.

6. Make sure you record your response properly.

7. In trying to determine the correct answer, you may find it helpful to cross out those options that you know are incorrect, and to make marks next to those you think might be correct. If you decide to skip the question and come back to it later, you will save yourself the time of reconsidering all the options.

8. Watch for the following key words in test questions:

all	generally	never	perhaps
always	however	none	rarely
but	may	not	seldom
except	must	often	sometimes
every	necessary	only	usually

When a question or answer option contains words such as always, every, only, never, and none, there can be no exceptions to the answer you choose. Use of words such as often, rarely, sometimes, and generally indicates that there may be some exceptions to the answer.

9. Do not waste your time looking for clues to right answers based on flaws in question wording or patterns in correct answers. Professionals at the College Board and ETS put

a great deal of effort into developing valid, reliable, fair tests. CLEP test development committees are composed of college faculty who are experts in the subject covered by the test and are appointed by the College Board to write test questions and to scrutinize each question that is included on a CLEP test. Committee members make every effort to ensure that the questions are not ambiguous, that they have only one correct answer, and that they cover college-level topics. These committees do not intentionally include trick questions. If you think a question is flawed, ask the test administrator to report it, or contact CLEP immediately.

Taking Free-Response or Essay Tests

If your college requires the optional free-response or essay portion of a CLEP Composition and Literature exams, you should do some additional preparation for your CLEP test. Taking an essay test is very different from taking a multiple-choice test, so you will need to use some other strategies.

The essay written as part of the English Composition and Essay exam is graded by English professors from a variety of colleges and universities. A process called holistic scoring is used to rate your writing ability.

The optional free-response essays, on the other hand, are graded by the faculty of the college you designate as a score recipient. Guidelines and criteria for grading essays are not specified by the College Board or ETS. You may find it helpful, therefore, to talk with someone at your college to find out what criteria will be used to determine whether you will get credit. If the test requires essay responses, ask how much emphasis will be placed on your writing ability and your ability to organize your thoughts as opposed to your knowledge of subject matter. Find out how much weight will be given to your multiple-choice test score in comparison with your free-response grade in determining whether you will get credit. This will give you an idea where you should expend the greatest effort in preparing for and taking the test.

Here are some strategies you will find useful in taking any essay test:

1. Before you begin to write, read all questions carefully and take a few minutes to jot down some ideas you might include in each answer.

2. If you are given a choice of questions to answer, choose the questions you think you can answer most clearly and knowledgeably.

3. Determine in what order you will answer the questions. Answer those you find the easiest first so that any extra time can be spent on the more difficult questions.

4. When you know which questions you will answer and in what order, determine how much testing time remains and estimate how many minutes you will devote to each question. Unless suggested times are given for the questions or one question appears to require more or less time than the others, allot an equal amount of time to each question.

5. Before answering each question, indicate the number of the question as it is given in the test book. You need not copy the entire question from the question sheet, but it will be helpful to you and to the person grading your test if you indicate briefly the topic you are addressing – particularly if you are not answering the questions in the order in which they appear on the test.

6. Before answering each question, read it again carefully to make sure you are interpreting it correctly. Underline key words, such as those listed below, that often appear in free-response questions. Be sure you know the exact meaning of these words before taking the test.

analyze	demonstrate	enumerate	list
apply	derive	explain	outline
assess	describe	generalize	prove
compare	determine	illustrate	rank
contrast	discuss	interpret	show
define	distinguish	justify	summarize

If a question asks you to outline, define, or summarize, do not write a detailed explanation; if a question asks you to analyze, explain, illustrate, interpret, or show, you must do more than briefly describe the topic.

For a current listing of CLEP Colleges

where you can get credit and be tested, write:

CLEP, P.O. Box 6600, Princeton, NJ 08541-6600

Or e-mail: clep@ets.org, or call: (609) 771-7865

GENERAL (INTRODUCTORY) PSYCHOLOGY

DESCRIPTION OF THE TEST
   The General Psychology examination covers material that is usually taught in a one-semester undergraduate course in introductory psychology. It stresses basic facts, concepts, and generally accepted principles. Among the topics included on the test are learning and cognition, behavior, personality, perception, motivation and emotion, life-span development, and social psychology.

   The test is 90 minutes long and contains approximately 95-100 multiple-choice questions to be answered in two separately timed 45-minute sections.

KNOWLEDGE AND SKILLS REQUIRED
The General Psychology examination requires knowledge of the following areas of psychology:

- Physiology and behavior
    - The nervous system
    - The endocrine system
    - Behavioral genetics
- Perceptual and sensory experience
    - Sensory functions (acuity, color zones, adaptation)
    - Contextual and psychological influences on perception
    - Altered consciousness
- Motivation and emotion
    - Sources and nature
    - Relation to performance
- Learning
    - Verbal and cognitive
    - Motor skills learning; memory and study
    - Classical and operant conditioning
- Cognition
    - Concept formation
    - Problem solving
    - Intelligence
    - Creativity
- Life-span development
    - Physical, behavioral, and cognitive
    - Theories
- Personality and adjustment
    - Major theories
    - Defense mechanisms
    - Stress, anxiety, and conflict
    - Psychosomatic factors
- Behavioral disorders
    - Types of disorders
    - Approaches to treatment

For instructional purposes from the official announcement ©CEEB

- ❖ Social psychology
    - Interpersonal relations
    - The socialization process (race, culture, sex)
    - Group processes
    - Attitudes and attitude change
- ❖ Measurement and statistics
    - Problems and techniques of measurement and assessment
    - Research methods
    - Interpretation of statistics
- ❖ History and philosophy
    - Major theories

Questions on the test require candidates to demonstrate either or both of the following:

- Knowledge of terminology, principles, theory
- Ability to comprehend, evaluate, or analyze problem situations and to apply knowledge to new situations

SAMPLE QUESTIONS

The 25 questions given here are similar to questions on the General Psychology examination, but they do not actually appear on the examination.

Before attempting to answer the sample questions, read all the information about the General Psychology examination given above.

Try to answer correctly as many questions as possible within 25 minutes. Then compare your answers with the correct answers on the last page.

Directions: Each of the questions or incomplete statements below is followed by five suggested answers or completions. Select the one that is BEST in each case.

1. The point of functional contact between two nerve cells is called
    A. feedback   B. threshold   C. axon   D. dendrite   E. synapse

2. Of the following species, which exhibits the GREATEST amount of variation in sexual behavior?
    A. Frog   B. Dog   C. Goldfish   D. Robin   E. Chimpanzee

3. The total number of chromosomes found in a human cell is
    A. 16   B. 20   C. 46   D. 86   E. 102

4. Shortly after learning to associate the word dog with certain four-legged furry animals, young children will frequently misidentify a cow or a horse as a dog. This phenomenon may be viewed as an example of
    A. differentiation
    B. negative transfer
    C. imprinting
    D. stimulus generalization
    E. linear perspective

5. In adults, total sensory deprivation for long periods of time (such as two or three days) produces
   A. a feeling of well-being similar to that achieved through meditation
   B. no change in emotions or cognition, provided the subject was mentally stable before the isolation
   C. increased efficiency in the senses of sight, hearing, and touch
   D. profound apathy and a subjective sensation of powerlessness
   E. hallucinations and impaired efficiency in all areas of intellectual functioning

5.____

6. The portion of the performance curve above marked X represents
   A. extinction
   B. a plateau
   C. spontaneous recovery
   D. serial position effect
   E. response generalization

6.____

7. Compared to boys, girls experience which of the following earlier?
   A. Moral maturity
   B. Growth spurt
   C. Intellectual achievement
   D. Athletic competence
   E. Self-actualization

7.____

8. Research on the effectiveness of psychotherapy has PRIMARILY indicated that
   A. psychotherapists differ among themselves as to what constitutes a cure
   B. nondirective techniques are generally superior to directive ones
   C. the effectiveness of a method depends on the length of time a therapist was trained in the method
   D. psychoanalysis is the most effective technique for eliminating behavior disorders
   E. psychoanalysis is the most effective technique for curing neuroses

8.____

9. If on the last day of a psychology class a student is asked to remember what was done in class each day during the term, she will likely be able to remember best the activities of the first and last class meetings.
   This situation is an example of
   A. retroactive inhibition
   B. positive transfer
   C. the serial position effect
   D. interference
   E. short-term memory

9.____

10. Frank's first impulse, when insulted by an acquaintance, was to strike the person. He was observed to yell loudly and to kick a door several times; after this he no longer seemed to feel like assaulting his acquaintance.
    This means of reducing aggressive impulses exemplifies which of the following?
    A. Repression
    B. Abreaction
    C. Displacement
    D. Cathexis
    E. Sublimation

10.____

11. Infant monkeys raised with two mother surrogates, one of bare wire and one of terry-cloth covered wire, spend more time with the mother surrogate that
    A. feeds them
    B. looks more like a monkey
    C. provides comforting contact
    D. is easier to cling to
    E. is more familiar to them

12. Studies concerning bystander intervention or help-giving in emergency situations suggest that a victim is MOST likely to receive help if
    A. the bystanders are of high intelligence
    B. the bystanders are of low intelligence
    C. several bystanders are present
    D. only a single bystander is present
    E. both male and female bystanders are present

13. Without repetition, material can be retained in short-term memory for maximum periods of several
    A. seconds
    B. minutes
    C. hours
    D. days
    E. weeks

14. Which of the following is usually true of a child's early imitation of adult speech? It
    A. is an exact replication of what was said
    B. does not include the less important words
    C. has changes in the order of the words that were said
    D. is an accurate replication of the first part but leaves off the last part
    E. is an accurate replication of the first part but leaves off the first part

15. Which of the following statements does NOT accurately describe the retina?
    A. The rods are more dense in the fovea than in the periphery.
    B. The blind spot is closer to the fovea than to the edge of the retina.
    C. The image on the retina is upside down.
    D. It is located at the back of the eye.
    E. It contains two kinds of receptors: rods and cones.

16. Which of the following is a TRUE statement about the relationship between test validity and test reliability?
    A. A test can be reliable without being valid.
    B. A test that has high face validity will have high reliability.
    C. A test that has low face validity will have low reliability.
    D. The higher the test's validity, the lower its reliability will be.
    E. The validity of a test always exceeds its reliability

17. Proactive inhibition describes a process by which
    A. people remember digits better than words
    B. people remember images better than words
    C. people remember elements in pairs
    D. prior learning interferes with subsequent learning
    E. subsequent learning interferes with prior learning

18. In the use of which of the following explanatory concepts do learning theory and psychoanalysis differ LEAST?
    A. Events that occurred in the individual's past
    B. Psychosexual conflicts that remain unresolved
    C. Intrapsychic forces
    D. Instinctive urges
    E. Complex conceptualizations of unobservable tendencies

19. The process of concealing insisting on the opposite unacceptable motivations is called by
    A. reaction formation
    B. denial
    C. conflict
    D. inhibition
    E. extinction

20. In an approach/avoidance conflict, which of the following increases MOST rapidly as the person nears the goal?
    A. Approach gradient
    B. Avoidance gradient
    C. Reinforcement potential
    D. Behavioral potential
    E. Valence

21. Which of the following correlation coefficients indicates the STRONGEST relationship between two variables?
    A. -.92   B. -.37   C. .02   D. .50   E. .8

22. *Give me a dozen healthy infants, well-formed, and my own specified world to bring them up in and I'll guarantee to take anyone at random and train him to become any type of specialist I might select ...*
    This statement was made by
    A. James
    B. Thorndike
    C. Watson
    D. Wertheimer
    E. Woodworth

23. If the old problem of heredity or environment is seen as essentially meaningless today in terms of understanding behavior, which of the following questions is also meaningless or of little import?
    A. Which of the various genetic potentialities will be activated as a result of the individual's life experience?
    B. What limits are placed on personality development by hereditary factors?
    C. Does heredity determine such complex characteristics as intelligence, emotional imbalance, and a mild disposition?
    D. How can one identify the presence of hereditary influence in a certain area?
    E. How does early experience influence perceptual development?

24. Terms such as apprehension, life space, self-actualization, free will, and decision are to be found in which of the following types of personality theories?
    A. Behavioristic
    B. Phenomenological
    C. Biological
    D. Cognitive dissonance
    E. Psychoanalytical

25. A young child breaks his cookie into a number of pieces and asserts that *now there is more to eat*.
    In Piaget's analysis, the child might well be giving evidence of
    A. formal logical operations
    B. concrete logical operations
    C. visual deficit
    D. preoperational thought
    E. sensorimotor analysis

25._____

KEY (CORRECT ANSWERS)

1. E	11. C
2. E	12. D
3. C	13. A
4. D	14. B
5. E	15. A
6. B	16. A
7. B	17. D
8. A	18. A
9. C	19. B
10. C	20. B

21. A
22. C
23. C
24. B
25. D

HOW TO TAKE A TEST

You have studied long, hard and conscientiously.

With your official admission card in hand, and your heart pounding, you have been admitted to the examination room.

You note that there are several hundred other applicants in the examination room waiting to take the same test.

They all appear to be equally well prepared.

You know that nothing but your best effort will suffice. The "moment of truth" is at hand: you now have to demonstrate objectively, in writing, your knowledge of content and your understanding of subject matter.

You are fighting the most important battle of your life—to pass and/or score high on an examination which will determine your career and provide the economic basis for your livelihood.

What extra, special things should you know and should you do in taking the examination?

I. YOU MUST PASS AN EXAMINATION

A. WHAT EVERY CANDIDATE SHOULD KNOW
Examination applicants often ask us for help in preparing for the written test. What can I study in advance? What kinds of questions will be asked? How will the test be given? How will the papers be graded?

B. HOW ARE EXAMS DEVELOPED?
Examinations are carefully written by trained technicians who are specialists in the field known as "psychological measurement," in consultation with recognized authorities in the field of work that the test will cover. These experts recommend the subject matter areas or skills to be tested; only those knowledges or skills important to your success on the job are included. The most reliable books and source materials available are used as references. Together, the experts and technicians judge the difficulty level of the questions.
Test technicians know how to phrase questions so that the problem is clearly stated. Their ethics do not permit "trick" or "catch" questions. Questions may have been tried out on sample groups, or subjected to statistical analysis, to determine their usefulness.
Written tests are often used in combination with performance tests, ratings of training and experience, and oral interviews. All of these measures combine to form the best-known means of finding the right person for the right job.

II. HOW TO PASS THE WRITTEN TEST

A. BASIC STEPS

1) Study the announcement

How, then, can you know what subjects to study? Our best answer is: "Learn as much as possible about the class of positions for which you've applied." The exam will test the knowledge, skills and abilities needed to do the work.

Your most valuable source of information about the position you want is the official exam announcement. This announcement lists the training and experience qualifications. Check these standards and apply only if you come reasonably close to meeting them. Many jurisdictions preview the written test in the exam announcement by including a section called "Knowledge and Abilities Required," "Scope of the Examination," or some similar heading. Here you will find out specifically what fields will be tested.

2) Choose appropriate study materials

If the position for which you are applying is technical or advanced, you will read more advanced, specialized material. If you are already familiar with the basic principles of your field, elementary textbooks would waste your time. Concentrate on advanced textbooks and technical periodicals. Think through the concepts and review difficult problems in your field.

These are all general sources. You can get more ideas on your own initiative, following these leads. For example, training manuals and publications of the government agency which employs workers in your field can be useful, particularly for technical and professional positions. A letter or visit to the government department involved may result in more specific study suggestions, and certainly will provide you with a more definite idea of the exact nature of the position you are seeking.

3) Study this book!

III. KINDS OF TESTS

Tests are used for purposes other than measuring knowledge and ability to perform specified duties. For some positions, it is equally important to test ability to make adjustments to new situations or to profit from training. In others, basic mental abilities not dependent on information are essential. Questions which test these things may not appear as pertinent to the duties of the position as those which test for knowledge and information. Yet they are often highly important parts of a fair examination. For very general questions, it is almost impossible to help you direct your study efforts. What we can do is to point out some of the more common of these general abilities needed in public service positions and describe some typical questions.

1) General information

Broad, general information has been found useful for predicting job success in some kinds of work. This is tested in a variety of ways, from vocabulary lists to questions about current events. Basic background in some field of work, such as sociology or economics, may be sampled in a group of questions. Often these are principles which have become familiar to most persons through exposure rather than through formal training. It is difficult to advise you how to study for these questions; being alert to the world around you is our best suggestion.

2) Verbal ability

An example of an ability needed in many positions is verbal or language ability. Verbal ability is, in brief, the ability to use and understand words. Vocabulary and grammar tests are typical measures of this ability. Reading comprehension or paragraph interpretation questions are common in many kinds of civil service tests. You are given a paragraph of written material and asked to find its central meaning.

IV. KINDS OF QUESTIONS

1. Multiple-choice Questions

Most popular of the short-answer questions is the "multiple choice" or "best answer" question. It can be used, for example, to test for factual knowledge, ability to solve problems or judgment in meeting situations found at work.

A multiple-choice question is normally one of three types:
- It can begin with an incomplete statement followed by several possible endings. You are to find the one ending which best completes the statement, although some of the others may not be entirely wrong.
- It can also be a complete statement in the form of a question which is answered by choosing one of the statements listed.
- It can be in the form of a problem – again you select the best answer.

Here is an example of a multiple-choice question with a discussion which should give you some clues as to the method for choosing the right answer:

When an employee has a complaint about his assignment, the action which will best help him overcome his difficulty is to
- A. discuss his difficulty with his coworkers
- B. take the problem to the head of the organization
- C. take the problem to the person who gave him the assignment
- D. say nothing to anyone about his complaint

In answering this question, you should study each of the choices to find which is best. Consider choice "A" – Certainly an employee may discuss his complaint with fellow employees, but no change or improvement can result, and the complaint remains unresolved. Choice "B" is a poor choice since the head of the organization probably does not know what assignment you have been given, and taking your problem to him is known as "going over the head" of the supervisor. The supervisor, or person who made the assignment, is the person who can clarify it or correct any injustice. Choice "C" is, therefore, correct. To say nothing, as in choice "D," is unwise. Supervisors have and interest in knowing the problems employees are facing, and the employee is seeking a solution to his problem.

2. True/False

3. Matching Questions

Matching an answer from a column of choices within another column.

V. RECORDING YOUR ANSWERS

Computer terminals are used more and more today for many different kinds of exams.

For an examination with very few applicants, you may be told to record your answers in the test booklet itself. Separate answer sheets are much more common. If this separate answer sheet is to be scored by machine – and this is often the case – it is highly important that you mark your answers correctly in order to get credit.

VI. BEFORE THE TEST

YOUR PHYSICAL CONDITION IS IMPORTANT

If you are not well, you can't do your best work on tests. If you are half asleep, you can't do your best either. Here are some tips:

1) Get about the same amount of sleep you usually get. Don't stay up all night before the test, either partying or worrying—DON'T DO IT!
2) If you wear glasses, be sure to wear them when you go to take the test. This goes for hearing aids, too.
3) If you have any physical problems that may keep you from doing your best, be sure to tell the person giving the test. If you are sick or in poor health, you relay cannot do your best on any test. You can always come back and take the test some other time.

Common sense will help you find procedures to follow to get ready for an examination. Too many of us, however, overlook these sensible measures. Indeed, nervousness and fatigue have been found to be the most serious reasons why applicants fail to do their best on civil service tests. Here is a list of reminders:

- Begin your preparation early – Don't wait until the last minute to go scurrying around for books and materials or to find out what the position is all about.
- Prepare continuously – An hour a night for a week is better than an all-night cram session. This has been definitely established. What is more, a night a week for a month will return better dividends than crowding your study into a shorter period of time.
- Locate the place of the exam – You have been sent a notice telling you when and where to report for the examination. If the location is in a different town or otherwise unfamiliar to you, it would be well to inquire the best route and learn something about the building.
- Relax the night before the test – Allow your mind to rest. Do not study at all that night. Plan some mild recreation or diversion; then go to bed early and get a good night's sleep.
- Get up early enough to make a leisurely trip to the place for the test – This way unforeseen events, traffic snarls, unfamiliar buildings, etc. will not upset you.
- Dress comfortably – A written test is not a fashion show. You will be known by number and not by name, so wear something comfortable.
- Leave excess paraphernalia at home – Shopping bags and odd bundles will get in your way. You need bring only the items mentioned in the official notice you received; usually everything you need is provided. Do not bring reference books to the exam. They will only confuse those last minutes and be taken away from you when in the test room.

- Arrive somewhat ahead of time – If because of transportation schedules you must get there very early, bring a newspaper or magazine to take your mind off yourself while waiting.
- Locate the examination room – When you have found the proper room, you will be directed to the seat or part of the room where you will sit. Sometimes you are given a sheet of instructions to read while you are waiting. Do not fill out any forms until you are told to do so; just read them and be prepared.
- Relax and prepare to listen to the instructions
- If you have any physical problem that may keep you from doing your best, be sure to tell the test administrator. If you are sick or in poor health, you really cannot do your best on the exam. You can come back and take the test some other time.

VII. AT THE TEST

The day of the test is here and you have the test booklet in your hand. The temptation to get going is very strong. Caution! There is more to success than knowing the right answers. You must know how to identify your papers and understand variations in the type of short-answer question used in this particular examination. Follow these suggestions for maximum results from your efforts:

1) Cooperate with the monitor

The test administrator has a duty to create a situation in which you can be as much at ease as possible. He will give instructions, tell you when to begin, check to see that you are marking your answer sheet correctly, and so on. He is not there to guard you, although he will see that your competitors do not take unfair advantage. He wants to help you do your best.

2) Listen to all instructions

Don't jump the gun! Wait until you understand all directions. In most civil service tests you get more time than you need to answer the questions. So don't be in a hurry. Read each word of instructions until you clearly understand the meaning. Study the examples, listen to all announcements and follow directions. Ask questions if you do not understand what to do.

3) Identify your papers

Civil service exams are usually identified by number only. You will be assigned a number; you must not put your name on your test papers. Be sure to copy your number correctly. Since more than one exam may be given, copy your exact examination title.

4) Plan your time

Unless you are told that a test is a "speed" or "rate of work" test, speed itself is usually not important. Time enough to answer all the questions will be provided, but this does not mean that you have all day. An overall time limit has been set. Divide the total time (in minutes) by the number of questions to determine the approximate time you have for each question.

5) Do not linger over difficult questions

If you come across a difficult question, mark it with a paper clip (useful to have along) and come back to it when you have been through the booklet. One caution if you do this – be sure to skip a number on your answer sheet as well. Check often to be sure that you have not lost your place and that you are marking in the row numbered the same as the question you are answering.

6) Read the questions
Be sure you know what the question asks! Many capable people are unsuccessful because they failed to read the questions correctly.

7) Answer all questions
Unless you have been instructed that a penalty will be deducted for incorrect answers, it is better to guess than to omit a question.

8) Speed tests
It is often better NOT to guess on speed tests. It has been found that on timed tests people are tempted to spend the last few seconds before time is called in marking answers at random – without even reading them – in the hope of picking up a few extra points. To discourage this practice, the instructions may warn you that your score will be "corrected" for guessing. That is, a penalty will be applied. The incorrect answers will be deducted from the correct ones, or some other penalty formula will be used.

9) Review your answers
If you finish before time is called, go back to the questions you guessed or omitted to give them further thought. Review other answers if you have time.

10) Return your test materials
If you are ready to leave before others have finished or time is called, take ALL your materials to the monitor and leave quietly. Never take any test material with you. The monitor can discover whose papers are not complete, and taking a test booklet may be grounds for disqualification.

VIII. EXAMINATION TECHNIQUES

1) Read the general instructions carefully. These are usually printed on the first page of the exam booklet. As a rule, these instructions refer to the timing of the examination; the fact that you should not start work until the signal and must stop work at a signal, etc. If there are any special instructions, such as a choice of questions to be answered, make sure that you note this instruction carefully.

2) When you are ready to start work on the examination, that is as soon as the signal has been given, read the instructions to each question booklet, underline any key words or phrases, such as least, best, outline, describe and the like. In this way you will tend to answer as requested rather than discover on reviewing your paper that you listed without describing, that you selected the worst choice rather than the best choice, etc.

3) If the examination is of the objective or multiple-choice type – that is, each question will also give a series of possible answers: A, B, C or D, and you are called upon to select the best answer and write the letter next to that answer on your answer paper – it is advisable to start answering each question in turn. There may be anywhere from 50 to 100 such questions in the three or four hours allotted and you can see how much time would be taken if you read through all the questions before beginning to answer any. Furthermore, if you

come across a question or group of questions which you know would be difficult to answer, it would undoubtedly affect your handling of all the other questions.

4) If the examination is of the essay type and contains but a few questions, it is a moot point as to whether you should read all the questions before starting to answer any one. Of course, if you are given a choice – say five out of seven and the like – then it is essential to read all the questions so you can eliminate the two that are most difficult. If, however, you are asked to answer all the questions, there may be danger in trying to answer the easiest one first because you may find that you will spend too much time on it. The best technique is to answer the first question, then proceed to the second, etc.

5) Time your answers. Before the exam begins, write down the time it started, then add the time allowed for the examination and write down the time it must be completed, then divide the time available somewhat as follows:
   - If 3-1/2 hours are allowed, that would be 210 minutes. If you have 80 objective-type questions, that would be an average of 2-1/2 minutes per question. Allow yourself no more than 2 minutes per question, or a total of 160 minutes, which will permit about 50 minutes to review.
   - If for the time allotment of 210 minutes there are 7 essay questions to answer, that would average about 30 minutes a question. Give yourself only 25 minutes per question so that you have about 35 minutes to review.

6) The most important instruction is to read each question and make sure you know what is wanted. The second most important instruction is to time yourself properly so that you answer every question. The third most important instruction is to answer every question. Guess if you have to but include something for each question. Remember that you will receive no credit for a blank and will probably receive some credit if you write something in answer to an essay question. If you guess a letter – say "B" for a multiple-choice question – you may have guessed right. If you leave a blank as an answer to a multiple-choice question, the examiners may respect your feelings but it will not add a point to your score. Some exams may penalize you for wrong answers, so in such cases only, you may not want to guess unless you have some basis for your answer.

7) Suggestions
   a. Objective-type questions
      1. Examine the question booklet for proper sequence of pages and questions
      2. Read all instructions carefully
      3. Skip any question which seems too difficult; return to it after all other questions have been answered
      4. Apportion your time properly; do not spend too much time on any single question or group of questions
      5. Note and underline key words – all, most, fewest, least, best, worst, same, opposite, etc.
      6. Pay particular attention to negatives
      7. Note unusual option, e.g., unduly long, short, complex, different or similar in content to the body of the question
      8. Observe the use of "hedging" words – probably, may, most likely, etc.

9. Make sure that your answer is put next to the same number as the question
10. Do not second-guess unless you have good reason to believe the second answer is definitely more correct
11. Cross out original answer if you decide another answer is more accurate; do not erase until you are ready to hand your paper in
12. Answer all questions; guess unless instructed otherwise
13. Leave time for review

b. Essay questions
   1. Read each question carefully
   2. Determine exactly what is wanted. Underline key words or phrases.
   3. Decide on outline or paragraph answer
   4. Include many different points and elements unless asked to develop any one or two points or elements
   5. Show impartiality by giving pros and cons unless directed to select one side only
   6. Make and write down any assumptions you find necessary to answer the questions
   7. Watch your English, grammar, punctuation and choice of words
   8. Time your answers; don't crowd material

8) Answering the essay question

Most essay questions can be answered by framing the specific response around several key words or ideas. Here are a few such key words or ideas:

M's: manpower, materials, methods, money, management
P's: purpose, program, policy, plan, procedure, practice, problems, pitfalls, personnel, public relations

a. Six basic steps in handling problems:
   1. Preliminary plan and background development
   2. Collect information, data and facts
   3. Analyze and interpret information, data and facts
   4. Analyze and develop solutions as well as make recommendations
   5. Prepare report and sell recommendations
   6. Install recommendations and follow up effectiveness

b. Pitfalls to avoid
1. Taking things for granted – A statement of the situation does not necessarily imply that each of the elements is necessarily true; for example, a complaint may be invalid and biased so that all that can be taken for granted is that a complaint has been registered
2. Considering only one side of a situation – Wherever possible, indicate several alternatives and then point out the reasons you selected the best one
3. Failing to indicate follow up – Whenever your answer indicates action on your part, make certain that you will take proper follow-up action to see how successful your recommendations, procedures or actions turn out to be
4. Taking too long in answering any single question – Remember to time your answers properly

EXAMINATION SECTION

EXAMINATION SECTION
TEST 1

DIRECTIONS: Each question or incomplete statement is followed by several suggested answers or completions. Select the one that BEST answers the question or completes the statement. *PRINT THE LETTER OF THE CORRECT ANSWER IN THE SPACE AT THE RIGHT.*

1. Arthur had always been extremely homesick whenever he was away from his parents. After graduation from high school, he attended a large university over 300 miles from his home but became so depressed and homesick he had to leave. He is now living at home and happily attending a local college.
   What is an objective evaluation of the situation described?
   A. This situation was handled by lowering the level of adjustment that the individual felt was necessary to cope effectively with the situation.
   B. This tension-producing situation was handled by making the individual feel better able to handle the situation.
   C. This indicates an escape or avoidance of the problem; e.g., the individual has not really solved the basic problem.

   1.____

2. A tree 100 yards away may project an image on the retina no larger than that of a toothpick a foot away. Despite this fact, the tree is perceived as being quite large.
   This paradox is MOST closely related to which of the following?
   A. We become adapted to ignore certain aspects of our environment, and these aspects will be defined largely by our cultural background.
   B. Knowing a magician's trick destroys the illusion.
   C. The size of the retinal image is a direct function of the size of the object and an inverse function of the distance of the object.
   D. Snow looks white even in poor illumination.

   2.____

3. A psychiatrist found that 90% of the patients receiving electro-shock treatment for involutional melancholia recovered within three weeks. He concluded that the treatment was useful in the treatment of this disease.
   In the study described above, which assumption was IMPLICITLY made by the investigator in arriving at his conclusion? (In other words, what assumption would one have to make in order to arrive at the conclusion he reached?)
   ASSUMPTIONS:
   I. No other type of treatment would have been so effective.
   II. No patient would have recovered in three weeks without the treatment.
   III. Involutional melancholia must be an organic disease if it can be treated with physical methods.
   IV. Electro-shock is more appropriate than other forms of treatment for this disease.
   V. Less than 90% would have recovered in three weeks without treatment.

   THE CORRECT assumption is:
   A. I   B. II   C. III   D. IV   E. V

   3.____

Questions 4-7.

DIRECTIONS: Questions 4 through 7 are to be answered on the basis of the following information.

An experiment was designed to determine whether noise will affect the amount of food that rats will eat in a given period. Two groups of twenty male rats, matched according to age, weight, and health, were chosen. For four weeks one group of rats was subjected to a loud noise while feeding and the other group was fed under regular conditions. The amount of food given each rat was carefully weighed before each feeding, and the amount uneaten was weighed after each feeding.
Select the CORRECT answer for each question from the following key:
I. The amount of time the rats took to eat.
II. The loud noise
III. The amount of food eaten
IV. The emotionality of the rats
V. The weight of the rats

4. The independent variable is
   A. I   B. II   C. III   D. IV   E. V

5. The dependent variable is
   A. I   B. II   C. III   D. IV   E. V

6. An uncontrolled variable of possible importance is
   A. I   B. II   C. III   D. IV   E. V

7. A controlled variable is
   A. I   B. II   C. III   D. IV   E. V

8. In an experiment to determine the influence of caffeine on learning ability, equal numbers of male and female subjects were used in the experimental and control groups. Constituting the groups in this manner illustrates
   A. the dependent variable
   B. that sex is assumed to have little to do with learning
   C. a controlled variable
   D. non-random sampling

9. You say "Hi Willie," to someone who, on second glance, turns out to be a complete stranger. This is an example of
   A. response generalization
   B. serial position effect
   C. competing response
   D. avoidance conditioning
   E. stimulus generalization

10. Which of these statements is the BEST advice from the standpoint of good mental health?
    A. Face the situation without involvement
    B. Accept your own feelings as something natural and normal
    C. Avoid conflicts
    D. Try not to think about our problems
    E. Don't worry pointlessly about problems

10.____

11. Your find, upon returning home, that Sasha, your new cocker spaniel puppy, has wet the carpet. You decide to punish him now for his breach of etiquette. You do this time after time. Sasha never becomes housebroken.
    Which of the following conditions of learning has NOT been met?
    A. Reinforcement   B. Repetition   C. Set   D. Contiguity

11.____

12. A certain college dean preferred to keep his watch in his vest pocket but his wife thought him old-fashioned and transferred the watch to his trousers pocket each morning. Although for a while he continued to fumble in his vest pocket when he wanted to know the time, he eventually made the correct movement. The MOST appropriate term to describe his behavior is
    A. avoidance conditioning   B. discrimination
    C. stimulus generalization   D. spontaneous recovery
    E. experimental extinction

12.____

Questions 13-17.

DIRECTIONS: Questions 13 through 17 are to be answered on the basis of the following statement to discover the writer's point of view.

Customs enshrined in the family in any tribe or nation are likely to be sensitively adjusted to the values and customs of each particular people. This is no mystic correspondence; the persons who make up the family are the same people who are the citizens of that nation – the businessmen, the farmers, the churchgoers or non-churchgoers, the readers of newspapers, and the listeners to the radio. In all their roles they are molded more or less surely into a people with certain habits, certain hopes, and a certain *esprit de corps*. Americans come to share certain slogans, behavior, and judgments which differ from those of Frenchmen or Czechs. This is inevitable. And in the process the role of the family also becomes different. By the same token, just as economic and political changes occur over a period of time in the United States or in France or in Czechoslovakia, the family also changes.

13. To the writer, the authoritarian family in the United States
    A. is more prevalent than any other type
    B. is necessary if the family as an institution is to be preserved
    C. is the most persistent form of daily organization
    D. is merely an ideal
    E. would be out of harmony with our other institutions

13.____

14. If the writer were to study the family in a particular culture, he would probably be MOST concerned with
    A. the internal power structure
    B. its performance of the traditional functions of the family
    C. its consistency with the general way of life
    D. the relative freedom granted to individual members
    E. the place of the family in the general culture pattern

15. In a dynamic society such as the United States, the changes which have taken place in the family are
    A. a consequence of the amalgamation of other cultures
    B. generally improvements
    C. the cause rather than the result of other social changes
    D. relatively slow
    E. to be expected

16. To the writer, the phrase "failure of the family" would PROBABLY
    A. accurately describe American society
    B. be reflected in our rising incidence of mental illness
    C. have no absolute meaning
    D. be the cause of most of our social ills
    E. be more true of the United States than France

17. The writer PROBABLY would be inclined to view our high divorce rate as a product of our
    A. lax divorce laws
    B. economic tensions
    C. marriage laws
    D. weakened moral standards
    E. emphasis on individualism

Questions 18-25.

DIRECTIONS: Questions 18 through 25 are to be answered on the basis of the following key:

Select answer
 I. If the problem is capable of empirical solution as stated
 II. If the problem requires some reformulation in order to be tested
 III. If the problem is, by its very nature, non-empirical and thus incapable of solution on the basis of factual evidence

18. Children from high-income families are more likely to develop social adaptability than children from low-income families.
    The CORRECT answer is:
    A. I   B. II   C. III

19. Can a randomly selected group without any special training communicate messages without the usual sensory and physical channels?
    The CORRECT answer is:
    A. I   B. II   C. III

20. Is light punishment the best way to discipline children? 20.____
    The CORRECT answer is:
    A. I   B. II   C. III

21. Is it wrong to spank children? 21.____
    The CORRECT answer is:
    A. I   B. II   C. III

22. Are amoebae capable of learning to move toward a source of light although 22.____
    they have no natural tendencies to do this?
    The CORRECT answer is:
    A. I   B. II   C. III

23. Is ability to memorize correlated with social adaptability? 23.____
    The CORRECT answer is:
    A. I   B. II   C. III

24. Since the images on our retinae are upside down, do we really perceive 24.____
    everything upside down without realizing it?
    The CORRECT answer is:
    A. I   B. II   C. III

25. Are ants as intelligent as frogs? 25.____
    The CORRECT answer is:
    A. I   B. II   C. III

26. John is convinced that one of his instructors "has it in for him" and is trying 26.____
    to make him flunk the course. His adviser has had difficulty in changing this
    idea even though there is apparently excellent evidence to the contrary.
    It would be MOST helpful if the adviser FIRST asked himself:
    A. What evidence does John have?
    B. What motive does John's idea satisfy?
    C. Could this be something psychological?
    D. What kind of evidence might change his opinion?

27. When a satiated animal is placed in a cage with another animal of the same 27.____
    species who is eating, the satiated animal begins to eat. This behavior
    indicates that
    A. hunger is not the sole determinant of eating behavior
    B. animals are naturally competitive
    C. animals are naturally imitative
    D. satiation, like deprivation, increases the level of motivation
    E. none of the above

28. Of the following, the technique that would be MOST promising for assessing 28.____
    unconscious or unverbalizable desires and motives is, for the reason given:
    A. Observation of expressive movements because they are unlearned
    B. Inference from body type because the method is objective and not prone
       to subjective error

C. Protective tests because they are indirect methods and use ambiguous stimuli and unrestricted response
D. Personality inventories because they are difficult to falsify
E. None of the above

Questions 29-30.

DIRECTIONS: Select from the following list the CORRECT defense mechanism to characterize the behaviors described in Questions 29 and 30.

    I.   Phobia
    II. Regression
    III. Delusion
    IV. Obsession
    V. Repression

29. Mr. Wood's work suffers because he is constantly thinking about an unpleasant experience which resulted from a foolish but not malicious blunder he made.
The CORRECT answer is:
A. I   B. II   C. III   D. IV   E. V

30. Whenever there is a forecast of rain, Bill is haunted by the idea that the windows are open and constantly checks them even though he knows he put them down.'
The CORRECT answer is:
A. I   B. II   C. III   D. IV   E. V

31. Which of the following MOST readily lends itself to experimental investigation?
A. The effect of lighting on efficiency
B. The meaning of dreams
C. The effect of home environment upon mental illness
D. The behavior of the queen be
E. Public opinion

32. A feature of repression that makes it important in the understanding of forgetting is that
A. it shows recognition to be more difficult than recall
B. it shows that some forgetting is motivated
C. it is a way of escaping an unpleasant situation
D. forgetting does not occur for events tinged with emotion

Questions 33-36.

DIRECTIONS: Questions 33 through 36 concern the following:

Below is a proposition about a psychological problem. Underneath the proposition are four statements about the results of investigations. All of these statements are to be accepted as true.
Select answer
I. If the statement tends to support the proposition
II. If the statement tends to refute the proposition
III. If the statement is irrelevant to the proposition

Proposition: Environment is the primary determinant of Q.

33. The Q's of identical twins reared apart are more similar than those of fraternal twins reared together.
The CORRECT answer is:
A. I   B. II   C. III

34. The Q's of Black boys showed a consistent positive relationship with the number of years they had lived in the city.
The CORRECT answer is:
A. I   B. II   C. III

35. The correlation between the Q's of children and their foster parents is lower than the correlation between the Q's of the same children and their real parents.
The CORRECT answer is:
A. I   B. II   C. III

36. Intelligence test scores are distributed normally in the population.
The CORRECT answer is:
A. I   B. II   C. III

37. A mental patient was brought to the hospital with symptoms of hallucinations. On the basis of this alone, he was diagnosed schizophrenic by the examining intern.
Indicate which one assumption was implicitly made by the investigator in arriving at his conclusion. (In other words, what assumption would one have to make in order to arrive at the conclusion which the investigator reached?)
ASSUMPTIONS:
I.   All schizophrenics show hallucinations.
II. Most people who show hallucinations are schizophrenic.
III. Schizophrenics often show hallucinations.
IV. It is necessary to know something about a patient's history in addition to his present symptoms in order to arrive at a diagnosis.

The CORRECT assumption is:
A. I   B. II   C. III   D. IV

38. Barbara, aged 7, was full after finishing an enormous Thanksgiving dinner including her favorite dessert, deep-dish apple pie. However, when she heard the familiar tinkle of the ice cream man's warning bell as his truck turned the corner, Barbara ran to her mother crying, "May I have an ice cream cone?"
This is an example of
   A. cues in the environment which can motivate behavior
   B. secondary reinforcement
   C. the fact that biological drives which activate behavior are not stable
   D. regression
   E. irrational drives

38.____

39. A way of seeing is also a way of not seeing.
Which of the following is NOT an illustration of this proposition?
   A. When we listen to our friend's conversation we don't hear other things.
   B. We see a physically bright light as brighter than a physically dim light.
   C. When hungry we see food objects; when sexy we see sex objects.
   D. We see a certain cluster of stars as a constellation, the Big Dipper.
   E. All of the above

39.____

Questions 40-44.

DIRECTIONS: Questions 40 through 44 concern the following:

The problem has been set and data have been collected. You are first to match each hypothesis in Section A with the experimental outcome in Section B which best supports it. Secondly, you are to select the hypothesis and matching experimental outcome which you think best explains the problem and data.

PROBLEM: What is the relation of emotional shock or trauma to juvenile delinquency?
DATA: One hundred and eight pairs of delinquent and non-delinquent children, each pair from the same family, were interviewed. Subjects were residents of New York, Philadelphia, and Bridgeport. In 92% of the cases, it was determined that the delinquent child of the pair had suffered some emotional shock or disappointment not suffered by the non-delinquent member of the pair.
HYPOTHESIS:
   W. Delinquency is directly traceable to emotional shock and not to slums and poverty.
   X. Delinquency can be traced largely to hereditary differences.
   Y. Delinquency is due to differences in training of children as between different families.
   Z. Delinquency is largely due to lack of educational and environmental opportunity.

B. EXPERIMENTAL OUTCOMES:
   I. A sample of orphan children of delinquent parents showed more delinquency than was present in a sample of orphan children with normal parents.
   II. Examination of records of delinquents showed that, in many cases, a severe emotional shock was present in the background of the subject.
   III. A random sample of children from the upper-income bracket and a random sample of children from the upper-income bracket, with both groups equated as to emotional shocks, showed a higher delinquency rate for the former group.

IV. The delinquency rate among children of foreign-born parents was higher than the rate among children of native parents.

Select the number of the Experimental Outcome that BEST supports each hypothesis.

40. Hypothesis W
    The CORRECT answer is:
    A. II   B. III   C. IV

41. Hypothesis X
    The CORRECT answer is:
    A. I   B. II   C. III   D. IV

42. Hypothesis Y
    The CORRECT answer is:
    A. I   B. II   C. III   D. IV

43. Hypothesis Z
    The CORRECT answer is:
    A. I   B. II   C. III   D. IV

44. The Hypothesis and Experimental Outcome which BEST explain the given problem and data are correctly matched in the answer to Question (Item)
    A. 40   B. 41   C. 42   D. 43

Questions 45-47.

DIRECTIONS: Questions 45 through 47 concern the following:

Fifty subjects were matched in pairs on Q scores. One of each pair practices for two hours on memorizing a ten-stanza poem. The other member of the pair practices one hour on the same materials. Twenty-four hours after the practice session, all subjects were then tested for the amount of the poem they remembered.

Select the CORRECT answer for each question from the following key:
I. I.Q.
II. Practice time
III. Length of poem
IV. Amount of poem remembered
V. Familiarity with poem

45. The major controlled variable is
    A. I   B. II   C. III   D. IV   E. V

46. The dependent variable is
    A. I   B. II   C. III   D. IV   E. V

47. The independent variable is
    A. I   B. II   C. III   D. IV   E. V

Questions 48-50.

DIRECTIONS: Questions 48 through 50 concern the following situation:

A group of four-year-old children were given practice for three months in tapping, gripping, and pulling. Other children, matched with these children in all other things, were given no practice at all during the three months. At the end of this period, all children who had been practicing did better than the other children in all three performances. Another three months elapsed during which none of the children had any practice. When tests of tapping and pulling were given, the children who had had no practice did practically as well as those who, previously, had had some practice. Both groups had improved. However, in tests of strength of grip, the practiced children maintained their advantage.

INSTRUCTIONS: For each of the following statements, select answer:
I. If the statement is supported by the data
II. If the statement is contradicted by the data
III. If the statement is a plausible hypothesis on the basis of the data but is neither supported nor contradicted by the data
IV. If the statement is irrelevant to the data

48. Training young children in physical activities makes then lastingly better in those activities than untrained children.
    The CORRECT answer is:
    A. I   B. II   C III   D. IV

49. In some activities, maturation as well as training brings about skill.
    The CORRECT answer is:
    A. I   B. II   C. III   D. IV

50. The relative strengths of maturation and training in developing skills vary with different activities.
    The CORRECT answer is:
    A. I   B. II   C. III   D. IV

KEY (CORRECT ANSWERS)

1. C	11. D	21. B	31. A	41. A
2. D	12. E	22. A	32. B	42. D
3. E	13. E	23. B	33. B	43. C
4. B	14. C	24. C	34. A	44. A
5. C	15. E	25. B	35. B	45. A
6. D	16. C	26. B	36. C	46. D
7. E	17. E	27. A	37. B	47. B
8. C	18. B	28. C	38. A	48. B
9. E	19. A	29. D	39. B	49. A
10. B	20. B	30. D	40. B	50. A

TEST 2

DIRECTIONS: Each question or incomplete statement is followed by several suggested answers or completions. Select the one that BEST answers the question or completes the statement. *PRINT THE LETTER OF THE CORRECT ANSWER IN THE SPACE AT THE RIGHT.*

Questions 1-4.

DIRECTIONS: Questions 1 through 4 are to be answered on the basis of the data in the following table. Select the CORRECT answer for each question from the following key:
    I. True statement supported by the data directly or by inference.
    II. Insufficient data furnished to come to this conclusion.
    III. False statement contradicted by the data directly or by inference.

Relative Importance for Employee Morale	As Ranked by Employee	As Ranked by Employer
Credit for work done	1	7
Interesting work	2	3
Fair pay	3	1
Understanding and appreciation	4	5
Counsel on personal problems	5	8
Promotion on merit	6	4
Good physical working condition	7	6
Job security	8	2

1. On the whole, employers have very good insight into the motivation of their employees.
 The CORRECT answer is:
 A. I   B. II   C. III

2. Workers tend to make unreasonable demands.
 The CORRECT answer is:
 A. I   B. II   C. III

3. The motive of economic fear is stronger in the worker than the motive of social recognition.
 The CORRECT answer is:
 A. I   B. II   C. III

4. Workers tend to favor promotion on merit while employers tend to favor promotion on the basis of seniority.
 The CORRECT answer is:
 A. I   B. II   C. III

2 (#2)

5. Whenever possible, psychologists prefer to make quantitative classifications rather than qualitative classifications. This is GENERALLY true for the reason that
   A. there is too much overlapping of categories when classes are qualitative
   B. qualitative information is only descriptive and cannot be used for effective control
   C. mathematical relationships must be determined before an acceptable theory can be established
   D. more powerful techniques are available for handling quantitative data than qualitative

5.____

Questions 6-10.

DIRECTIONS: In each of Questions 6 through 10, select the one item, among those listed, that does not belong; i.e., it is not in the same class or it is the only one relevant (or irrelevant), or it is the only one right (or wrong), etc. The one that does NOT belong is:

6. A. Reaction formation   B. Displacement   6.____
    C. Projection   D. Hostility

7. A. Conditioned response   B. Motor skill   7.____
    C. Insight   D. Maze behavior

8. A. A gull's warning to her chicks   B. Language of the bees   8.____
    C. Courtship pattern of the stickleback   D. A dog's begging

9. A. Salivation at the sight of food   9.____
    B. Eye-watering with grit in eye
    C. Sweating in warm room
    D. Contraction of eye pupils in bright light

10. A. Theorizing based on behavior   10.____
    B. Inference from brain anatomy
    C. Observing one's own consciousness
    D. Conclusions from brain stimulation

Questions 11-25.

DIRECTIONS: Each of Questions 11 through 25 may have more than one correct alternative. That is, for a given question, from zero to all five alternatives may be correct. You must identify all the correct alternatives or items in order to achieve a correct answer. Select the letter of the CORRECT answer.

11. Which of the following are *stimulus* factors used (or measured) in conformity experiments?
    I. Size of the group
    II. Early experiences of the stooges
    III. Personality structure of the critical subject
    IV. Personality structure of the group
    V. Presence or absence of a group of stooges
    The CORRECT combination is:
       A. I only   B. II, III   C. IV, V
       D. V only   E. None of the above

12. Skinner's experiments with animals
    I. suggest that pigeons cannot easily be taught such complex tasks as bowling or playing ping pong
    II. have little relevance to the understanding or control of human behavior
    III. show that pigeons can be made "superstitious" if the training conditions are right
    IV. suggest that reinforcement should be given immediately if one wishes to control behavior
    V. suggest that the principle of successive approximation is of little value in training animals such as pigeons
    The CORRECT combination is:
       A. II, IV   B. I, III   C. III, IV
       D. I, V   E. None of the above

13. Giving a person an adequate paycheck at the end of the month is an example of
    I. primary positive reinforcement
    II. secondary negative reinforcement
    III. immediate primary reinforcement
    IV. delayed primary reinforcement
    V. delayed negative secondary reinforcement
    The CORRECT combination is:
       A. IV, V   B. I, III   C. I, IV
       D. III, V   E. None of the above

14. Pavlov's findings concerning "transmarginal excitation" suggest that
    I. in the equilibrium state, the animal reacts to weak stimuli the same as to strong stimuli
    II. in the ultra-paradoxical state, the animal over-reacts to average stimuli, but does not react to weak stimuli
    III. in the paradoxical state, the animal reacts to weak stimuli, but not to strong stimuli
    IV. in the paradoxical state, the animal reacts to average stimuli, but not to strong stimuli
    V. the cycle of events following the "transmarginal excitation" is more difficult to elicit the second time than the first

The CORRECT combination is:
A. I, II, III
B. I, II
C. II only
D. IV, V
E. None of the above

15. According to various studies:
    I. When the activity in one's nervous system (that is, the neural firing) becomes too intense, old patterns of firing (habits) become interrupted and do not operate for a period of time
    II. Immediately following over-excitation of the nervous system, the organism enters a brief plastic pattern in which it can learn new habits more rapidly than is normally the case
    III. Children can learn a foreign language easier than adults, at least in part, because the children have fewer interfering habit patterns than do the adults
    IV. There is a characteristic body posture in humans associated with over-excitation of the nervous system or "transmarginal excitation"
    V. Laboratory studies tell us very little about what really goes on in a human's nervous system when that human experiences a true religious "conversion"
    The CORRECT combination is:
    A. I, IV
    B. I, II, III
    C. II, III, IV, V
    D. I, II, III, IV, V
    E. None of the above

15.____

16. Various experiments on "group pressures toward conformity" suggest that
    I. the more the material that the subject must judge deals with concrete objects in the real world (as opposed to material which merely calls for an opinion about an unobservable quantity), the more likely it is that the subject will be influenced by the group
    II. judgments of fact are easier to shift than are attitudes, it is easier to shift personal preferences than it is to shift judgments of vague facts
    III. the easier the task set before the subject, the more likely it is the group will be able to influence the subject's behavior
    IV. if the subject is asked to make judgments of material from memory, he yields less readily than if he is allowed to judge on the basis of immediate perception of the material
    The CORRECT combination is:
    A. I only
    B. II, III
    C. I, II, III
    D. All of the above
    E. None of the above

16.____

17. Various experiments on "group pressures toward conformity" suggest that
    I. the vaguer the instructions the subject is given, the more likely it is that he will conform to group opinion
    II. in general, the more information the subject has concerning the group, the more influence the group will have on him
    III. most experimenters have found that maximum conformity is induced when the group has at least seven or eight members
    IV. it is quite important that all members of the reference group be unanimous (or nearly so) in their judgments if pressure to conform is to be induced in the subject

17.____

V. up to a point, the larger the discrepancy between the subject's personal judgment and that of the group, the less the subject is influenced by the group

The CORRECT combination is:
A. I only
B. I, II, III
C. II, III, IV
D. I, II, IV
E. II, IV, V

18. Various experiments on "group pressures toward conformity" suggest that
    I. the subject is more likely to yield to group pressures if the members of the group are physically present than if the subject merely hears their voices
    II. the more prestige or competence members of the group are seen as having, the more powerful agents they become in influencing the subject
    III. subjects typically yield more to groups composed of strangers than to groups composed of people they are acquainted with
    IV. subjects typically yield more to hostile groups than to friendly groups
    V. subjects typically yield more to groups towards which they (the subjects) are hostile than to groups they like

    The CORRECT combination is:
    A. I only
    B. II only
    C. III only
    D. IV only
    E. III, IV

19. Various experiments on "group pressures toward conformity" suggest that
    I. the more "out in the open" the subject is forced to be in making his judgments, the more likely it is he will resist group pressures
    II. the subject will be more likely to yield if he is told that the whole group must come to a unanimous decision on the matter at hand
    III. in general, the more important the judgments that the subject must make are said to be, the less likely it is that the subject will take the rest of the group into account
    IV. conforming behavior is difficult to predict even in experimental situations
    V. situational or "background" factors are of little importance in producing conformity behavior

    The CORRECT combination is:
    A. I, II
    B. III only
    C. II only
    D. II, IV
    E. IV, V

20. In order to encourage a subject to resist group pressures,
    I. one should reward him for non-conforming behavior
    II. make him think himself an expert in the task at hand
    III. give him one or two brief failure experiences in the task at hand prior to inducing group pressures
    IV. make him aware of the penalties for anti-social behavior
    V. make him believe that the group is actually quite hostile towards him and then let him make his judgments in private

    The CORRECT combination is:
    A. I only
    B. I, V
    C. II, III, IV
    D. I, III
    E. I, II, V

21. The pattern for most "religious" or other "conversion" experiences USUALLY includes
    I. the climax of some great emotional experience
    II. the "great experience" or the "conversion-inducing" experience
    III. some sort of sensory deficit (such as hysterical blindness)
    IV. a plastic period immediately following the above during which indoctrination typically takes place
    V. the occurrence of a true behavioral conversion, if all of the above happen
    The CORRECT combination is:
    A. I, II, III   B. I, III   C. I, IV, V
    D. I, II   E. I, II, III, IV, V

22. Electro-convulsive shock
    I. has been shown to be quite an effective form of therapy for most types of mental illness
    II. is seldom used by mental hospitals today
    III. induces "retrograde amnesia" for events occurring just prior to the shock
    IV. causes little physical damage to the subject's brain even if used extensively
    V. can snap a severely depressed patient out of his depression for at least a limited period of time
    The CORRECT combination is:
    A. III, V   B. III, IV, V   C. I only
    D. II only   E. None of the above

23. Experiments by Pavlov indicated that
    I. what he called "transmarginal excitation" in dogs had many of the characteristics of the "great experience" in humans
    II. "experimental neurosis" could be induced in dogs even if no real punishment was given to the animals
    III. dogs cannot be made into "masochists"
    IV. following "transmarginal excitation," dogs tended to lose most of their conditioned responses, for a period of time
    V. the "transmarginal excitation" could later be re-induced in his animals even if only some small part of the original exciting conditions were presented to the animals
    The CORRECT combination is:
    A. I, II   B. II, IV   C. IV, V
    D. I, II, IV, V   E. None of the above

24. In classical conditioning, the
    I. CS always follows the UCS
    II. animal does not need to be trained to make the CR to the CS
    III. animal does not need to be trained to make the UCR to the UCS
    IV. CS is typically said to be "neutral" at the beginning of the experiment
    V. stronger or more intense the CS is, in general, the faster the conditioning takes place

The CORRECT combination is:
A. I, II
B. I, IV
C. III, IV, V
D. I, IV, V
E. None of the above

25. Which of the following are *residual* factors used (or measured) in conformity experiments?
   I. Personality structure of the group
   II. Personality structure of the critical subject
   III. Presence or absence of a group of stooges
   IV. Difficulty of judgment of task
   V. Concreteness of material to be judged
   The CORRECT combination is:
   A. I only
   B. II only
   C. III only
   D. IV only
   E. V only

26. Which of the following is NOT a criterion for distinguishing deviant from normal behavior?
   A. Personal distress
   B. Disabling behavior tendencies
   C. Poor reality contact
   D. Statistical infrequency
   E. All of the above

27. A middle-aged man wears tennis shoes consistently to church on Sunday. This behavior would BEST be described as
   A. neurotic
   B. eccentric
   C. crazy
   D. psychotic
   E. pathological

28. The behavior defining psychosis in the implicit sense (loss of reality contact) may be exhibited in which of the following?
   A. Sensory-perceptual anomalies
   B. Disorientation as to time, person, or place
   C. Thought disorder
   D. Motor anomalies
   E. All of the above

29. What model does society currently use as a basis for the terms and concepts to be applied to deviant behavior?
   A. Statistical
   B. Moral
   C. Medical
   D. Behavioral
   E. Dynamic

30. Patterns of bodily symptoms which tend to occur together are known as
   A. syncreases
   B. syndromes
   C. profiles
   D. pathological formations
   E. anagrams

31. Which of the following difficulties are encountered with the *dynamic* model for the study and treatment of deviant behavior?
    A. Failure to comprehend the distinction between inference and observation
    B. Language of this model is largely figurative
    C. Absence of quantification
    D. All of the above
    E. Both A and C only

32. Reduction of the rate, speed, or magnitude of a conditioned response by eliminating the reinforcement related to the response is known as
    A. counterconditioning
    B. spontaneous recovery
    C. learning
    D. operant conditioning
    E. extinction

Questions 33-36.

DIRECTIONS: Questions 33 through 36 are to be answered on the basis of the following:

With reference to the numbered parts in the following experimental situation, select the respective number if it is a(n)
 I. conditioned stimulus
 II. unconditioned response
 III. unconditioned stimulus
 IV. conditioned response

A human subject is placed in a chair. A puff of air (33) is directed toward one eye for one second and the subject blinks (34). Contiguous with the air puff a light, of itself not able to elicit a blink (35), is switched on in view of the subject. Eventually, the subject comes to the light (36) when it is unpaired with the air puff.

33. The CORRECT answer is:
    A. I   B. II   C. III   D. IV

34. The CORRECT answer is:
    A. I   B. II   C. III   D. IV

35. The CORRECT answer is:
    A. I   B. II   C. III   D. IV

36. The CORRECT answer is:
    A. I   B. II   C. III   D. IV

37. The experimental situation described in Questions 33 through 36 is an example of which of the following forms of conditioning?
    A. Classical conditioning
    B. Semantic conditioning
    C. Operant conditioning
    D. Counter-conditioning
    E. All of the above

38. **A STIMULUS GENERALIZATION GRADIENT**

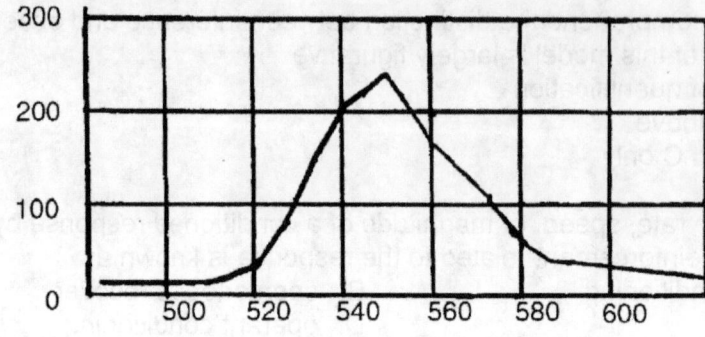

In the original conditioning session, a subject was conditioned to respond to a single wavelength of light. Assuming that the above graph represents the strength of response of that subject to test stimuli of various wavelengths, what is the MOST likely wavelength value of the single stimulus used in the original conditioning?
A. 510   B. 540   C. 550   D. 560   E. 570

39. Under which of the following conditions will retention of the same learned material, as measured by a recall test, be BEST?
A. When the material supports an idea held by the learner
B. When the material is at variance with an idea held by the learner
C. When the material is neutral to the learner (neither supporting nor contradicting his ideas)
D. All of the above
E. None of the above

40. Which of the following is evidence for the notion that it is possible for human learning to take place without the subject's being able to verbalize what has been learned (learning without awareness)?
A. Eyeblink conditioning in infants
B. The "Greenspoon Effect"
C. Conditioning of the pupillary response
D. All of the above
E. Only A and C

41. Which of the following curves BEST represents the motivation-efficiency relationship?   41.____

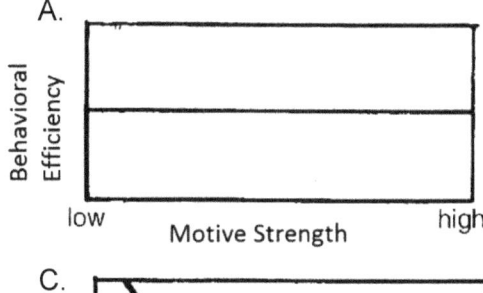
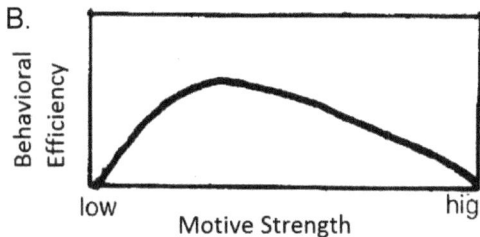
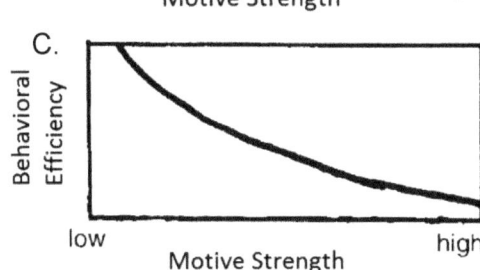
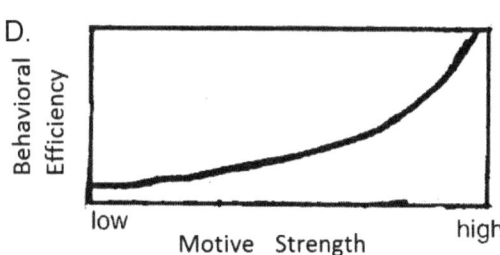

42. Subject A is offered $1 for each red paper square he can pick up from a moving conveyor belt. Subject B is merely told to do the same task as accurately and quickly as he can. At the end of the experiment, Subject A does not recall the colors of the paper squares other than the red ones. Subject B does remember and can report the other colors. The principle that BEST describes this situation is: 42.____
    A. The higher the motivation, the more selectively the individual attends to relevant stimuli only
    B. The principle of perceptual defense
    C. The principal of rigidity
    D. Decline in efficiency as an accompaniment to extreme motivation or unusually high arousal

43. A little old lady Sunday school teacher is reading a novel and registers the sentence, "Goddam lights!" as "Guard, dim the lights!" The principle that BEST describes this situation is: 43.____
    A. The higher the motivation, the more selectively the individual attends to relevant stimuli only
    B. The principle of perceptual defense
    C. The principal of rigidity
    D. Decline in efficiency as an accompaniment to extreme motivation or unusually high arousal

44. A 13-year-old boy goes to the candy machine he frequents and drops in his dime, although the prices have risen since he last used the machine to 15, and the sign on the machine says so. The boy keeps pulling on the knob, getting angrier and angrier until, finally, a clerk points out the rather obvious sign on the machine that prices are now a nickel more.   44.____
    The principle that BEST describes this situation is:
    A. The higher the motivation, the more selectively the individual attends to relevant stimuli only

B. The principle of perceptual defense
C. The principal of rigidity
D. Decline in efficiency as an accompaniment to extreme motivation or unusually high arousal

45. "Our boy" is on the line with two foul shots to make. The score is tied and there will be only two seconds left to play in the game after his second shot. He has to make at least one basket to ensure our winning the game. He feels the crowd is tense, and he is so anxious to sink one that he misses both. The principle that BEST describes this situation is:
    A. The higher the motivation, the more selectively the individual attends to relevant stimuli only
    B. The principle of perceptual defense
    C. The principal of rigidity
    D. Decline in efficiency as an accompaniment to extreme motivation or unusually high arousal

46. Although the image on your retina of a stop sign a block away is much smaller than that of the same sign at a distance of five feet, you do not judge the sign to actually grow larger as you approach it. This is an example of the phenomena of
    A. retinal disparity
    B. psychophysical equality
    C. size constancy
    D. visual compensation
    E. audio compensation

47. Exposure to prolonged stress may bring about irreversible changes in the functioning of certain bodily systems. This statement is
    A. true
    B. false
    C. sometimes true, sometimes false
    D. not determinable from the information given

48. Organic disorders produced by psychological stressors are known as
    A. psychosomatic disorders
    B. hallucinogenic disorders
    C. parasympathetic disorders
    D. carcinogenic disorders
    E. none of the above

49. Research on the effects of adrenalin and noradrenalin in relation to emotion gives evidence for which of the following?
    A. There are hormonal differences in the two states of emotion, anger and fear
    B. There are individual differences in the typical hormonal reaction to threat and, therefore, in the accompanying emotion
    C. The emotional states of anger and fear are hormonally indiscriminable
    D. Both A and B
    E. Both A and C

50. Effects of the parasympathetic and sympathetic nervous system functions are _____ with respect to the responses of visceral organs (responses such as rates of function, secretions, etc.).

    A. the same
    B. opposite
    C. unknown
    D. variable
    E. unrelated

50._____

KEY (CORRECT ANSWERS)

1.	C	11.	E	21.	E	31.	D	41.	B
2.	B	12.	C	22.	A	32.	E	42.	A
3.	A	13.	E	23.	D	33.	C	43.	B
4.	B	14.	A	24.	C	34.	B	44.	C
5.	D	15.	D	25.	B	35.	A	45.	D
6.	D	16.	E	26.	D	36.	D	46.	C
7.	C	17.	D	27.	B	37.	A	47.	A
8.	D	18.	B	28.	E	38.	C	48.	A
9.	A	19.	C	29.	C	39.	A	49.	D
10.	C	20.	E	30.	B	40.	D	50.	B

TEST 3

DIRECTIONS: Each question or incomplete statement is followed by several suggested answers or completions. Select the one that BEST answers the question or completes the statement. *PRINT THE LETTER OF THE CORRECT ANSWER IN THE SPACE AT THE RIGHT.*

1. Investigations of psychiatric patients with somatic complaints support the notion of
   A. response specificity (the patient with cardiovascular symptoms shows more heart rate changes than muscular responses to experimental stimulation, for example)
   B. response generality (the patients show overall higher sensitivity to experimental stimulation than the normals)
   C. both A and B; sometimes A, sometimes B
   D. neither A nor B

   1.____

2. Increased frequency and lowered amplitude of brain waves (EEG) are typical of a body state of
   A. alertness
   B. deep sleep
   C. desynchronization
   D. relaxation

   2.____

3. The data from clinical EEG is as yet of little use in diagnosing psychopathology, but the EEG is useful in diagnosing epilepsy.
   This statement is
   A. true
   B. false
   C. sometimes true, sometimes false
   D. indeterminable from the information given

   3.____

4. Which of the following is NOT a measure of arousal?
   A. Synchronization of the EEG
   B. Desynchronization of the EEG
   C. Palmar conductance
   D. Muscle tension

   4.____

5. Central to the physiology of arousal is the reticular activating system. Which of the following statements about the RAS is FALSE?
   A. The RAS has two functional parts, the ascending RAS and the descending RAS
   B. Direct stimulation, destruction, or inactivation of the RAS may lead to disruption in the power of other stimuli to produce arousal
   C. Some of the main structures involved in the RAS are the reticular formation and parts of the hypothalamus and thalamus
   D. None of the above statements are false

   5.____

6. A demonstration that LSD will cause some psychotic-like reactions or experiences in a normal person is an example of which of the following analogues?
   A. Experimental   B. Behavioral   C. Situation   D. Subject

   6.____

7. The FIRST step in going from casual to controlled clinical observation involves operationalization of the hypotheses. Which of the following definitions would be an operational definition of depression? Depression
   A. shall be indicated by a score of 50 or less on a standardized activity preference test
   B. is gloominess, dejection, low-spiritedness
   C. is an emotional condition, either normal or pathological
   D. is the result of excessive early emphasis on moral values

8. The difference between idiographic and nomothetic methods in the study of personality is largely one of specificity of the prediction that is being made, nomothetic predictions being more gene4ral and idiographic predictions more particular.
   This statement is
   A. true
   B. false
   C. sometimes true, sometimes false
   D. indeterminable from the information given

9. The concept of the control is a vital one in any psychological research. When two groups (e.g., brain-injured and manic-depressives) are being compared for similarities and they are both found to differ from the control group, the conclusion to be CORRECTLY drawn is:
   A. The similarities between brain-injured and depressives are due to the fact that both groups are "organic"
   B. The similarities are due to the fact that both groups present behavior pathologies
   C. Appropriate controls should include other psychopathological patients, handicapped patients, and equally hospitalized patients before a reason for the brain-injured/depressive similarities can be adduced
   D. None of the above

10. Psychopharmacologists are interested PRIMARILY in which of the following relationships?
    A. Shock-behavior
    B. Drug-behavior
    C. Ablation-behavior
    D. Environment behavior
    E. Medical history-behavior

11. An experimenter gives a subject a drugless sugar pill but tells him the pill contains a drug that will make him feel extremely drowsy. The subject indeed falls asleep five minutes after taking the pill. This is an instance of
    A. autosuggestion
    B. drugged sleep
    C. the placebo effect
    D. hypnosis

12. Which of the following will affect the effect of drugs in the experimental situation?
    A. Dosage level
    B. Dosage sequences
    C. Method of drug administration
    D. All of the above

13. In genetic studies, the use of fraternal twins is almost as good as that of identical twins since age, birth order, and parentage are the same for both types of twins, and these are the important considerations in genetic research. This statement is
    A. true
    B. false
    C. sometimes true, sometimes false
    D. indeterminable from the information given

14. If the occurrence rate for a disease in the population at large and the concordance rate between first cousins for the disease are the same, our BEST conclusion is that
    A. no special importance of an hereditary factor with respect to this disease seems indicated
    B. there is a definite possibility that the disease is inheritable
    C. the disease may be inheritable, but we have no good evidence to support one interpretation or the other (heredity or non-heredity)
    D. all of the above are false

15. The elicitation of deviant responses in conditioning situations requiring a very difficult discrimination or other conflict in response is evidence for the phenomenon called experimental
    A. neurosis   B. psychosis   C. necrosis   D. psittacosis

16. The basic determinant of experimentally produced behavior deviations may be defined as any pattern of stimulation presented to an organism which has the power to elicit two or more incompatible responses, the strengths of which are functionally equal. This determinant is
    A. discrimination   B. fear   C. conflict   D. generalization

17.

The above figure illustrates what type of gradient? (This illustration is for a rat running toward food in a straight alley.)
    A. Generalization   B. Avoidance   C. Probability   D. Goal

18. Statement 1:   The tendency to approach a goal is stronger the farther the subject is from it.
    Statement 2:   The tendency to avoid a feared stimulus is stronger the nearer the subject is to it.
    With respect to these two statements, it is CORRECT to say that Statement 1 is

A. true and Statement 2 is true
B. false and Statement 2 is false
C. true and Statement 2 is false
D. false and Statement 2 is true

19.

Strength of tendency to approach or avoid

Gradient of avoidance
Gradient of approach

w x y z
Near   Far
Distance from feared goal

Consider the above representation of an approach-avoidance conflict. What would be the prediction from the Miller model of the reaction of a subject placed at the point X distance from the feared goal? (Note: The prediction from Miller's model is required here; it is true that some experimental data gathered would refute Miller's model.)
A. A retreat to point Y, where approach and avoidance are in equilibrium
B. An advance to point W, since it is closest to the goal
C. A retreat to point Z, where approach and avoidance are not in disproportion
D. A freezing in fear at point X

20. Of the varieties of conflict, which is the EASIEST to resolve, the one type for which there are very few situations that the conflict would produce neurotic behavior in?
A. Approach-approach
B. Avoidance-Avoidance
C. Approach-avoidance
D. Double approach-avoidance

21. When an individual is prevented from carrying out some activity in relation to another object or person, he may, instead, carry out the same activity toward some irrelevant target. Or, when a subject is prevented from engaging in one activity, he may engage in an entirely different one.
This type of behavior is termed
A. replacement
B. displacement
C. conflict
D. substitute solution

22. The man at the office party, conflicted between his desire to flirt with an attractive secretary and his fear of being discovered by his fiancée in this flirtation, gets a cup of water from the cooler, flips through a magazine on a desk, shuts a window, lights a cigarette. His activities with each of the articles is appropriate to that thing but irrelevant to his anxiety.
This man is exhibiting behavior called
A. objective displacement
B. activity displacement
C. cognitive displacement
D. draining away of energy

23. Not thinking or not remembering events that are related to the arousal of a conflict is termed
    A. perceptual defense
    B. repression
    C. stereotyped behavior
    D. somatic escape
    E. specific fear

24. The central problem in the extinction of behavior pathology is the reduction of conflict.
    This statement is
    A. true
    B. false
    C. sometimes true, sometimes false
    D. indeterminable from the information given

25. Several hypotheses listed below have been offered as techniques for resolving conflict or reducing anxiety. The hypotheses are those of psychosurgery, electroconvulsive shock, time effects, and increasing approach motivation. Of these four, which has INDISPUTABLE human experimental evidence in its favor?
    A. Psychosurgery
    B. Electroconvulsive shock
    C. Time effects
    D. Increasing approach motivation
    E. None of the above

26. The phenomenon of an anxiety response seeming to gain strength during a period of time when there are no additional stresses present is termed
    A. generalization   B. trauma   C. incubation   D. transition

27. All anxiety develops on the basis of some original painful trauma.
    This statement is
    A. true
    B. false
    C. sometimes true, sometimes false
    D. indeterminable from the information given

28. Taylor's original experiment comparing high- and low-anxious subjects (as determined by MAS scores) in a conditioned eye-blink response, found that the highs produced the conditioned response significantly sooner than the lows, and were also somewhat slower to extinguish. In a logical extension of these findings, Spence and Taylor conducted yet another similar experiment, this time comparing psychotics and neurotics with normals.
    Their prediction (from the results of the original experiment) was that
    A. higher rates of conditioning should be found in neurotic and psychotic subjects than in normals
    B. lower rates of conditioning should be found in neurotic and psychotic subjects than in normals
    C. approximately equivalent rates of conditioning should be found in neurotic and psychotic subjects as in normals
    D. higher rates of conditioning should be found in normals than in neurotic and psychotic subjects

29. Failure to make adequate discriminations by making old responses where new ones are called for is termed
    A. homeostasis
    B. rigidity
    C. stasis
    D. fixation
    E. neurotic paradox

30. One type of anxiety measure is a sentence completion task in which the first word or phrase is supplied by the experimenter or test booklet. This anxiety measure is termed
    A. the semiprojective method
    B. the biological method
    C. the method of automatic feedback perception
    D. measurement in the natural habitat

31. Pretense of the nonexistence of a threatening situation is a neurotic state called
    A. hypochondria pattern
    B. denial pattern
    C. repetitive pattern
    D. reparative response

32. Compulsive acts are universally accompanied by obsessive thoughts.
    This statement is
    A. true
    B. false
    C. sometimes true, sometimes false
    D. indeterminable from the information given

33. Obsessive-compulsive patients generally complain of the discomfort of guilt feelings.
    This statement is
    A. true
    B. false
    C. sometimes true, sometimes false
    D. indeterminable from the information given

34. Which of the following is a major factor in the subsequent development of obsessive-compulsive patterns of neurosis?
    A. Permissive moral training
    B. Repressive moral training
    C. Hereditary susceptibility
    D. All of the above

35. Disorders in which the symptoms may or may not involve bodily functions, but where minute examination of the malfunctioning organ reveals no physical defect at all are called
    A. psychosomatic
    B. hysterical
    C. somatopsychological
    D. pathological

36. Which of the following experimental approaches to psychosomatic disorders is based on the position that psychosomatic responses represent learned reaction to stimuli that are themselves intrinsically innocuous?
    A. The conditioning of psychosomatic responses
    B. Hypnotically induced psychosomatic responses
    C. Raynaud disease attitude approach
    D. Personality correlates approach

36.____

37. Which of the following psychosomatic symptoms is characteristic of the patient who sees himself as being mistreated and is preoccupied with what is happening to him, not with retaliation?
    A. Urticaria (hives)   B. Asthma   C. Diarrhea
    D. Constipation   E. Duodenal ulcer

37.____

38. A lesion of the lining of the stomach or duodenum which may be of psychosomatic origin is called
    A. bulimia   B. gastritic   C. peptic ulcer
    D. anorexia   E. colitis

38.____

39. Several striking demonstrations have been made of the way in which ulcers may be produced experimentally. One of the best known is the study of ulcers in "executive monkeys" conducted by Brady, et al. From the data obtained, Brady suggests the hypothesis that emotional stress brings on ulcers under which of the following conditions?
    I. When the stress is intermittent rather than continuous
    II. When the stress is continuous rather than intermittent
    III. When the period of the stress's occurrence coincides with the natural periodicity of gastric secretions under normal conditions
    The CORRECT combination is:
    A. I only   B. II only   C. II, III
    D. I, III   E. I, II, III

39.____

40. Which of the following is the BEST scientific hypothesis yet offered for the understanding of the psychosomatic origin of asthma?
    A. Aquaphobia
    B. Repressed weeping
    C. Physiological concomitant of introjection
    D. Physiological concomitant of projection
    E. None of the above

40.____

41. In a well-described series of experiments, differences in autonomic responses in newborn infants were measured. Detailed examination of the form of the cardiac responses supported which of the following views? That
    A. stable individual differences in response are to be found in newborn infants
    B. fluctuating individual differences in response are to be found in newborn infants
    C. no significant individual differences are to be found in newborn infants
    D. such information was incapable of measurement

41.____

42. A serendipitous creative solution is facilitated when
    A. a mediating idea brings two associative elements into contiguity
    B. the co-occurrence of two objects in the environment causes the ideas representing these objects to be contiguous in consciousness
    C. the remote elements are combined because of their similarity
    D. remote associations are combined
    E. all of the above

43. The Remote Associates Test score can be said to be related to
    A. the size of an individual's associative hierarchy
    B. the slope of an individual's associative hierarchy
    C. an individual's ability to relate distant stimuli
    D. all of the above
    E. none of the above

44. The source of all mental acts in the Freudian theory of the mind is the
    A. conscious   B. preconscious   C. unconscious
    D. superego   E. all of the above

45. Repressed material is found ONLY in the
    A. conscious   B. preconscious   C. unconscious
    D. superego   E. all of the above

46. Which of the following may be used as evidence to support Freud's concept of the unconscious?
    A. Dreams   B. Psychotic behavior   C. Creative thinking
    D. Disconnected thoughts   E. All of the above

47. The censor in Freud's theory of the mind can be found between the
    A. id and the unconscious   B. superego and the id
    C. ego and the superego   D. conscious and the preconscious
    E. preconscious and the unconscious

48. The superego MAINLY is
    A. conscious   B. preconscious   C. unconscious
    D. all of the above E. none of the above

49. The ability to delay gratification is characteristic of
    A. primary process B. secondary process   C. unconscious
    D. id   E. none of the above

50. Immediate gratification is characteristic of
    A. id   B. primary process
    C. pleasure-pain principle   D. secondary process
    E. none of the above

KEY (CORRECT ANSWERS)

1.	A	11.	C	21.	B	31.	B	41.	A
2.	A	12.	D	22.	B	32.	B	42.	B
3.	A	13.	B	23.	B	33.	B	43.	D
4.	A	14.	A	24.	A	34.	B	44.	C
5.	D	15.	A	25.	E	35.	B	45.	C
6.	B	16.	C	26.	C	36.	A	46.	E
7.	A	17.	D	27.	B	37.	A	47.	E
8.	A	18.	D	28.	A	38.	C	48.	C
9.	C	19.	A	29.	B	39.	D	49.	B
10.	B	20.	A	30.	A	40.	E	50.	B

TEST 4

DIRECTIONS: Each question or incomplete statement is followed by several suggested answers or completions. Select the one that BEST answers the question or completes the statement. *PRINT THE LETTER OF THE CORRECT ANSWER IN THE SPACE AT THE RIGHT.*

1. Regulation by the pleasure-pain principle is a characteristic of ideas in which of the following systems of the mental apparatus?
   A. Unconscious   B. Preconscious   C. Conscious
   D. Ego   E. Superego

   1.____

2. Racial discrimination can be PARTLY seen as a form of
   A. repression   B. projection   C. displacement
   D. reaction-formation   E. isolation

   2.____

3. If a man comes home from work after his boss has fired him and argues with his wife who in turn hits her son who then kicks the dog, we would say that this behavior is characteristic of
   A. projection   B. displacement   C. repression
   D. reaction-formation   E. acting out

   3.____

4. Repression is the MAJOR mechanism employed in
   A. anxiety neurosis   B. manic-depressive psychosis
   C. obsessional neurosis   D. schizophrenia
   E. hysteria

   4.____

5. Hypernormal reflexes, chronic muscle contraction, tense posture, and hand tremor are symptoms COMMONLY found in
   A. phobia   B. anxiety neurosis
   C. obsessional neurosis   D. hysteria
   E. character disorders

   5.____

6. Conflict between the superego and the ego will MOST likely result in
   A. depression   B. conduct disorders
   C. phobia   D. psychosomatic disorders
   E. hysteria

   6.____

7. Behavior characterized by rushing around, self-condemnation, guilt, and unreasonableness is seen in
   A. agitated depression   B. retarded depression
   C. hypomania   D. hypermania
   E. paranoia

   7.____

8. In an experiment studying repression, severe trauma was associated with the learning of nonsense material, the following results were found immediately after the trauma:
   A. Retention was higher in the control group
   B. Retention was higher in the trauma group
   C. Retention was the same in both groups
   D. No repression was found in either group
   E. None of the above

8.____

9. The MOST commonly used defense mechanism is
   A. displacement   B. projection   C. repression
   D. suppression   E. identification

9.____

10. The difference between primal repression and repression proper is that in the latter case the material repressed
    A. was once easily available to consciousness
    B. never relates to the mother
    C. originates in the id
    D. originates in the superego
    E. originates in the pleasure center

10.____

11. The dog does not stop jumping over when the electricity is turned off and no shock is possible. He continues to jump because
    A. he is anxious sine the shock was so strong
    B. he has concomitant hunger drive
    C. he is reinforced by termination of shock
    D. of curiosity drive
    E. he is reinforced by reduction of fear

11.____

12. For a good experimental demonstration of repression, which of the following is LEAST important?
    A. Must demonstrate that the individual has learned or could recall material
    B. Some painful experience must be associated with the material
    C. The repressed idea will strive for expression
    D. The learned material must be verbal
    E. Proper therapy should bring the idea to consciousness

12.____

13. The creative child in the classroom
    A. tends to work alone
    B. clowns when he presents his ideas
    C. often has his ideas later attributed to a less creative group member
    D. produces more ideas than the other children
    E. all of the above

13.____

Questions 14-17.

DIRECTIONS: Questions 14 through 17 are to be answered based on a well-described study of creativity.

14. In the study, high IQ-low creative (A) and "low" IQ-high creative (B) students were studied. When their school achievement was tested, it was found that
    A. A was higher than B
    B. B was higher than A
    C. A was about as high as B
    D. none of the above

15. In the operant conditioning study of the creatives, it was shown that they have a(n) _____ novelty.
    A. need for
    B. preference for
    C. dislike of
    D. avoidance reaction to
    E. association to

16. In this operant conditioning study of creatives, the reinforcement used was
    A. candy pellets
    B. avoidance of shock
    C. escape from shock
    D. improbable associates
    E. dominant associates

17. In the operant conditioning study of creatives, the low creative individuals
    I. avoided novelty
    II. were reinforced by commonness
    III. avoided commonness
    The CORRECT combination is:
    A. I only
    B. II only
    C. I and III
    D. I and II
    E. III only

18. The creative process consists of the combining of mutually remote ideas. "The lion's ferocious chrysanthemum head" illustrates which method?
    A. Serendipity
    B. Mediation
    C. Similarity
    D. Novelty
    E. Repetitiveness

19. A creative individual typically has a(n) _____ associative hierarchy.
    A. steep
    B. augmented
    C. reduced
    D. flat
    E. restricted

20. MOST typically repressed material is
    I. sexual
    II. hostile
    III. lost forever to memory
    The CORRECT combination is:
    A. I only
    B. II only
    C. I and III
    D. I and II
    E. III only

21. The defense of denial USUALLY is tied to
    A. screen memories
    B. homosexuality
    C. displacement
    D. need for novelty
    E. repression

22. Individuals who suffer from a severe depressive episode
    A. recover and do not suffer a relapse
    B. recover and suffer a relapse in about 25% of the cases
    C. recover and suffer a relapse in about 50% of the cases
    D. recover and suffer a relapse in about 70% of the cases
    E. none of the above

23. The authoritarian personality attempts to escape loneliness by
    I. seeking out relationships in which he can be dominant
    II. seeking out relationships in which he can be submissive
    III. seeking out relationships in which he can feel on an equal footing
    The CORRECT combination is:
    A. I only   B. II only   C. II and III
    D. I and II   E. III only

24. It is not possible to produce attacks of asthma in the laboratory without introducing the specific substance to which the individual is allergic.
    This statement is
    A. true   B. false
    C. sometimes true   D. sometimes false

25. It is believed that asthma is associated with personality patterns characterized by a great deal of concern over an intense need to maintain a strong bond with the mother.
    This statement is
    A. true
    B. false
    C. sometimes true
    D. indeterminable from the information given

26. Most of the neuroses are defenses against anxiety, even in _____, where the undisturbed clinical picture is one of bland indifference.
    A. phobic reaction   B. obsessive-compulsive reaction
    C. conversion reaction   D. anxiety reaction
    E. depressive condition

27. One characteristic of ALL anxiety reactions is that
    A. infantile experiences themselves become conscious
    B. patients are aware only of being vigilant and exhausted and constantly alert for something they can't identify
    C. patients are usually calm between attacks
    D. acute psychotic episodes usually occur, especially when the anxiety is of the chronic type
    E. patients seldom have frightening dreams, although their daytime experience is marked by apprehension

28. A popular myth is that only successful behavior remains in the long run, yet patients, for example, persist in fruitless, self-defeating repetitions of nonadaptive behavior. How is this accounted for? As due to
    A. instinct
    B. accident
    C. the effort of the neurotic to revive childhood object relations in adult situations
    D. lack of intelligence
    E. a uniquely human characteristic of reliance on magic and ritual, which is still carried on today by educated people as, for example, to ritualistically control health and prosperity

29. In becoming functionally disabled, the conversion patient may discover he enjoys his privileged status as an invalid more than he enjoyed the freedom of being well, illustrating the concept of
    A. primary gain
    B. primary anxiety
    C. secondary gain
    D. secondary anxiety
    E. concept illustration

30. To carry out literally the wish "to get away from it all just to go away and forget everything" illustrates
    A. fugue
    B. psychogenic stupor
    C. trance state
    D. hysterical convulsion
    E. conversion reaction

31. Obsessive compulsives often use magical thinking in the sense that their rituals are techniques for removing their guilt, illustrating
    A. undoing
    B. reaction formation
    C. confabulation
    D. isolation
    E. emotional ambivalence

32. John Smith washed his hands after a contaminating act, attitude, or fantasy, illustrating
    A. obsessive rumination
    B. rigidity
    C. defective repression
    D. undoing
    E. ego-splitting

33. In obsessive compulsive disorders, one frequently sees
    A. "la belle indifference"
    B. an absence of sadomasochism
    C. conscious experience of a struggle against conscious impulses
    D. unconscious primary process thinking
    E. fugue states

34. A disorder in which the unconscious conflicts are crystallized in the altered function of some specific body part is
    A. anxiety reaction
    B. panic attack
    C. phobias
    D. conversion reaction
    E. dissociative reaction

35. In one subtype of schizophrenia, diagnostic emphasis is on a motor disturbance; at one time the patient may be in a disorganized excitement, and at another extreme he may be mute and motionless.
    This is called
    A. chronic undifferentiated type B. simple
    C. hebephrenic D. catatonic
    E. paranoid

36. A conversion reaction with loss of appetite and refusal to eat is
    A. anorexia B. bulimia
    C. spasmodic torticollis D. hemiplegia
    E. psychosomatic disorder

37. Schizophrenics often tell of something terrible that is happening to them, or of something frightful they have done, without approaching the emotional participation that the normal person expects.
    This is called
    A. affective flattening B. estrangement
    C. somatic delusions D. disturbance in object relations
    E. disturbance in role-taking skills

38. A disorder in which the patient reacts to stress, tension, and anxiety with direct physiological malfunction, which may lead to irreversible organ or tissue damage, is called
    A. involutional disorder B. personality disorder
    C. psychosomatic disorder D. acute brain disorder
    E. inadequate personality disorder

39. Which one of the following symptoms is likely to dispose of tension and anxiety MOST completely?
    A. Anxiety reaction B. Panic attack
    C. Phobic reaction D. Conversion reaction
    E. Counterphobic reaction

40. A soldier who recently killed an enemy in combat found that his right arm was paralyzed. It was neurophysiologically normal and the soldier had suffered no injuries. He was PROBABLY suffering from
    A. panic reaction B. phobia
    C. conversion reaction D. dissociative reaction
    E. fugue state

41. A schizophrenic girl became frightened when her violin case was mislaid. She was immediately sure that she had swallowed it, illustrating
    A. projection B. denial
    C. introjection D. defective repression
    E. an hallucination

42. Hallucinations are difficult to explain
    A. and they occur only in cases of extreme psychopathology
    B. but are within the reach of almost everyone
    C. and cannot be produced by experimental methods
    D. and occur only when there is a neurological complication
    E. but apparently require a toxic agent in the bloodstream

43. Schizophrenics show disturbance in language and thought, and sometimes new words appear in the talk of some patients, illustrating
    A. logical justification   B. scatter
    C. neologisms   D. condensations
    E. expressive languages

44. In about what percent of the persons suffering from chronic high blood pressure can no organic etiology be found?
    A. 98-100%   B. 0-2%   C. 10-15%   D. 20-25%   E. 75-80%

45. According to Alexander's Theory, if destructive impulses are inhibited in the fantasy stage of development, when planning and visual imagery are active, then
    A. migraine headaches are more likely than some other psychosomatic disorders
    B. essential hypertension is more likely than some other psychosomatic disorders
    C. rheumatical arthritis is more likely than some other psychosomatic disorders
    D. it is unlikely that a psychosomatic disorder will develop
    E. a skin disorder is more likely than some other psychosomatic disorder

46. According to Cameron, sexual dysfunction
    A. is limited to the psychosomatic disorders
    B. occurs in males but not in females
    C. can usually be traced dynamically to events which occur in the first year of life
    D. is a rare form of symptom in modern society
    E. is almost universal in neurotic, psychotic, and personality disorders

47. According to Machiavelli in THE PRINCE:
    I. Whoever is the cause of another's coming to power, falls himself, for that power is built up either by art or force, both of which are suspect to the one who has become powerful.
    II. The nature of people is fickle, and it is easy to persuade them of something but difficult to keep them in that persuasion.
    III. It is better to hire mercenaries than to conscript one's own people and force them into fighting.
    IV. When two powerful neighboring states go to war, the wise prince strives to maintain strict neutrality.
    V. No state is safe unless it has its own arms.

The CORRECT combination is:
A. I, II, IV   B. I, II, III   C. II, III, IV
D. II, III, V   E. I, II, V

48. According to Machiavelli in THE PRINCE:
    I. How we live is so different from how we ought to live that he who studies what ought to be done rather than what is done will learn the way to his downfall rather than to his preservation.
    II. It is much safer to be loved than to be feared, if one must choose between the two.
    III. In the actions of all men and especially princes, where there is no court of appeal, the end is all that counts.
    IV. Princes should leave the function of distributing charges and burdens to others and preserve for themselves the office of dispensing favors and pardons.
    V. Unless men are compelled to be bad, they will invariably turn out good.
    The CORRECT combination is:
    A. I, II, III   B. II, III, IV   C. I, III, V
    D. I, III, IV   E. I, IV, V

49. According to various studies, the "yielder"
    I. appears to be self-deprecating
    II. probably had very permissive parents
    III. typically had late "independence training"
    IV. if a man, probably scores as being more "feminine" than average on masculinity tests
    V. typically considers himself as being helpful in interpersonal relations
    The CORRECT combination is:
    A. I, II, III   B. I, II, III, IV   C. I, III, V
    D. II, III, IV, V   E. I, III, IV, V

50. According to various studies, the "yielder"
    I. is judged as having a less "complex" personality than a non-yielder as measured by various projective tests
    II. considers himself as being stable and healthy-minded
    III. considers himself as having personal effectiveness
    IV. on objective ratings, scores as being rigid and conventional
    V. on objective ratings, scores as being inconsistent, anxious, and moralistic
    The CORRECT combination is:
    A. I, II   B. I, II, III   C. I, II, III, IV
    D. II, III   E. I, II, III, IV, V

KEY (CORRECT ANSWERS)

1. A	11. E	21. A	31. A	41. C
2. C	12. D	22. D	32. D	42. B
3. B	13. E	23. D	33. C	43. C
4. E	14. C	24. B	34. D	44. E
5. B	15. A	25. A	35. D	45. A
6. A	16. D	26. C	36. A	46. E
7. A	17. D	27. B	37. A	47. E
8. A	18. B	28. C	38. C	48. D
9. C	19. D	29. C	39. D	49. E
10. A	20. D	30. A	40. C	50. E

TEST 5

DIRECTIONS: Each question or incomplete statement is followed by several suggested answers or completions. Select the one that BEST answers the question or completes the statement. *PRINT THE LETTER OF THE CORRECT ANSWER IN THE SPACE AT THE RIGHT.*

1. According to various studies: 1.____
   I. Conformity is learned.
   II. "Reference groups" influence our behavior by providing comparison points which we use in evaluating ourselves and others.
   III. "Reference groups" influence our behavior by setting standards and enforcing them by rewarding or punishing individuals who conform or do not conform to these standards.
   IV. There is both positive and negative conformity.
   V. We know more about why group pressures are effective in changing behavior than about how group pressures can be established in experimental situations.
   The CORRECT combination is:
   A. I only   B. I, II   C. I, II, III
   D. I, II, III, IV E. I, II, III, IV, V

2. Various studies on group pressures suggest that 2.____
   I. the longer a subject resists before finally yielding, the less he will conform after yielding
   II. the stronger the pressure put on a subject, the longer the conformity will last when the subject finally does conform
   III. the greater the shift in the subject's judgment towards the group norm, the more of the shift he will retain afterwards
   IV. group pressures can induce psychosomatic symptoms if the pressures are great enough
   V. the negative conformer is actually as influenced by group pressures as is the positive conformer
   The CORRECT combination is:
   A. I, II, III, IV, V   B. I, II, III, IV   C. II, III, IV, V
   D. III, IV, V   E. I, III, IV, V

3. The "programmed textbook" or "teaching machine" 3.____
   I. was first designed (in prototype) by B.F. Skinner
   II. makes use of the principle of successive approximation
   III. is typically liked more by the brightest and dullest students than by the average student
   IV. typically gives the students primary enforcement if they get the correct answer
   V. typically delays reinforcement until the end of a given section of material rather than presenting it after each response the student must make
   The CORRECT combination is:
   A. II, III   B. I, II   C. III, IV
   D. IV, V   E. II, IV

4. In general, the "programmed textbook" or "teaching machine"
   I. is easier to write or create than a standard textbook
   II. is of little use in getting educators to consider what the real goals of the educational process are
   III. cannot be written or arranged to take into account the differing abilities of the students
   IV. eliminates the need for any discussion of the subject material presented
   V. cannot teach factual material as well as can a human teacher
   The CORRECT combination is:
   A. I, II B. I, II, III C. I, II, III, IV
   D. All of the above E. None of the above

5. According to various authorities,
   I. there exist no specific curricular patterns, no model syllabi for courses, no pedigree of instructor, and no wizardry of instructional method that should be patented for their impact on the values of students
   II. potency to affect student values is found in the distinctive climate of just a few American institutions
   III. potency to affect student values is found only in the teacher who has very strong value-commitments of his own
   IV. in terms of persuading students to change their values or attitudes, the effective teacher is one who always lets the students know what behavioral changes he expects from them
   V. those American colleges and universities that are effective in changing student values are typically institutions noted for their permissive attitudes towards student behavior and their encouragement of a heterogeneity of student values
   The CORRECT combination is:
   A. II, III B. III, IV, V C. II, III, IV, V
   D. I, II, III, IV E. I, II, III, IV, V

6. Adaptation Level Theory was FIRST developed by
   I. Robert Blake II. James McConnell III. Philip E. Jacob
   IV. Nancy Moutin V. Ian Fleming
   The CORRECT combination is:
   A. All of the above B. None of the above C. I, II
   D. V E. II only

7. In Adaptation Level Theory,
   I. the stimulus factors cannot be measured
   II. the background factors cannot be measured
   III. the residual (personality) factors cannot be measured
   IV. the subject's prior experience is of little importance
   V. psychophysical events (such as the perception of lifted weights) can be predicted but the theory is of little use in the accurate prediction of social behavior
   The CORRECT combination is:
   A. All of the above B. None of the above C. I, III
   D. II, IV E. III only

8. Experiences produce lasting changes in a person by consolidating and elaborating the perceptual organizations and their imagery. It is in this sense that Cameron speaks of
    A. oral imagery
    B. cognition
    C. oral discrimination
    D. internalization
    E. oral anticipation

8._____

9. The compulsive character is a personality type that is assumed to result from a pathological fixation at the _____ phase of development. The missing word is
    A. oral   B. anal   C. phallic   D. genital   E. latency

9._____

10. Studies of newborns indicate that there is(are)
    A. no difference between children at birth
    B. consistent differences in tension level between different children
    C. differences between children in tension only after approximately one month of age
    D. a similarity in the degree to which common stress will disturb the equilibrium of different children
    E. differences in tension level but similarity in the characteristic modes of internal organ functioning

10._____

11. The peer culture allows the child to progressively develop
    A. role-differentiation
    B. conscience
    C. formalized relationships
    D. reciprocal inhibition
    E. all of the above

11._____

12. In order to develop adequately in accordance with the reality principle, it is necessary for the child to
    A. avoid as much frustration as possible
    B. encounter both frustration and some delay of gratification
    C. develop in a state of constant equilibrium
    D. have uninterrupted need-satisfaction sequences
    E. encounter severe frustration at some time

12._____

13. The ability to delay gratification is a function of what part of the personality structure?
    A. Superego
    B. Id
    C. Ego
    D. Preconscious
    E. Frustration tolerance level organization

13._____

14. The defensive aspect of ego functions is BEST seen as belonging to
    A. the conscious ego system
    B. the readily available preconscious ego system
    C. the conflict-free sphere
    D. the autonomous ego sphere
    E. none of the above

14._____

15. An arrest of personality development at some phase, as for example, in overindulgence that makes further efforts at the time to mature, unattractive to the child, is known as
    A. regression
    B. reaction formation
    C. conversion
    D. fixation
    E. none of the above

16. Most contemporary psychopathology theories place a great deal of emphasis on
    A. learning
    B. the talion principle
    C. sexual impulses
    D. anxiety
    E. regression

17. The Strassman, Thaler, and Schein paper on prisoners of war concluded that
    A. soldiers who became apathetic tended to refuses repatriation
    B. in general, memories of home reinforced the high morale of American soldiers in Korean POW camps
    C. only by fighting incipient apathy could POW's maintain personality integration
    D. the apathy syndrome serves to maintain personality integration in the face of severe reality and psychological stress
    E. all of the above were true

18. Lykken's study of anxiety in the sociopathic personality concluded that "primary sociopaths" showed
    A. significant less anxiety on a questionnaire device
    B. less GSR reactivity to a "conditioned" stimulus associated with shock
    C. less avoidance of punished responses on a test of avoidance learning
    D. a high degree of oedipal guilt
    E. A, B, and C above

19. The adolescent is MOST likely to find emotional support and understanding from
    A. his parents
    B. his peer culture
    C. isolated activity
    D. heterosexual interactions
    E. heroin

20. The ego operates to bind cathexes into stable organizations in accordance with
    A. somatic reality
    B. the talion principle
    C. the reality principle
    D. the pleasure principle
    E. the ego-ideal

KEY (CORRECT ANSWERS)

1.	D	11.	E
2.	C	12.	B
3.	A	13.	C
4.	E	14.	E
5.	D	15.	D
6.	B	16.	D
7.	B	17.	D
8.	D	18.	E
9.	B	19.	B
10.	B	20.	C

EXAMINATION SECTION
TEST 1

DIRECTIONS: Each question or incomplete statement is followed by several suggested answers or completions. Select the one that BEST answers the question or completes the statement. *PRINT THE LETTER OF THE CORRECT ANSWER IN THE SPACE AT THE RIGHT.*

1. Which of the following fears is found MORE frequently in children 5 to 12 years of age than in younger children?
   A. Animals
   B. Noises
   C. Threat of injury
   D. Strange objects or persons

   1.____

2. Which of the following types of conflict is EASIEST to resolve?
   A. Approach-approach
   B. Approach-avoidance
   C. Avoidance-avoidance
   D. Double approach-avoidance

   2.____

3. Transfer from one subject to another or to life situations will be increased if
   A. techniques and applications are emphasized
   B. the first subject is very difficult
   C. a good deal of drill is given in the first subject
   D. the situations seem quite different

   3.____

4. Attributing our own thoughts or desires to others is called
   A. compensation   B. fantasy   C. rationalizing   D. projection

   4.____

5. Reverting to an earlier learned response after a later learned response has been frustrated is called
   A. repression   B. regression   C. remission   D. resolution

   5.____

6. Bird migration is set off by the effect of increases or decreases in daily illumination on the bird's output of _____ hormones.
   A. adrenal   B. thyroid   C. gonadal   D. pineal

   6.____

7. After conditioning has occurred, stimuli similar to the conditioning one also arouse the unconditioned response. This is known as
   A. spontaneous recovery
   B. backward conditioning
   C. higher-order conditioning
   D. generalization

   7.____

8. Shaping of behavior is accomplished through
   A. classical procedure
   B. secondary reinforcement
   C. primary enforcement
   D. reinforcing successive approximations

   8.____

9. By "learning a place" we mean that the rat
   A. associates certain stimuli with the food location
   B. always makes the same responses to get to the same place
   C. is disturbed if we change the location of the food
   D. none of the above

9.____

10. Kohler is ESPECIALLY noted for his work with
    A. trial and error
    B. instrumentation
    C. rats
    D. all of the above

10.____

11. Learning to learn is demonstrated when
    A. insight occurs
    B. a detour is solved
    C. successive problems are learned more efficiently
    D. all of the above

11.____

12. The MOST clearly and generally established principle of economic learning is that involving
    A. whole versus part learning
    B. the value of guidance
    C. the effectiveness of repetition
    D. distribution of effort

12.____

13. By "reactive inhibition" we mean that the organism is
    A. fatigued after a long work period
    B. resistant to repetition of a response
    C. likely to drop other responses in favor of one just recently made
    D. subject to lapses of memory following extensive recitation

13.____

14. Responses that are not reinforced tend to be
    A. weak   B. perseverant   C. extinguished   D. repressed

14.____

15. In reproducing forms from memory, the individual is likely to
    A. retain the general scheme
    B. make the reproduction less conventional
    C. add more details than he omits
    D. none of the above

15.____

16. Testimony concerning events witnessed is
    A. about 85 percent accurate
    B. subject to errors in perception
    C. inaccurate only because of forgetting
    D. distorted by eidetic factors

16.____

17. Memories have been revived experimentally through
    A. electric shock
    B. stimulating parts of the brain
    C. cutting interfering neural circuits
    D. use of tranquilizers

17.____

18. Of the following general statements about deterioration in mental patients, which is the MOST questionable one?
    A. More recently acquired forms of reaction are lost before those formed earlier in life.
    B. Generalization and abstraction in psychoses is qualitatively the same as that in the young child.
    C. Deterioration in many cases regarded as hopeless appears to be reversible.
    D. The responses of a deteriorated person show generally a definite patterning which tends to mask his defects.

19. The Zeigarnik experiment showed that
    A. completed tasks were recalled better than interrupted tasks
    B. interrupted tasks were recalled better than completed ones
    C. both completed and interrupted tasks were recalled equally well
    D. resumed tasks were recalled better than unresumed tasks

20. In further experiments on the Zeigarnik effect, it was found that Zeigarnik's results could be duplicated only by
    A. using children as subjects   B. under ego-orienting instructions
    C. under task-orienting instructions   D. none of the above

21. The explanation given to account for the superiority of retention after sleep was the operation of _____ inhibition.
    A. proactive   B. reactive   C. anterograde   D. retroactive

22. In forming concepts, it is important that otherwise different things are in, at least one respect,
    A. identical   B. different   C. similar   D. abstract

23. Which one of the following is essential in reading?
    A. Verbalization   B. Retention of earlier experience
    C. Imagery   D. Free association

24. The periphery of the retina is more sensitive to light than the fovea because it
    A. has more rods than the central area
    B. has cones packed more tightly than in the central area
    C. has ore free nerve endings
    D. is closer to the blind spot

25. The Purkinje phenomenon is evident as one changes from
    A. rod to cone vision   B. cone to rod vision
    C. achromatic to chromatic vision D. surface color to film color vision

26. High intelligence is positively correlated with a high occupational level and   26.____
    with the amount of education completed. This proves that
    A. social factors are more important than biological factors in the
       determination of intelligence
    B. intelligent parents almost always have intelligent children
    C. both A and B are true
    D. neither A nor B is true

27. Children's I.Q.'s correlate with their fathers' occupational levels   27.____
    A. only when the father provides part of the child's environment
    B. in northern industrial cities but not in the south
    C. even though neither the father nor the mother provides the child's
       environment
    D. provided that both parents are at least normal in intelligence

28. Current research on physique and temperament claims   28.____
    A. distinct physical types and temperamental types
    B. correlated dimensions of physique and temperament
    C. differences in temperament which are directly caused by different
       physiques
    D. a perfect correlation between physique and temperament

29. The "halo effect" is the result of   29.____
    A. extremely complex ratings
    B. favoritism
    C. an inability to separate the trait to be rated from the person's other
       characteristics
    D. willingness to see the best in people

30. When making up a questionnaire-type personality inventory, the MAIN   30.____
    consideration in selecting questions is whether or not
    A. the subjects will refuse to answer
    B. persons who answer the questions differently are actually different with
       respect to the trait being tested
    C. the answers can be categorized
    D. the questions are sufficiently ambiguous

31. Questionnaire-type personality inventories are   31.____
    A. of greatest value when used as screening devices
    B. most useful in the understanding of individual cases
    C. the earliest form of projective test
    D. usually poorly standardized

32. Center of distribution is to spread of distribution as mean is to   32.____
    A. average   B. standard score
    C. normal distribution   D. standard deviation

33. A percentile score of 60 on an intelligence test means that a person
    A. is equaled or exceeded by 60 percent of the persons tested
    B. has an intelligence equal to or higher than that of 60 percent of those tested
    C. has an intelligence equal to or higher than 40 percent of those tested
    D. has an intelligence quotient no better than average

34. When will 50 percent of a group be below the median for the group?
    A. Always, regardless of the distribution
    B. When the distribution is bimodal
    C. When the mean and median coincide
    D. Only when the distribution is skewed

35. In a normal distribution, the 75th centile point will lie between the mean and one standard deviation above the mean
    A. all of the time
    B. none of the time
    C. when the standard deviation is large
    D. when the standard deviation is small

36. Suppose we make up two tests, each designed to measure a different ability. We then find zero correlation between scores on the two tests. This indicates that
    A. persons scoring high on the first test are as likely to be below average as above average on the other test
    B. if we know that a person possesses a lot of one ability, it is most reasonable to think he has more than an average amount of the other
    C. the lowest person on one test is quite unlikely to be above average on the other test
    D. the highest person on one test is likely to be the lowest on the second test

37. In setting a critical minimum score on an aptitude test,
    A. all who will fail in the job are eliminated
    B. most potential failures are eliminated
    C. all who will succeed are given a chance
    D. interests are weighted equally with aptitudes

38. The ability to predict vocational success from aptitude tests is shown by
    A. the sigma of the distribution
    B. a high validity coefficient
    C. a measure of central tendency
    D. a small standard deviation

39. An aptitude test differs from an ability test in that an aptitude test
    A. measures largely the amount of education (training) a person has received
    B. is used mainly for predictive purposes
    C. measures present achievement in a given field
    D. measures interests and/or values

40. If a test yields consistent scores for the same individual when administered on different occasions, it is said to be
    A. valid   B. reliable   C. standardized   D. stable

41. What interpretation, if any, can be given to a raw score of 70 on an intelligence test?
    A. No interpretation can be given to the score without further information.
    B. The person is below average in intelligence.
    C. The person has exceeded 30 percent of the people in that test.
    D. The person has exceeded 70 percent of the people in that test.

42. What effect does unlimited training have upon individual differences in an ability?
    A. It emphasizes individual differences in most cases.
    B. It minimizes individual differences in most cases.
    C. Individuals remain the same relative to each other in most cases.
    D. It depends entirely upon the ability-minimizing differences in some abilities and emphasizing differences in others.

43. Unlike the M.A., the I.Q. by itself indicates
    A. brightness or dullness
    B. chronological age
    C. factors in intelligence
    D. the level of absolute intelligence achieved

44. Terman's study with gifted children showed that the gifted child was
    A. physically inferior to the average
    B. better adjusted on personality and character tests than the average
    C. more uneven in his educational achievements
    D. more prone to mental disease than the average

45. In order to assure that intelligence items are fair,
    A. all items must be unfamiliar to those taking the test
    B. all items must be familiar to those taking the test
    C. items must be either unfamiliar or assuredly familiar
    D. novelty or familiarity of items does not count

46. Intelligence quotients from different tests are
    A. directly comparable
    B. invariably different in size
    C. similar in meaning but not identical
    D. inversely comparable

47. The study of adult performance of Terman's high I.Q. children showed that
    A. the more successful the adult, the higher his childhood score had been
    B. the more successful adults differed most from the less successful ones on the verbal scale
    C. personal factor of adjustment were more important than intellectual factors
    D. childhood ability is a relatively poor predictor of adult success

48. The difficulty of items in the Binet-Simon tests was based upon the
    A. opinion of experts in all fields
    B. judgment of educators and psychologists
    C. percentage passing at different ages
    D. scores made by superior children

49. The Stanford-Binet and the Wechsler-Bellevue tests have this in common: both are _____ tests.
    A. principally verbal
    B. group
    C. individual
    D. maze

50. A child has an M.A. of 8 years, and his C.A. is just 6 years. If his I.Q. remains constant, his M.A. at the age of 12 years will be
    A. 15 years, 8 months
    B. 16 years
    C. 16 years, 4 months
    D. 17 years

KEY (CORRECT ANSWERS)

1. C	11. D	21. B	31. D	41. A
2. C	12. D	22. C	32. D	42. C
3. A	13. B	23. B	33. B	43. A
4. D	14. C	24. A	34. C	44. C
5. B	15. A	25. B	35. A	45. C
6. C	16. B	26. D	36. A	46. C
7. D	17. B	27. A	37. B	47. C
8. D	18. B	28. C	38. B	48. C
9. D	19. B	29. C	39. B	49. C
10. A	20. C	30. B	40. B	50. B

TEST 2

DIRECTIONS: Each question or incomplete statement is followed by several suggested answers or completions. Select the one that BEST answers the question or completes the statement. *PRINT THE LETTER OF THE CORRECT ANSWER IN THE SPACE AT THE RIGHT.*

1. The free-association technique is MOST closely associated with 1.____
   A. Cattell B. Janet C. Freud D. Charcot

2. Psychology can BEST be characterized as 2.____
   A. philosophical B. biosocial C. physiological D. practical

3. Experimental reports on the transfer of training indicate that the degree of transfer varies with the intelligence of pupils 3.____
   A. not at all
   B. slightly
   C. to a great extent
   D. inversely

4. The history of hypnosis is MOST closely tied to the treatment of 4.____
   A. hysteria
   B. the insane
   C. psychotic people
   D. organic disorders

5. Placebos are used to 5.____
   A. control attitudes
   B. relieve tensions in a subject
   C. quantify the results of an experiment
   D. counterbalance controlled conditions

6. The principle of the conditioned response as formulated by E.L. Thorndike was referred to as the law of 6.____
   A. associative shifting
   B. recency
   C. exercise
   D. readiness

7. A study of language development in the child would be designated 7.____
   A. comparative B. ontogenetic C. experimental D. phylogenetic

8. A phobia is _____ anxiety. 8.____
   A. less specific than
   B. more specific than
   C. synonymous with an
   D. less acute than

9. Anything which initiates an organic activity is 9.____
   A. an independent variable
   B. qualitative
   C. external
   D. a stimulus

10. Pseudopods are comparable, in a primitive way, with 10.____
    A. receptors
    B. auditory organs
    C. organs of equilibrium
    D. effectors

2 (#2)

11. Neurons beginning in receptors are 11.____
    A. afferent   B. effectors   C. efferent   D. connectors

12. The all-or-nothing principle means that 12.____
    A. all neurons entering a synapse discharge at the same time or not at all
    B. different intensities of stimulation above threshold have the same effect upon the unit activated
    C. a nerve is completely refractory or not at all
    D. all fibers in a nerve are simultaneously activated, or none is

13. Egocentricity, irritability, selfishness, and moroseness are MOST characteristic of which one of the following personality types? 13.____
    A. Paranoid   B. Epileptoid   C. Cycloid   D. Schizoid

14. The pyramidal cells give rise to 14.____
    A. ascending tracts
    B. descending tracts
    C. fibers particularly concerned with form discrimination
    D. the law of "roots"

15. The part of the body which FIRST becomes responsive to tactual stimulation is the 15.____
    A. head   B. hand   C. foot   D. abdomen

16. Which of the following has been shown in the laboratory to result in loss of critical ability, including the capacity for self-criticism? 16.____
    A. Aphasia   B. Aphonia   C. Ataxia   D. Anoxia

17. Studies of successful foster homes point to the conclusion that the discipline in such homes tends to be 17.____
    A. lenient   B. strict   C. consistent   D. self-imposed

18. According to studies of the success of foster home placement, which of the following combinations of factors is MOST likely to be associated with successful placement? 18.____
    A. Under nine years of age at placement, and average intelligence
    B. Over thirteen years of age at placement, and very superior intelligence
    C. Under nine years of age at placement, and very superior mentality
    D. Over thirteen years of age at placement, and average mentality

19. For clinical purposes, projective techniques are considered by many psychologists to be superior to personality rating scales because projective techniques are 19.____
    A. easier to administer   B. take less of the examiner's time
    C. more interesting to the subject   D. less subject to conscious control

20. The amount of relationship between variables is indicated by 20.____
    A. frequency polygon   B. correlation coefficient
    C. ratio scale   D. mean

21. There is less variability in a _____ curve.
    A. high and narrow
    B. high and broad
    C. low and narrow
    D. low and broad

22. If both male and female rats had one dominant and one recessive gene (Rr), the percentage of offsprings with two recessive genes (rr) would be
    A. 25
    B. 50
    C. 75
    D. 100

23. The effect of familiarity in the case of inter-racial attitudes is
    A. dependent upon the nature of the contact
    B. a tendency to breed contempt
    C. greater understanding and acceptance
    D. of little importance one way or the other

24. Intelligence is
    A. measured directly
    B. inferred from performance
    C. symbolic reasoning
    D. not characteristic of animals

25. If the M.A. is greater than the C.A., the I.Q. will be
    A. average
    B. below average
    C. above average
    D. meaningless

26. When performance and verbal tests of intelligence are correlated, the coefficient is
    A. negative and high
    B. negative and low
    C. positive and high
    D. positive and low

27. Terman's research indicates that as gifted children grow older, they
    A. lose their high level of intelligence
    B. achieve more than the general population
    C. are poorly adjusted
    D. all of the above

28. Cretinism is caused by
    A. inadequate prenatal environment
    B. hypothyroidism
    C. excess cerebrospinal fluid
    D. no known physiological cause

29. Improving the environment of samples of American Indians tends to
    A. leave their I.Q. scores unchanged
    B. decrease their I.Q. scores
    C. increase their I.Q. scores to the same level as whites
    D. increase their scores to a level significantly above whites

30. A large number of aptitude tests can be factored into
    A. one specific factor
    B. fifteen specific factors
    C. several factors
    D. as many factors as there are tests

31. An item is considered valid if it
    A. is of high difficulty compared to some external criterion
    B. discriminates between high and low groups on some external criterion
    C. has face validity
    D. is interesting

32. The FIRST stage of developing aptitude tests is
    A. job analysis
    B. standardization
    C. test evaluation
    D. item selection

33. Valid tests of vocational selection can help
    A. determine the probability of future success
    B. in guidance
    C. eliminate potentially unsuccessful candidates
    D. all of the above

34. In the first months of an infant's life, the baby's reflex responses are
    A. almost the only reactions the baby shows
    B. virtually absent from behavior
    C. more accurate than later in life
    D. less conspicuous than generalized mass reactions

35. Play and reading interests of boys and girls will be found to be MOST different at the age of _____ years.
    A. three
    B. six
    C. twelve
    D. eighteen

36. The unsociability often reported for very bright children is MOST likely due to
    A. their biological makeup
    B. their complete absorption in intellectual pursuits
    C. their lack of personal attractiveness
    D. the absence of suitable companions

37. If we measure a number of individuals upon a variety of complex mental functions, we will find that the different functions show
    A. a negative relationship
    B. no relationship
    C. a fairly high degree of positive relationship
    D. practically a perfect positive relationship

38. As children in groups with very limited environments, such as canal-boat dwellers, "hollow-folk," etc., grow older, their I.Q. is found to
    A. increase
    B. stay the same
    C. decrease
    D. vary widely and irregularly

39. Forgetting curves are characterized by
    A. a more rapid initial drop followed by slower forgetting
    B. a constant rate of loss
    C. a slow drop at first, with more rapid loss
    D. none of the above

40. Formulation of rules, definitions, and verbal generalizations
    A. has virtually no place in the process of learning
    B. should be the final outcome of learning
    C. should accompany and be accompanied by actual experience
    D. should be the first step in any learning

41. Human infants allowed to choose their own foods in a "cafeteria" feeding experiment
    A. ate an excess of sugar
    B. showed weight losses
    C. selected a balanced diet
    D. developed a temporary salt deficiency

42. Sexual behavior in human females is
    A. largely instinctive
    B. directly regulated by hormones
    C. regulated by the estrus cycle
    D. primarily a function of learned habits, attitudes, and fears

43. The Arapesh man may be characterized as having a strong _____ motive.
    A. cooperative   B. assertive   C. acquisitive   D. achievement

44. The level of aspiration tends to be set _____ actual performance.
    A. far above   B. slightly above
    C. slightly below   D. far below

45. According to Freud's concept of motivation, man's PRIMARY motives are
    A. mostly conscious   B. mostly unconscious
    C. all sexual   D. learned

46. The type of attitude test that attempts to get at attitudes indirectly in order to get around the subject's defensiveness is called
    A. projective   B. questionnaire
    C. self-rating   D. sneaky

47. Which of the following is the MOST likely example of a "functionally autonomous" motive? A
    A. hungry rat pressing a bar to get food
    B. man who enjoys working after retirement even though he doesn't need the money
    C. young sexually mature male standing on the street corner "watching all the girls go by"
    D. man who changes jobs to earn more money

48. Which emotion is the later developing one? 48.____
    A. Anger B. Jealousy C. Fright D. Fear

49. Which nervous system is MOST involved in emotional response? 49.____
    A. Somatic B. Parasympathetic
    C. Sympathetic D. Peripheral

50. Which is TRUE? Blind-deaf children 50.____
    A. do not have the usual emotional expressions
    B. express the emotion of anger but not the emotion of joy
    C. express the emotion of joy but not that of anger
    D. express both emotions of anger and emotions of joy

KEY (CORRECT ANSWERS)

1. C	11. A	21. A	31. B	41. C
2. B	12. B	22. A	32. A	42. D
3. C	13. B	23. A	33. D	43. A
4. A	14. B	24. B	34. D	44. B
5. D	15. A	25. C	35. C	45. B
6. A	16. D	26. C	36. D	46. A
7. B	17. C	27. B	37. C	47. B
8. B	18. A	28. B	38. C	48. B
9. D	19. D	29. C	39. A	49. C
10. D	20. B	30. C	40. C	50. D

TEST 3

DIRECTIONS: Each question or incomplete statement is followed by several suggested answers or completions. Select the one that BEST answers the question or completes the statement. *PRINT THE LETTER OF THE CORRECT ANSWER IN THE SPACE AT THE RIGHT.*

1. If identical twins are separated early in life, one going to an average environment and the other to an intellectually impoverished environment,
   A. their I.Q.'s would probably not differ by more than one point
   B. there would be a larger difference in I.Q. than if they were fraternal twins
   C. the twin in the impoverished environment would be handicapped in all later learning
   D. the twin in the average environment would have an average I.Q.

1.____

2. One of the following is not necessarily involved in the standardization of an aptitude test. Which is NOT necessary?
   A. Factor analysis
   B. Job analysis
   C. Some measure of success on the job
   D. Validation

2.____

3. In selecting tests for measuring aptitude, the MOST important thing to consider is their
   A. face validity
   B. ease of administration
   C. ease of scoring
   D. correlation with measures of success

3.____

4. Scholastic aptitude is MOST closely related to
   A. general intelligence   B. personality
   C. interest inventory   D. clerical aptitude

4.____

5. When a fertilized cell divides, its chromosomes
   A. change their chemical constitution   B. are duplicated
   C. undergo multiplication   D. lose certain genes

5.____

6. The spread of a distribution of scores is a measure of
   A. multimodality   B. skewness   C. overlapping   D. variability

6.____

7. Class intervals are used to
   A. group scores
   B. find the range
   C. determine the normality of a distribution
   D. determine whether or not a distribution is bimodal

7.____

8. We sometimes repeat a test administration in order to
   A. develop a ratio scale   B. determine absolute zero
   C. find the relative zero point   D. discover reliability

8.____

9. The only scale with an absolute zero point is the
   A. interval   B. ratio   C. ordinal   D. rating

10. A strong stimulus tends to
    A. accelerate the nerve impulse
    B. activate more fibers
    C. prolong the relative refractory period
    D. interfere with the propagation

11. Muscles, tendons, and joints contain organs which mediate what sense?
    A. Touch   B. Equilibrium   C. Kinesthesis   D. Pressure

12. The contacts of organisms with their environment are mediated by
    A. effectors   B. connectors
    C. receptors   D. reciprocal innervation

13. Split litters are for the purpose of controlling
    A. the effects of isolation on behavior   B. drug effects on performance
    C. counterbalanced conditions   D. the effects of heredity

14. The intervening variable inferred to account for the neural basis of memory is called
    A. redintegration   B. association
    C. associative strength   D. an engram

15. Which of the following statements BEST summarizes the outcomes of experiments in which subjects heard a narrative and later attempted to reproduce it?
    A. About 90% of the original material is retained.
    B. The theme tends to persist.
    C. 50% of the details are distorted.
    D. Elaboration of detail is absent.

16. Resistance to extinction is due to
    A. libido   B. emotion
    C. drive strength   D. homeostasis

17. The so-called "need for affection" may be a need for
    A. stimulation   B. love   C. warmth   D. activity

18. The "oldest of mental provinces," as quoted from Freud, refers to
    A. the ego   B. emotions
    C. consciousness   D. the id

19. Morphine addiction
    A. is caused by the absence of homeostasis
    B. is a motive that only human beings can develop
    C. illustrates an acquired need
    D. is hereditary

20. A child's level of aspiration should be encouraged depending upon
    A. his interests
    B. his aptitudes
    C. the culture in which he lives
    D. his parents' socio-economic level

21. Aggressiveness is conceived as PRIMARILY based upon
    A. frustration   B. competition   C. jealousy   D. rivalry

22. Identification can BEST be related to
    A. sympathy   B. happiness   C. anger   D. fear

23. On what basis have emotions in some cases been differentiated physiologically?
    A. EEG
    B. Blood sugar level
    C. Intestinal activity
    D. Tremors

24. Expecting an increasingly unpleasant situation will MOST likely bring on
    A. fear   B. anger   C. startle   D. anxiety

25. Apathy stems from injury to the
    A. spinal cord
    B. cerebellum
    C. hypothalamus
    D. parasympathetic system

26. Pavlov's concept of the basis of neurosis was that it stemmed from
    A. conflict between positive and negative response tendencies
    B. low frustration tolerance
    C. loss of positive goal orientation
    D. aggression

27. An employee who is fired throws himself on the floor, shouts, and kicks his feet. This is an example of
    A. effective behavior
    B. behavior which is goal-motivated
    C. projection
    D. regression

28. Psychosomatic disorders are MOST likely produced by or related to
    A. an injury to the associative tissue of the cortex
    B. drugs
    C. compensation
    D. anxiety

29. Neurosis
    A. is an organic condition
    B. can be experimentally induced in animals
    C. is an exclusively human reaction
    D. is due mainly to the complexity of cultures

30. The parts of speech which predominate at first are
    A. vowel sounds
    B. holophrases
    C. verbs
    D. consonants

31. A test with a *RIGHT, RIGHT, LEFT, LEFT* sequence may be used to discover whether or not an infant can
    A. recall   B. imitate   C. verbalize   D. reason

    31.____

32. In co-twin control experiments, what we wish to control is
    A. exercise   B. maturation
    C. past experience   D. sex differences

    32.____

33. If a child of C.A. 6 has an M.A. of 9, its I.Q. is
    A. very superior   B. normal
    C. likely to remain constant D. inferior

    33.____

34. In Spearman's treatment of test results, *g* stands for
    A. the growth factor
    B. the degree of genius exhibited in test performance
    C. general ability
    D. so-called group factors

    34.____

35. Two tests are regarded as measuring the same factor when they
    A. are uncorrelated
    B. are intercorrelated to a low degree
    C. are highly correlated
    D. highly correlated with other tests but uncorrelated to each other

    35.____

36. Anticipatory responses
    A. precede the conditioned stimulus
    B. follow the unconditioned stimulus
    C. follow the conditioned stimulus
    D. occur without any relation to the stimulating conditions

    36.____

37. The MOST efficient reinforcement is
    A. continuous   B. intermittent
    C. secondary   D. variable interval

    37.____

38. Differential conditioning provides us with a tool for studying
    A. motor process   B. sensory discrimination
    C. maturation of behavior D. the higher learning processes

    38.____

39. The token reward experiment illustrates _____ reinforcement.
    A. variable ratio   B. fixed interval
    C. intermittent   D. secondary

    39.____

40. All learning curves have a
    A. plateau   B. potential physiological limit
    C. more or less steady rise D. great degree of fluctuation

    40.____

41. Detour problems provide us especially with information concerning
    A. insight   B. trial-and-error
    C. motor coordination D. memory

    41.____

42. Learning how to learn is an example of
   A. positive transfer
   B. bilateral transfer
   C. verbal-to-motor transfer
   D. insight

43. In all instances of learning, however, different, the outcomes have in common the following feature: all
   A. involve modifications of the organism
   B. are examples of operant conditioning
   C. involve acquisition of skill
   D. involve primary reinforcement

44. The theory of mass action implies that, in the learning of complex mazes, the degree of retardation is related to the
   A. extent of brain damage
   B. location of brain damage
   C. size of the maze pathway
   D. extent to which the sense of vision is disturbed

45. Differential forgetting may be used to account for the effectiveness of
   A. recitation
   B. distributed learning
   C. perseveration
   D. whole learning

46. The relearning method is otherwise known as the _____ method.
   A. anticipation   B. reproduction   C. saving   D. retention

47. The experimental group learns list A, learns list B, and then recalls list A. The control group learns list A, rests, and then recalls list A. This is the research design of experiments on
   A. proactive inhibition
   B. distributed learning
   C. negative transfer of verbal learning
   D. retroactive inhibition

48. The LOWEST level of intelligence is characteristic of
   A. hydrocephaly
   B. mongolianism
   C. microcephaly
   D. cretinism

49. The metal growth curve shows
   A. a slow rise followed by successively larger increments
   B. about the same increment from year to year until the early twenties
   C. smaller increments during the late teens than occurred during the preceding years
   D. no difference in slope for those above and below average ability

50. If Blacks and Whites with the same average intelligence at birth were given equal educational opportunities, their I.Q.'s would, by the teen age, be
   A. equal
   B. different and in favor of Whites
   C. different and in favor of Blacks
   D. unpredictable

KEY (CORRECT ANSWERS)

1. C	11. C	21. A	31. D	41. A
2. A	12. C	22. A	32. D	42. A
3. D	13. D	23. B	33. A	43. A
4. A	14. D	24. D	34. C	44. A
5. B	15. B	25. D	35. C	45. C
6. D	16. C	26. A	36. C	46. C
7. A	17. A	27. D	37. B	47. D
8. D	18. D	28. D	38. B	48. D
9. B	19. C	29. B	39. D	49. C
10. B	20. B	30. A	40. B	50. D

TEST 4

DIRECTIONS: Each question or incomplete statement is followed by several suggested answers or completions. Select the one that BEST answers the question or completes the statement. *PRINT THE LETTER OF THE CORRECT ANSWER IN THE SPACE AT THE RIGHT.*

1. Autistic thinking is characterized by 1.____
   A. dominance by the reality principle
   B. wishes and desires, without regard to realistic considerations
   C. regression to the mean
   D. Aristotelian logic
   E. none of the above

2. In Freudian theory, the pre-conscious differs from the unconscious in that 2.____
   A. the pre-conscious contains what may easily be made conscious
   B. the pre-conscious represents a higher level of cortical development
   C. the pre-conscious is equivalent to the super-ego and the unconscious is equivalent to the id
   D. the pre-conscious is an earlier development
   E. none of the above

3. In Freudian theory, an instinct is characterized by 3.____
   A. an aim   B. impetus or intensity   C. a source
   D. an object   E. all of the above

4. Thinking, as Freud conceived of it, is 4.____
   A. only found in rational adults
   B. characterized by primary and secondary processes
   C. produced by the reality principle
   D. unaffected by defense mechanisms
   E. none of the above

5. Which of the following was(were) associated with hypnosis? 5.____
   A. Charcot   B. Mesmer   C. Braid
   D. Bernheim   E. All of the above

6. Gall and Spurzheim were associated with 6.____
   A. philosophical psychology
   B. localization of cortical function
   C. the effect of ductless glands on behavior
   D. the doctrine of phrenology
   E. the development of the cephalic index

7. Anamnesis refers to 7.____
   A. the patient's history prior to the onset of a mental disorder
   B. a rare form of memory loss
   C. disruption of normal associative processes
   D. personality changes produced by a lesion of the parietal lobe
   E. a metabolic disease that causes mental deficiency

8. Clang associations are
    A. often found in psychotics
    B. usually neologisms
    C. words which resemble the sound of another word
    D. all of the above
    E. none of the above

9. Differentiation between organically caused hemiplegia and hysterically caused hemiplegia is made on the basis that in the hysterical state
    A. symptoms do not follow neurological patterns
    B. the patient gains advantages by his symptoms
    C. symptoms are often exaggerated
    D. all of the above
    E. none of the above

10. Ideas of reference
    A. are often found in hysterical personalities
    B. do not usually occur in paranoid states
    C. are not a common feature of psychoses
    D. all of the above
    E. none of the above

11. Which of the following does NOT belong?
    A. Insulin coma therapy   B. Psychosurgery
    C. Psychotherapy   D. Metrazol therapy
    E. Electro-convulsive shock therapy

12. Which of the following does NOT belong?
    A. Lying   B. Denial   C. Repression
    D. Isolation   E. Projection

13. The life style
    A. is a concept proposed by Alfred Adler
    B. is not determined by genetic factors
    C. refers to a person's mode of attempting to achieve life goals
    D. all of the above
    E. none of the above

14. Maskelyne's dismissal of his assistant Kinnebrook is an example of
    A. the personal equation in scientific work
    B. sublimated sadism
    C. the need for accurate recording instruments
    D. perceptual distortion
    E. none of the above

15. Explaining an event or phenomenon in its simplest terms or with the fewest assumptions is called
    A. Occam's razor
    B. Morgan's canon
    C. the law of parsimony
    D. all of the above
    E. none of the above

16. Parapsychology is
    A. another name for metapsychological formulations
    B. an alternate approach to problems in ego psychology
    C. typified in Wilhelm Reich's work on Orgone theory
    D. all of the above
    E. none of the above

17. When a person responds to one situation with feelings that arise from another situation in his past, this is called
    A. reaction-formation
    B. conceptual diffusion
    C. regression
    D. all of the above
    E. none of the above

18. Dementia praecox is a term that was once widely used to describe the condition that is now designated as
    A. melancholia
    B. schizophrenia
    C. neurasthenia
    D. psychasthenia
    E. none of the above

19. When the distinction is made, the idiopathic epilepsies are regarded by writers on the subject as differing from the symptomatic epilepsies in that the former are
    A. manifested in petit mal rather than grand mal attacks
    B. those in which gross lesions cannot be demonstrated
    C. pseudo-epilepsies whose symptoms are of hysterical origin\
    D. accompanied by mental deterioration
    E. none of the above

20. Cretinism is associated with which one of the following types of glandular disfunctioning?
    A. Hyperthyroidism
    B. Hypothyroidism
    C. Hyperpituitarism
    D. Hypopituitarism
    E. None of the above

21. Psychologically, the whole is more than the sum of its parts, is a statement which has been quoted most as a tenet of which of the following schools of psychological thought?
    A. Sensationalism
    B. Configurationalism
    C. Psychoanalysis
    D. Structuralism
    E. None of the above

22. Somatic manifestations of personality disorders are BEST characterized as those which are
    A. hereditary in origin
    B. indicative of structural alteration
    C. revealed in physical functioning
    D. environmentally acquired
    E. none of the above

23. Of the following characteristics, the one that is MOST common to all types of epilepsy is
    A. recurring lapses of consciousness   B. mental deterioration
    C. convulsive manifestations   D. localized brain lesions
    E. none of the above

24. A child develops a headache every time a particularly distasteful task is announced. This type of reaction is characterized as
    A. hysterical   B. rationalization   C. projection
    D. physiological   E. none of the above

25. Eidetic images are
    A. subjective visual, auditory, and similar phenomena which assume a perceptual character
    B. pure sensory impressions free of the meaning derived from recognition of objects perceived
    C. hallucinations manifested by adults who, except for this special departure from reality, are normally adjusted
    D. hallucinations manifested by highly suggestible pre-psychotic children
    E. none of the above

26. The term used to refer to a blue that is as blue as it can be is
    A. chromatic   B. ethereal   C. bright
    D. luminous   E. saturated

27. Which one of the following is comparable with the film in a camera?
    A. Iris   B. Retina   C. choroid coat
    D. fovea   E. lens

28. A deuteranope has
    A. normal color vision
    B. red-green blindness
    C. a color weakness in the red end of the spectrum
    D. all of the above
    E. none of the above

29. According to the Young-Helmholtz theory, stimulation with blue, which is then removed, would produce a negative after-image of the following hue:
    A. red   B. green   C. yellow   D. purple   E. orange

30. Night blindness is due to a defect in the
    A. rods   B. cones   C. optic chiasma
    D. occipital lobes   E. medulla oblongata

31. The difference between a frequency of 1000 cycles played on, respectively, a harp and a French horn is PRIMARILY one of
    A. amplitude   B. timbre   C. volume
    D. aural harmonics   E. frequency

32. The MOST indispensable aspect of the auditory mechanism is the
    A. tectorial membrane
    B. basilar membrane
    C. tympanic membrane
    D. stirrup
    E. none of the above

33. The disease known as tabes dorsalis involves which of the following senses?
    A. Organic
    B. Static
    C. Kinesthetic
    D. Cutaneous
    E. All of the above

34. Which one of the following is NOT a primary taste experience?
    A. Sour
    B. Bitter
    C. Sweet
    D. Burnt
    E. All of the above

35. Vascular changes are theorized to relate to
    A. pain sensitivity
    B. tactile sensitivity
    C. olfaction
    D. gustatory sensitivity
    E. temperature sensitivity

36. Evidence against the motor theory of thinking is provided by which of the following?
    A. Action currents are found in certain muscles when the subject is thinking
    B. Cases of sensory aphasia
    C. Observations on a curarized human subject
    D. Observation on the thinking process in deaf-mutes
    E. None of the above

37. For which of the following types of thinking is language MOST necessary?
    A. Concept formation
    B. Logical thinking
    C. Problem-solving
    D. Discovery of a principle
    E. All of the above

38. Double alternation differs from sensory discrimination in that
    A. external cues are absent
    B. verbalization is necessary
    C. only human subjects can succeed in the task
    D. retention of previous experience is necessary
    E. verbalization is unnecessary

39. Which of the following is NOT necessary for concept formation?
    A. Generalization
    B. Abstraction
    C. Discrimination
    D. Verbalization
    E. Deduction

40. A basic element in most problems which test for insight is
    A. language skills
    B. a detour
    C. rote memory
    D. instrumental conditioning
    E. concept formation

41. Which of the following perceptions depends on the phi phenomenon?
    A. The apparent backward movement of the landscape seen from a moving train
    B. The negative after-effect of movement
    C. The apparent movement of a stationary pinpoint of light in a dark room
    D. The moving headlines on the New York Times Building
    E. All of the above

42. The tendency to see objects as stable and unchanging in spite of changes in retinal stimulation is known as
    A. mind set
    B. perceptual set
    C. primitive organization
    D. relational discrimination
    E. perceptual constancy

43. If cues to distance were eliminated or distorted,
    A. size constancy would break down
    B. brightness constancy would break down
    C. knowledge of the real size of the stimulus object would re-establish size constancy
    D. all of the above
    E. none of the above

44.

    An animal is trained to respond to (x) and not to (y), then is presented with (y) and a smaller triangle (z). Which of the following is CORRECT about the responses to y and z?
    A. Only absolute responses are made.
    B. Only few relational responses are made.
    C. Animals cannot be trained to make absolute responses.
    D. Relational responses are more easily demonstrated.
    E. Relational responses and absolute responses are made.

45. If the eyes were 8 inches, instead of 2 ½ inches apart, retinal disparity would be
    A. the same
    B. ineffective as a cue for depth
    C. greater
    D. less
    E. variable

46. Evidence that visual depth perception in some animals may be unlearned is provided by
    A. visual cliff experiments
    B. studies of chimpanzees deprived of light stimulation
    C. experiments on conventional cataract cases in humans
    D. all of the above
    E. none of the above

47. When interrupted tasks are recalled more readily than completed tasks, we have an illustration of the
    A. autokinetic effect
    B. Zeigarnik effect
    C. law of least effort
    D. law of effect
    E. irrational effect

48. Under which one of the following conditions will interrupted tasks be recalled more readily than completed tasks? The subject
    A. is ego-oriented
    B. displays an ego-defensive motive
    C. is task-oriented
    D. is of below-average intelligence
    E. is of above-average intelligence

49. A person who sleeps for six hours after learning a list of ten nonsense syllables is likely to remember more of this list, upon awakening, than a person who has
    A. slept for eight hours
    B. been awake for eight hours
    C. slept for four hours
    D. memorized a list of meaningful words and then slept for six hours
    E. not slept

50. Retroactive inhibition is
    A. the inhibiting effect exerted upon the retention of any activity or material by other activities intervening between the original learning and the retention test
    B. a shrinkage of nerve cells, for whatever reason, that are involved in memory processes
    C. the effect of sleep upon the retention of material learned in the waking stage
    D. the process by which material learned earlier facilitates the later learning of new material
    E. the inhibiting effect exerted upon the retention of material learned in the sleeping stage

KEY (CORRECT ANSWERS)

1.	B	11.	C	21.	B	31.	B	41.	D
2.	A	12.	A	22.	C	32.	B	42.	E
3.	E	13.	D	23.	A	33.	C	43.	A
4.	B	14.	A	24.	A	34.	D	44.	D
5.	E	15.	D	25.	A	35.	E	45.	C
6.	D	16.	E	26.	E	36.	C	46.	C
7.	A	17.	E	27.	B	37.	C	47.	B
8.	D	18.	B	28.	D	38.	A	48.	A
9.	D	19.	B	29.	C	39.	D	49.	D
10.	E	20.	B	30.	A	40.	B	50.	A

TEST 5

DIRECTIONS: Each question or incomplete statement is followed by several suggested answers or completions. Select the one that BEST answers the question or completes the statement. *PRINT THE LETTER OF THE CORRECT ANSWER IN THE SPACE AT THE RIGHT.*

1. When one eye is stimulated only with red and the other only with green, the resultant effect is of which hue?
   A. Purple B. Aquamarine C. Yellow
   D. Blue E. None of the above

   1.____

2. If a pressure wave is aperiodic, an observer would hear
   A. a tone B. a purple sine wave C. noise
   D. a complex tone E. none of the above

   2.____

3. The otolith organs are important to the sense of
   A. smell B. balance C. audition
   D. kinesthesia E. none of the above

   3.____

4. In which of the following abilities do dull and gifted children tend to differ MOST markedly?
   A. Arithmetical computation B. Drawing
   C. Reading comprehension D. Spelling
   E. Music

   4.____

5. Although the retinal image is relatively flat, it contains _____ of the various aspects of the external world.
   A. replicas B. images C. correlates
   D. residues E. none of the above

   5.____

6. In the experiment on perception of obstacles by the blind, cutaneous stimulation of exposed areas of skin is
   A. a necessary condition
   B. a sufficient condition
   C. a necessary and sufficient condition
   D. unimportant in the perception of obstacles
   E. none of the above

   6.____

7. In the experiments on perception of obstacles by the blind, the performance of the normal subjects was
   A. better than that of the blind subjects
   B. always inferior to that of the blind subjects
   C. improved considerably with practice
   D. was not directly comparable to that of the blind subjects
   E. none of the above

   7.____

8. The critical ration refers to
   A. a difference that is greater than change variation
   B. a minimum cutting score on an aptitude test
   C. the size of the class interval in a frequency distribution
   D. a type of scale involving an absolute zero point
   E. none of the above

9. The presence of the absolute refractory period indicates
   A. that the axon has just been stimulated
   B. damage to the cell membrane
   C. that the nerve has just fired
   D. that the relative refractory period has just passed
   E. none of the above

10. A low innervation ratio means that
    A. fewer muscle fibers are connected to a neuron
    B. dextrous movement is possible
    C. a muscle is likely to be fatigued more quickly
    D. a muscle is not likely to be so powerful as most others
    E. a muscle is likely to be more powerful than most others

11. The sequence of irritability in a nerve just after a stimulation is:
    I. supernormal period   II. relative refractory period
    III. absolute refractory period   IV. period of latent addition
    V. subnormal period
    The CORRECT sequence is:
    A. I, II, III, IV, V   B. IV, II, III, V, I   C. III, II, I, IV, V
    D. IV, III, II, I, V   E. III, IV, II, I, V

12. The loss of the ability to speak in a person suffering from aphasia
    A. is a reaction formation to aggressive impulses
    B. arises from damage to the pre-frontal lobes
    C. stems from a brain lesion and means a permanent and total loss of speech
    D. arises from cerebellar ataxia
    E. none of the above

13. The presence of a Babinski reflex in an adult indicates a
    A. lesion of the hypothalamus   B. lesion of the occipital lobe
    C. lesion of the pre-frontal lobes D. regression towards childhood
    E. none of the above

14. Striated muscles are
    A. under voluntary control   B. capable of quick motion
    C. arranged antagonistically   D. all of the above
    E. none of the above

15. Which of the following forms of mental retardation are believed to have a physiological base?
    A. Cretinism
    B. Mongoloidism
    C. Tay-Sachs disease
    D. all of the above
    E. none of the above

16. The neuron is characterized by
    A. easy fatigability
    B. differential degree of response
    C. ready regeneration after injury
    D. all of the above
    E. none of the above

17. The cerebrum consists of the
    A. occipital lobe
    B. temporal lobe
    C. frontal lobe
    D. parietal lobe
    E. all of the above

18. Which of the following does NOT belong with the others?
    A. General paresis
    B. Huntington's chorea
    C. Gil de la Tourette's disease
    D. Cretinism
    E. Hebephrenic schizophrenia

19. Korsakoff's syndrome is caused by
    A. congenital syphilis
    B. acute hypothyroidism
    C. a functional psychosis
    D. acute alcoholism
    E. none of the above

20. The concept of the collective unconscious is MAINLY associated with
    A. Sigmund Freud
    B. Adolph Meyer
    C. Alfred Adler
    D. Earnest Jones
    E. none of the above

21. Projective tests entail
    A. free choice of response
    B. relatively unstructured stimuli
    C. relatively unspecific directions
    D. all of the above
    E. none of the above

22. In Freudian theory, the ego
    A. is identical with the self-dynamism in Sullivan's theory
    B. is contiguous with consciousness
    C. is under the control of the super-ego
    D. all of the above
    E. none of the above

23. The ego, in Freudian theory,
    A. is partly conscious and partly unconscious
    B. is considered to mediate between id drives, super-ego demands and reality
    C. is considered to maintain contact with reality
    D. all of the above
    E. none of the above

24. The von Frey hairs are
    A. a neurotic disorder characterized by extreme skin sensitivity
    B. a rare psychiatric diagnosis
    C. a procedure designed to measure sensitivity to pressure
    D. all of the above
    E. none of the above

25. Factor analytic techniques
    A. indicate the least number of factors necessary to explain intercorrelations among test scores
    B. are employed when regular psychoanalytic techniques fail
    C. are used in blood serum analyses
    D. demonstrate the effect of genetic factors upon behavior
    E. none of the above

26. Studies of intelligence differences between Blacks and Whites have shown that
    A. Whites are generally superior when Black educational opportunities are higher than Whites
    B. there is a large overlap between the two groups
    C. Blacks are generally superior when educational opportunities are equal
    D. Whites are superior on verbal scales and Blacks are superior on performance scales
    E. none of the above

27. Identical twins are more alike in intelligence than are fraternal twins. This fact indicates that
    A. heredity has a part in determining intelligence
    B. intelligence is not an inherited characteristic
    C. the environment of fraternal twins is more alike than the environment of identical twins
    D. intelligence is determined partly by prenatal nutrition
    E. all of the above

28. Studies of foster children indicate that
    A. I.Q. tends to rise as a result of more favorable environment
    B. I.Q. tends to drop as a result of emotional readjustment
    C. there is no relation between I.Q. and environment
    D. mental age is affected by placement in a good foster home, but I.Q. is not
    E. none of the above

29. Where data exist on intelligence test scores for both biological and foster mothers of children, it is clear that the children's scores are
    A. more like the true mother's
    B. more like the foster mother's
    C. about midway between the two
    D. determined by the socioeconomic status of the foster mother
    E. none of the above

30. The relationship between parental-intelligence and true child-intelligence scores suggests that
    A. paternal scores are more highly related
    B. maternal scores are more highly related
    C. they are related to about the same degree
    D. the major factor is the difference between the intelligence level of the parents which throws the relationship toward one or the other of them
    E. none of the above

31. Both the mean and the median
    A. are good measures of central tendency in skewed distributions
    B. can be manipulated algebraically
    C. are used equally in advanced statistical techniques
    D. will be similar in symmetrical distributions
    E. all of the above

32. The pioneer in the study of verbal learning was
    A. Galton
    B. Cattell
    C. Ebbinghaus
    D. Wundt
    E. none of the above

33. Functionalism was essentially a psychology of
    A. development
    B. adjustment
    C. experience
    D. meaning
    E. none of the above

34. Physiological homeostasis represents an attempt to maintain
    A. constancy of the internal environment
    B. reticular balance
    C. organic potency
    D. virility
    E. none of the above

35. So-called pleasure areas are found in the
    A. cortex
    B. pituitary gland
    C. septal region
    D. reticular structure
    E. none of the above

36. After removal of gonads in mature human beings,
    A. sexual motivation is not present anymore
    B. there is an increase in the thirst drive
    C. food cannot be used as an incentive in learning experiments
    D. sexual motivation may still continue
    E. none of the above

37. The CHIEF point of the anecdote about the dispute over the number of teeth possessed by a horse was that
    A. many facts can be achieved through a reasoning process
    B. it is out of philosophical disputes that advances in knowledge are made
    C. scientific procedure requires observation
    D. truth is to be sought through application of basic principles
    E. none of the above

38. Attributing human traits to animals is known as
    A. animism
    B. anthropomorphism
    C. subjective inference
    D. anecdotalism
    E. none of the above

39. Functional psychoses
    A. are due to brain injuries
    B. have not been traced to structural damage
    C. are still regarded as incurable
    D. are a form of hysteria
    E. none of the above

40. Mental hygiene is concerned, for the most part, with
    A. the cure of psychotic people
    B. the prevention of behavior disorders
    C. custodial treatment of the mentally ill
    D. the psychotherapy of neurotic behavior
    E. none of the above

41. In an experiment on how alcohol influences learning, the dependent variable might be
    A. some aspect of learning
    B. variable amounts of alcohol
    C. a controlled amount of alcohol
    D. the subject's previous learning experience
    E. none of the above

42. The standard deviation is USUALLY preferred as a measure of variation because
    A. it can be manipulated algebraically
    B. it is usually a stable measure
    C. it is less subject to influence by extreme scores than the quartile
    D. A and B above are correct
    E. A and C above are correct

43. Making a Type I or a Type II error,
    A. involves one or another type of error in problem solving
    B. involves accepting or rejecting an hypothesis erroneously
    C. means a type of error has been made in the administration of a test
    D. all of the above
    E. none of the above

44. A correlation coefficient of 1.17 means
    A. a computational mistake was made
    B. a low degree of relationship
    C. a high degree of relationship
    D. a mistake was made in the experiment
    E. the data is homoscedastic

45. A correlation coefficient is a number that
    A. indicates the degree of variation of each variable
    B. how much homoscedasticity is present
    C. indicates the amount of association between two variables
    D. shows the critical ratio between two distributions
    E. all of the above

46. Kurtosis
    A. refers to an emotional disorder that is more severe than an ordinary neurosis
    B. is a brain lesion of the frontal lobes that causes personality changes
    C. is the name of one of the scales on the Minnesota Multi-phasic Personality Inventory
    D. refers to one of Kretschmer's body types
    E. refers to the shape of a frequency distribution

47. The standard deviation
    A. is a measure of variability about the mean
    B. indicates the degree of variation about the median
    C. is a measure of variability between two scores
    D. is usually smarter than the average deviation
    E. is the square of the variance

48. The middle score of a skewed distribution is found at the
    A. mean   B. mean   C. mode
    D. interquartile range   E. standard deviation

49. A coefficient of correlation may be computed by
    A. the Pearson Product-Moment method
    B. the Spearman Rank-Order method
    C. the Bi-serial method
    D. all of the above
    E. none of the above

50. About one-half of the population is below average in intelligence
    A. because of an increase in the number of mental defectives born
    B. because of a decrease in the standards for education
    C. because of the loss of more intelligent people in wars
    D. because of the difficulty of the test
    E. none of the above

KEY (CORRECT ANSWERS)

1. C	11. D	21. D	31. D	41. A
2. C	12. E	22. E	32. C	42. D
3. A	13. E	23. D	33. D	43. B
4. C	14. D	24. C	34. A	44. A
5. B	15. D	25. A	35. D	45. C
6. D	16. E	26. B	36. D	46. E
7. C	17. E	27. A	37. C	47. A
8. A	18. E	28. A	38. B	48. B
9. C	19. D	29. D	39. B	49. D
10. A	20. E	30. C	40. B	50. E

EXAMINATION SECTION
TEST 1

DIRECTIONS: Each question or incomplete statement is followed by several suggested answers or completions. Select the one that BEST answers the question or completes the statement. *PRINT THE LETTER OF THE CORRECT ANSWER IN THE SPACE AT THE RIGHT.*

1. Discerning the common elements in situations that are otherwise different is referred to as

    A. cue reduction
    B. discrimination
    C. relevant grouping
    D. generalizing
    E. abstracting

2. Closed system thinking is BEST illustrated by

    A. solving a series of addition problems
    B. determining the best route to a new location
    C. writing a novel
    D. devising a new formula
    E. inventing a better mousetrap

3. Distribution of practice is especially relevant to

    A. weakening of incorrect responses
    B. slowing down performance
    C. increased tension
    D. reducing accuracy of performance
    E. reducing motivation

4. Directive therapy may be BEST described as a therapy in which

    A. the subject selects his own goals
    B. past experiences are given primary attention in problem solving
    C. the therapist prescribes
    D. the individual, not the present problem, is the focus
    E. the emotional rather than intellectual factors are emphasized

5. Drugs which produce behavior resembling psychoses are called

    A. psychotherapeutic drugs
    B. tranquilizers
    C. sulfa-drugs
    D. antibiotics
    E. psychotomimetic drugs

6. A characteristic wave pattern of waking-sleeping is shown by the record made by a

    A. compass
    B. thermometer
    C. kymograph
    D. galvanometer
    E. electroencephalograph

7. A woman with strong maternal tendencies is found incapable of bearing children and is in no position to adopt one. The behavior that would be MOST valuable to her is

    A. sublimation
    B. rationalization
    C. regression
    D. projection
    E. fantasy

8. That part of the process of concept formation where the individual learns to respond only to certain properties that objects have in common is called

   A. differentiation   B. assimilation   C. abstraction
   D. generalization   E. adaptation

9. An abscissa would be found in

   A. the nervous system
   B. the eye
   C. a human ear
   D. the reactions of a schizophrenic
   E. a graph

10. Genes for blue eyes are said to be recessive. Mr. and Mrs. Jones have blue eyes. If they have eight children, the number having blue eyes should be

    A. 6   B. 2   C. 4   D. 8   E. 0

11. The subjectively established unit of measure of visual intensity is called

    A. bril   B. fissure   C. pyknic   D. veg   E. rho

12. Stating that a mental disorder is functional means that it

    A. can best be treated by surgery or drugs
    B. is concerned with the personality only
    C. is a product of imagination only
    D. has been learned
    E. produces no physical symptoms

13. A temporary flat place in a learning curve is called

    A. a fatigue index   B. an ordinate
    C. a plateau   D. an abscissa
    E. skewedness

14. An experimental procedure which involves reinforcement of one stimulus and extinction of all others will eventually lead to

    A. generalization
    B. latent learning
    C. higher order conditioning
    D. conditioned discrimination
    E. negative adaptation

15. The refractory period has reference to

    A. nerve functioning   B. retroactive inhibition
    C. reverberating circuits D. regressive tendencies
    E. retinal images

16. Self-understanding is aided MOST by

    A. repressing threatening memories
    B. attempting to understand one's own motives
    C. the use of defense mechanisms

D. avoiding anxiety-producing situations
E. venting one's emotions whenever one feels like it

17. Ossicles are found in the 17._____

   A. kidneys   B. eyes   C. heart   D. ears   E. lungs

18. The MOST important factor in producing apparent motion in the absence of actual motion is 18._____

   A. time interval between stimuli
   B. fatigue
   C. size of stimuli
   D. intensity of stimuli
   E. actual movement of stimuli

19. Negative transfer of training means that when something has been previously learned, it 19._____

   A. hinders recall
   B. reinforces new learning
   C. makes one forget old learning
   D. aids learning in a new situation
   E. hinders new learning

20. Mrs. Jones did not want her third child and has never been able to really care about it, but she shows excessive affection toward the child.
    This is an example of 20._____

   A. rationalization   B. repression
   C. sublimation   D. reaction formation
   E. projection

21. The SIMPLEST form of learning is generally regarded as a form of 21._____

   A. conditioning   B. rote memory
   C. associative process   D. functional learning
   E. discrimination

22. A defense mechanism MOST apt to do harm to others is that of 22._____

   A. rationalization   B. reaction formation
   C. compensation   D. projection
   E. sublimation

23. The term insanity as viewed by the psychological world 23._____

   A. is synonymous with neurosis
   B. is synonymous with psychosis
   C. is a legal term
   D. means disorganization of the ego structure
   E. refers to loss of contact with reality

24. When the brain is exposed and the somesthetic area is stimulated directly by a micro-electrode, subjects report no pain since pain is 24._____

   A. an abnormal condition
   B. a function of the thalamus

C. not a brain function
D. a product of the imagination
E. a function of the cortex

25. There would be no galvanic skin reflex if there were

A. no sweat gland activity
B. no cortical stimulation
C. damage to the occipital lobe
D. no creative thought
E. no reminiscence

KEY (CORRECT ANSWERS)

1. E
2. A
3. A
4. C
5. E

6. E
7. A
8. C
9. E
10. D

11. A
12. D
13. C
14. D
15. A

16. B
17. D
18. A
19. E
20. D

21. A
22. D
23. C
24. B
25. A

TEST 2

DIRECTIONS: Each question or incomplete statement is followed by several suggested answers or completions. Select the one that BEST answers the question or completes the statement. *PRINT THE LETTER OF THE CORRECT ANSWER IN THE SPACE AT THE RIGHT.*

1. Persons who hold prejudices against minority groups MOST likely retain their negative attitudes as a result of

    A. proven inferiority of minority groups
    B. wide reading and studying
    C. general distrust or dislike of persons who are different
    D. personal experiences
    E. logical thinking

2. The temporary nature of the extinction of a previously conditioned response is BEST exemplified by

    A. relearning
    B. stimulus generalization
    C. conditioned discrimination
    D. spontaneous recovery
    E. higher order conditioning

3. Putting two or more elements of past experience together to make something new is called

    A. differentiation
    B. reasoning
    C. abstracting
    D. learning set
    E. solution by reduced cues

4. The simultaneous contraction and relaxation of antagonistic muscles is called

    A. reciprocal inhibition
    B. general inhibition
    C. extension reflex
    D. reflex action
    E. flexion reflex

5. Pavlov's experiments in which he used one conditioned response to build another conditioned response is an example of

    A. secondary conditioning
    B. higher-order conditioning
    C. classical conditioning
    D. reinforcement
    E. advanced conditioning

6. If a child born does not have enough oxygen for a long period of time, or has no oxygen at all for a short period of time, and still lives, he is likely to

    A. become extremely active in early childhood
    B. become an invalid
    C. recover completely in a long time

2 (#2)

D. recover completely in a short time
E. have a marked loss in intelligence

7. In emotional states, the sympathetic part of the autonomic nervous system   7.____

A. reduces the discharge of adrenalin
B. decreases heart rate
C. causes irregular breathing
D. contracts the pupil of the eye
E. speeds up the flow of saliva

8. A defense mechanism is a device adopted unconsciously by the individual   8.____

A. in order to achieve beyond his level of aspiration
B. for the deception of authority figures
C. so that he may solve his basic problems
D. so that he may engage in fantasy
E. for fooling himself about his motivational conflicts

9. We can expect to find the MOST elaborate social structures in   9.____

A. societies with few natural resources
B. highly industrialized societies
C. societies with strict child-rearing techniques
D. primitive societies
E. the oldest cultures

10. A regression to childish levels of behavior occurs in a type of schizophrenia called   10.____

A. hebephrenic   B. dementia praecox
C. simple   D. paranoid
E. catatonic

11. Letters of recommendation when used for selecting employees are usually regarded as being   11.____

A. unbiased evaluations of employees
B. of doubtful value
C. highly reliable
D. rarely stereotyped
E. good discriminators between qualified and unqualified persons

12. One of the MOST obvious characteristics of perception is its   12.____

A. resistance to shifting
B. all inclusive quality
C. agreement with the physical world
D. selective nature
E. unique sameness from person to person

13. In the conditioning experiments of Pavlov with the dog, bell, and food, the dependent variable was the   13.____

A. condition of the dog B. amount of salivation
C. time element D. ringing of the bell
E. presenting of food

14. We could not form concepts if we could not 14.____

    A. see colors
    B. vocalize
    C. read
    D. discriminate
    E. form clear mental images

15. The use of psychological methods and techniques by employers to select and retain the 15.____
    BEST employees is a branch of psychology known as _____ psychology.

    A. social B. industrial C. general
    D. vocational E. clinical

16. One of Freud's MAIN contributions to psychology was 16.____

    A. the classification of mental disorders
    B. his theory of personality
    C. the use of the experimental method
    D. the use of scientific techniques
    E. his use of phenomenology

17. The MOST immediate cause of pain is probably 17.____

    A. tissue damage
    B. continuous stimulation
    C. pressure in the cerebral cortex
    D. excessive release of nerve energy
    E. overstimulation

18. Typically, there is least hostility, most enjoyment, and most constructive work in groups 18.____
    where the leadership is

    A. formal B. laissez-faire C. informal
    D. autocratic E. democratic

19. When people reproduce things from memory, a general characteristic is that remem- 19.____
    bered items are changed by

    A. becoming less familiar in detail
    B. omission of details
    C. becoming less symmetrical
    D. substitution of details
    E. addition of details

20. The Young-Helmholtz theory of color vision holds that seeing the color yellow results 20.____
    from the simultaneous stimulation of _____ cones.

    A. red and white B. blue and red C. blue and green
    D. red and green E. green and white

21. When ESP experiments have been done by different investigators under rigidly controlled conditions, the results

    A. simply have not agreed
    B. have been useless
    C. prove conclusively that some people have extra-sensory perception
    D. always have agreed
    E. rule out ESP even as a possibility

22. A person interested in the study of the physiology of taste would also be interested in

    A. tabes dorsalis
    B. kinesthesis
    C. alkaloids
    D. papillae
    E. free nerve endings

23. Generally, theories of color vision regard the eye as an instrument that

    A. integrates and mixes effects of light
    B. mixes light much as we mix colors in paint
    C. has separate receptors for each hue
    D. reflects light like a mirror
    E. reduces light to its color elements

24. Rest periods should come at

    A. mid-afternoon
    B. immediately after production begins to drop
    C. late morning
    D. mid-morning
    E. just before production falls off

25. The process of building up and breaking down stores of energy in the body is referred to as

    A. homeostasis
    B. hyperphaglia
    C. ambiversion
    D. opsin
    E. metabolism

KEY (CORRECT ANSWERS)

1. C
2. D
3. B
4. A
5. B

6. E
7. C
8. E
9. B
10. E

11. C
12. D
13. B
14. D
15. B

16. B
17. A
18. E
19. B
20. D

21. A
22. D
23. A
24. E
25. E

TEST 3

DIRECTIONS: Each question or incomplete statement is followed by several suggested answers or completions. Select the one that BEST answers the question or completes the statement. *PRINT THE LETTER OF THE CORRECT ANSWER IN THE SPACE AT THE RIGHT.*

1. Any improvement in memory that occurs from memorizing nonsense syllables will be the result of

   A. exercise of the brain
   B. direct transfer
   C. reduced resistance to memorizing
   D. building of permanent neural connections for memory
   E. improved methods of memorizing

2. A primary group is one which is characterized by

   A. lack of prejudice
   B. democratic procedures
   C. natural leadership
   D. concern for people
   E. face-to-face relationships

3. In psychoanalysis, the importance of dreams lies in their

   A. continuity of content
   B. variety of content
   C. latent content
   D. freedom of expression
   E. manifest content

4. When events occur together in space and/or time, they are said to be

   A. antithetical
   B. contiguous
   C. conflicting
   D. identical
   E. conditioned

5. A psychotherapist whose patient has an extreme fear of parties arranges to get the patient to attend a party where he suffers no embarrassment and really likes and enjoys the party.
   This type of therapy is called

   A. supportive
   B. desensitization
   C. insight
   D. re-education
   E. hypnotic

6. At full maturity, Bill's height was only forty-six inches. Of the following glands, the one which was MOST likely involved in causing Bill's lack of growth is.

   A. gonads
   B. pituitary
   C. thyroid
   D. pancreas
   E. parathyroid

7. The development of irrational fears (phobias) in people is an illustration of

   A. extinction
   B. stimulus generalization
   C. partial reinforcement
   D. reinforcement
   E. instrumental learning

8. When two sets of measures (two factors) correlate highly, this means that 8.____

   A. scores on the two factors will be in the same rank order
   B. the two factors tend to vary together
   C. scores will be the same on both factors
   D. one factor causes the other
   E. none of the above

9. Spearman found that the different parts of tests used to measure intelligence are inter-correlated. He concluded that this common element is basic to the total intellectual functioning of the individual.
   He called this element 9.____

   A. basic aptitude   B. *g*
   C. intelligence   D. reasoning potential
   E. *s*

10. The inborn aspect of intelligence is BEST represented by the term 10.____

    A. flexibility   B. ability   C. versatility
    D. adaptation   E. capacity

11. If we are trying to predict success or failure after training in a specific line of work, we would MOST likely administer a test of 11.____

    A. aptitude   B. achievement   C. intelligence
    D. personality   E. interest

12. The psychoanalytic process by which the patient regards the therapist in the same emotional context as he regarded his father is known as 12.____

    A. contemporary causation   B. resistance
    C. free association   D. functional autonomy
    E. transference

13. Emotions are MOST closely similar to 13.____

    A. perceptions   B. aspirations   C. images
    D. habits   E. drives

14. The LOWEST type of feeblemindedness is known as 14.____

    A. low normal   B. imbecile   C. idiot
    D. borderline   E. moron

15. The MOST generally accepted explanation of forgetting is that it results from 15.____

    A. conscious repression
    B. interference by new learnings
    C. inadequate original learning
    D. reduced motivation
    E. the passing of time

16. The central nervous system is located 16.____

    A. within the skull and spinal column
    B. near the surface of the body
    C. in ganglion centers

D. only within the spinal column
E. within the whole body excluding extremities

17. The Thematic Apperception Test is made up of a series of

    A. situational events
    B. cartoons with the captions left off
    C. geometric forms
    D. ambiguous pictures
    E. ink blots on a white background

18. Since fear motivates behavior, it must be considered

    A. a drive
    B. always constructive
    C. as always overly observable
    D. a positive goal
    E. a weak response

19. The area of study which has provided the MOST information on cultures is

    A. physiology   B. dermatology   C. psychology
    D. anthropology   E. sociology

20. Learning consists of relatively permanent changes in behavior that are the result of

    A. spontaneous recovery   B. gradients
    C. experience   D. maturation
    E. inherited tendencies

21. The psychoanalytic technique which requires the patient to say whatever comes to his mind regardless of how irrelevant or objectionable it may seem is called

    A. cathexis   B. dream analysis
    C. transference   D. free association
    E. catharsis

22. Present evaluation of psychosurgery is that

    A. it causes too little change in emotional reactions
    B. it should be employed more extensively
    C. less drastic and more effective treatment methods are now available
    D. its effects are too temporary
    E. it is the best technique for treating schizophrenia

23. The study reporting the results of various combinations of time spent in recitation as contrasted with time spent in reading found the MOST rewarding combination of reading and recitation to be

    A. 60 percent reading, 40 percent recitation
    B. 40 percent reading, 60 percent recitation
    C. 80 percent recitation, 20 percent reading
    D. 30 percent recitation, 70 percent reading
    E. 50-50 split

24. One of the CHIEF characteristics of functionalism as a system of psychology was its emphasis on

   A. the study of the subconscious
   B. learned rather than unlearned behavior
   C. the study of the total behavior and experience of an individual
   D. the study of animal behavior
   E. the study of mental content

25. When compared with extremely intelligent children, on the average, normal children are found to be

   A. taller and heavier
   B. better adjusted socially
   C. more stable emotionally
   D. physically weaker
   E. healthier

KEY (CORRECT ANSWERS)

1.	E	11.	A
2.	E	12.	E
3.	C	13.	E
4.	B	14.	C
5.	C	15.	B
6.	B	16.	A
7.	B	17.	D
8.	B	18.	A
9.	B	19.	D
10.	E	20.	C

21.	D
22.	C
23.	C
24.	C
25.	D

TEST 4

DIRECTIONS: Each question or incomplete statement is followed by several suggested answers or completions. Select the one that BEST answers the question or completes the statement. *PRINT THE LETTER OF THE CORRECT ANSWER IN THE SPACE AT THE RIGHT.*

1. A situation in which an organism slowly becomes accustomed to a fear-invoking stimulus and acts less and less frightened is known as

    A. habituation
    B. imprinting
    C. pseudo-conditioning
    D. inhibition
    E. sensitization

    1.____

2. Vision is to retinal disparity as sound is to

    A. ear
    B. stereophonic
    C. eyeball
    D. facial vision
    E. brightness

    2.____

3. The MAIN value of learning a general theory is that it helps one to

    A. demonstrate knowledge of a subject
    B. integrate a number of separate facts
    C. make mental associations
    D. express ideas easily
    E. avoid being specific

    3.____

4. In a summary of several surveys, the MOST important item that workers said they wanted in a job was

    A. comfortable working conditions
    B. a good employer
    C. high pay
    D. opportunity for advancement
    E. job security

    4.____

5. Hyperthyroidism causes

    A. mental deficiency
    B. sleepiness
    C. over-activity
    D. inactivity
    E. sluggishness

    5.____

6. A detailed account of all the facts pertinent to a job is a

    A. employment table
    B. job analysis
    C. occupational index
    D. job list
    E. job description

    6.____

7. The normal curve is an example of a

    A. pie chart
    B. histogram
    C. bar graph
    D. frequency polygon
    E. skewed distribution

    7.____

8. The metabolic process is MOST dependent upon 8.____

   A. nitrogen B. hydrogen
   C. carbon dioxide D. oxygen
   E. carbon monoxide

9. Casual observation by a researcher led him to hypothesize that most drivers obey a certain traffic signal at an intersection. He then systematically observed traffic at the intersection in order to test his hypothesis. 9.____
   One may infer that the research was based on

   A. both inductive and deductive reasoning
   B. inductive reasoning
   C. deductive reasoning
   D. improper controls
   E. insufficient evidence

10. Experimental studies on transfer of training have caused psychologists to reject the principle of 10.____

    A. trial-and-error B. instrumental learning
    C. formal discipline D. S-R bonds
    E. negative transfer

11. Contiguity is especially relevant to 11.____

    A. size constancy
    B. the occurrence of two items closely together in time and place
    C. accommodation of the lens
    D. reduced cues
    E. perception

12. In the early days of psychotherapy, the MOST widely used technique was 12.____

    A. directive B. psychoanalytic
    C. client-centered D. non-directive
    E. eclectic

13. In evaluating the TAT and the Rorschach as measuring devices for personality characteristics, one may say correctly that they are 13.____

    A. nonverbal
    B. easily administered
    C. group tests
    D. objectively scored
    E. subtle kinds of interviews

14. If we were to learn the meaning of a word by hearing or seeing it used in different ways, we would have an example of concept formation by the method called 14.____

    A. definition B. context
    C. generalization D. classification
    E. discriminative learning

15. The term *equivalence of function* means that when a part of the brain is injured, very often the function of the damaged area 15.____

A. is completely lost to the animal
B. can be restored in the same area
C. is of so little importance it is not missed
D. appears as a malfunction in another brain area
E. is taken over by another area of the brain

16. Presenting the conditioning stimulus without reinforcement to an organism previously conditioned leads to

   A. spontaneous discrimination
   B. conditioned discrimination
   C. extinction
   D. spontaneous recovery
   E. stimulus generalization

17. Studies which correlate the beliefs of a child with beliefs of parents show _____ correlation.

   A. no positive
   B. significant positive
   C. no significant
   D. low negative
   E. perfect negative

18. Scientists have long been inclined to believe that the immediate stimulus for the sensation of pain is

   A. overtaxing of cells
   B. disturbed chemical balance
   C. tissue injury
   D. pressure
   E. touching of certain nerve endings

19. The fact that the cerebral cortex is NOT functioning at birth means that

   A. learning of complex behavior is delayed
   B. the child will be developmentally retarded
   C. all reflex behavior is impossible
   D. crying is prevented
   E. muscular movements cannot be made

20. A specialized psychotherapeutic technique designed to permit patients to act out roles, situations, and fantasies related to their problems is called

   A. group therapy
   B. play therapy
   C. client-centered therapy
   D. psychoanalysis
   E. psychodrama

21. A person who is disturbed by groupings made of dots or dashes where some of the dots or dashes are missing is PROBABLY responding to the innate grouping factor called

   A. illusion
   B. proximity
   C. similarity
   D. continuation
   E. symmetry

22. Aphasia means

   A. loss of olfactory sensitivity
   B. loss of ability to understand what is heard or read
   C. word blindness
   D. muscular incoordination
   E. loss of memory

23. In psychoanalytic theory, that part of the personality conceived as a storehouse of motives and instinctual reactions is called the

   A. sexual syndrome   B. self   C. ego
   D. id   E. superego

24. In psychoanalytic theory, that part of the personality which reconciles pleasure-seeking impulses with the reality of society is called the

   A. libido   B. ego   C. conscience
   D. superego   E. id

25. The Bard-Cannon theory of emotions assumes that

   A. all emotions are emergency reactions
   B. feelings and bodily changes are simultaneously initiated through the hypothalamus
   C. emotion is completely under intellectual control
   D. feelings are the result of bodily changes
   E. expressions of emotion are produced by feelings

KEY (CORRECT ANSWERS)

1. A
2. B
3. B
4. E
5. C

6. E
7. D
8. D
9. A
10. C

11. B
12. A
13. E
14. B
15. E

16. C
17. B
18. C
19. A
20. E

21. D
22. B
23. D
24. B
25. B

TEST 5

DIRECTIONS: Each question or incomplete statement is followed by several suggested answers or completions. Select the one that BEST answers the question or completes the statement. *PRINT THE LETTER OF THE CORRECT ANSWER IN THE SPACE AT THE RIGHT.*

1. If one were to punish an individual who is expressing anger, we could expect that person's level of anger to

    A. increase
    B. fluctuate in an unpredictable way
    C. drop to zero
    D. decrease
    E. remain relatively the same

    1.____

2. Tranquilizers have the general characteristics of

    A. giving intellectual vigor
    B. keeping one awake in emergency situations
    C. reducing anxiety
    D. giving athletes more energy
    E. making one feel exhilarated

    2.____

3. Gestalt psychology is characterized by

    A. analysis of sensations
    B. free association
    C. organization and configurations
    D. the study of conditioned reflexes
    E. an emphasis on introspection as in structuralism

    3.____

4. Personal maladjustment is MOST likely to occur when the perceived self is

    A. radically different from the real self
    B. the individual's awareness of his own personality
    C. the result of past experiences
    D. traced to early infancy
    E. greatly influenced by learning

    4.____

5. The research finding that the intelligence of fraternal twins correlates significantly HIGHER than that of sibling pairs indicates that

    A. fraternal twins are more intelligent than siblings
    B. environment is a factor
    C. heredity is a factor
    D. intelligence measures are unreliable
    E. siblings are more intelligent than fraternal twins

    5.____

6. A reflex is

    A. exemplified in a recurrent nerve circuit
    B. an unlearned response to a stimulus
    C. the same as reaction time

    6.____

D. the same as an instinct
E. any rapid response

7. An attribute is

   A. unrelated to the physical aspects of a stimulus
   B. in the stimulus rather than the observer
   C. the total quality of a stimulus
   D. a perceived aspect of a stimulus
   E. exemplified by a tone

8. Sexual perversions are the result of

   A. inadequate physical development
   B. learning
   C. lack of appropriate hormones
   D. instinctive patterning
   E. overly strong sex drive

9. At the synapse,

   A. nerve impulses may reverse direction and travel back through the excited neuron
   B. the nerve impulse from one neuron initiates an impulse in the adjoining neuron
   C. direct neural connection is made with the spinal cord
   D. nerve impulses pass from one neuron to the next
   E. there is speeding up of the nerve impulse

10. Research tends to support the conclusion that thirst is the result of

    A. cycling by action of the kidneys
    B. loss of salt through sweating
    C. dehydration of body cells
    D. dryness of the mouth and throat
    E. a shortage of water in the stomach

11. A probability of .01 would indicate that the obtained difference could be expected to occur by chance only once in _____ times.

    A. 10   B. 100   C. 1,000   D. 10,000   E. 100,000

12. Differences in reaction time are MOST dependent upon the

    A. diameter of the nerves involved
    B. length of the nerves involved
    C. number of synapses involved
    D. amount of nerve energy involved
    E. age of the person

13. Children in a family tend to have the same attitudes and beliefs as their parents because of

    A. family loyalty   B. socio-economic status
    C. discipline   D. hereditary factors
    E. learning

14. A differential threshold should also be recognized as

    A. a just noticeable difference
    B. a proportion
    C. maximal discrimination
    D. a ratio
    E. a constant

15. If one child is 8 and another is 10 and both have an I.Q. of 120, the 10-year-old child is

    A. a near genius
    B. of the same intelligence as the 8 year old
    C. less intelligent
    D. brighter
    E. higher in mental age

16. The one essential for problem solving by the insight method is

    A. rote learning
    B. previous experience
    C. ability to use language
    D. to be over 12 years of age
    E. formal schooling

17. A trait is any aspect of personality that is

    A. easily observable but not necessarily quantifiable
    B. reasonably characteristic and distinctive
    C. observable and quantifiable on a ratio scale
    D. overt as well as covert
    E. factorially impure

18. With reference to interpretation of sex differences, research evidence shows that

    A. average differences between groups are small compared to differences within groups
    B. most intelligence tests discriminate against girls and in favor of boys
    C. girls are superior to boys in overall intelligence
    D. variability is not a factor when comparisons are made between groups
    E. boys are superior to girls in overall intelligence

19. A concept is generally learned more easily if it is

    A. pictured   B. concrete   C. abstract
    D. printed   E. new

20. The scatter diagram for a correlation coefficient of +1.00 can be described BEST as

    A. either a straight line or a circle
    B. either an ellipse or a straight line
    C. a straight line
    D. elliptical
    E. circular

21. Variations in expressions of emotions are MOST evident in   21._____

    A. chimpanzees   B. the Japanese
    C. human children   D. human adults
    E. monkeys

22. The median should be recognized as the   22._____

    A. 25th percentile
    B. 75th percentile
    C. score that cuts a distribution in half
    D. average
    E. most frequently occurring score in a distribution

23. The organic psychosis which sometimes occurs as the result of syphilitic infection is   23._____
    known as

    A. dementia praecox   B. neurasthenia
    C. asphasia   D. general paresis
    E. apraxia

24. If the items of a test are too difficult for the students taking it, a plotted curve of the distri-   24._____
    bution of the scores would be

    A. rectangular
    B. normal
    C. bulged up in the center
    D. skewed positively
    E. skewed negatively

25. Unconscious problem solving is often assumed to take place during   25._____

    A. trial-and-error   B. illumination
    C. incubation   D. hypnosis
    E. preparation

KEY (CORRECT ANSWERS)

1. A
2. C
3. C
4. A
5. B
6. B
7. D
8. B
9. B
10. C
11. B
12. C
13. E
14. A
15. E
16. B
17. B
18. A
19. B
20. C
21. D
22. C
23. D
24. D
25. C

EXAMINATION SECTION
TEST 1

DIRECTIONS: Each question or incomplete statement is followed by several suggested answers or completions. Select the one that BEST answers the question or completes the statement. *PRINT THE LETTER OF THE CORRECT ANSWER IN THE SPACE AT THE RIGHT.*

1. Because studies of learning show that events occurring close together in time are easier to associate than those occurring at widely different times, parents should PROBABLY avoid _____ punishment. 1.____

    A. corporal   B. mild   C. consistent
    D. inescapable   E. delay of

2. According to Abraham Maslow's hierarchy of needs, which of the following statements is TRUE? 2.____

    A. Individuals may have peak experiences when meeting physiological needs.
    B. Self-actualization will always precede the meeting of needs for esteem.
    C. There are cultural differences in the rate at which individuals attain self-actualization.
    D. Women are more likely to reach self-actualization than men are.
    E. Physiological needs must be met before an individual achieves self-actualization.

3. A teenager would MOST probably draw on which of the following to recall her tenth birthday party? 3.____

    A. Episodic memory
    B. Semantic memory
    C. Echoic memory
    D. Eidetic imagery
    E. State-dependent learning

4. Leadership, job satisfaction, and employee motivation are all studied in _____ psychology. 4.____

    A. human factors   B. industrial-organizational
    C. community   D. counseling
    E. experimental

5. According to the ethical guidelines set by the American Psychological Association (APA), of the following, it is TRUE that psychological research in which animals are used as subjects 5.____

    A. must not involve the use of surgical procedures
    B. is no longer permitted by the APA without special authorization
    C. should conform to all APA ethical guidelines for animal research
    D. must be limited to investigations that use correlational procedures
    E. may not be conducted by psychologists who do not have a license

6. Which of the following is INCORRECTLY matched with the hormone that it secretes?

   A. Thyroid gland - thyroxine
   B. Adrenal gland - epinephrine
   C. Pituitary gland - prolactin
   D. Pancreas - insulin
   E. Ovary - testosterone

7. Hunger and eating are PRIMARILY regulated by which of the following?

   A. Androgens
   B. Estrogens
   C. The hypothalamus
   D. The kidneys
   E. The medulla oblongata

8. Elena is presented with a list of 20 numbers. When asked to recall this list, she remembers more numbers from the beginning than from the end of the list.
   This phenomenon demonstrates which of the following types of effect?

   A. Mnemonic
   B. Primacy
   C. Recency
   D. Secondary
   E. Clustering

9. A prototype is BEST defined as

   A. an example of habituation
   B. an example of bottom-up processing
   C. the equivalent of feature abstraction
   D. the hypothetical *most typical* instance of a category
   E. an essential element of category membership

10. Theories of motivation that assert the existence of biological motives to maintain the body in a steady state are called

    A. mechanistic
    B. homeostatic
    C. reductionistic
    D. genetic
    E. instinctual

11. According to attribution theory, Pablo is MOST likely to attribute his high score on a difficult exam to

    A. good luck
    B. his intelligence
    C. his instructor's teaching ability
    D. the low level of difficulty of the exam
    E. his classmates' inadequate preparation for the exam

12. In which of the following types of research are the same children tested periodically at different points in their development?

    A. Clinical case study
    B. Between subjects
    C. Cross-sectional
    D. Ethnographic
    E. Longitudinal

13. The occipital lobes contain the

    A. primary visual cortex
    B. prefrontal cortex
    C. somatosensory cortex

D. pons
E. sensory and motor connections to other brain regions

14. Eleanor Gibson and her colleagues have used the visual cliff to measure an infant's ability to perceive

   A. patterns
   B. depth
   C. size constancy
   D. shape constancy
   E. different hues

15. The MOST well-adjusted and socially competent children tend to come from homes where parents employ which of the following parental styles?

   A. Minimal supervision
   B. Authoritarian
   C. Authoritative
   D. Indulgent
   E. Permissive

16. Which of the following approaches to psychology emphasizes observable responses over inner experiences when accounting for behavior?

   A. Behaviorist
   B. Cognitive
   C. Existentialist
   D. Psychodynamic
   E. Structuralist

17. Carla tutors other students because she likes to be helpful, whereas Jane tutors classmates strictly for pay. Their behaviors demonstrate the difference between

   A. primary and secondary drives
   B. instinctive and derived drives
   C. appetitive and aversive motivation
   D. intrinsic and extrinsic motivation
   E. positive and negative reinforcement

18. The view that human emotions are universal has been supported by studies of

   A. facial expressions
   B. body language
   C. linguistic structures
   D. hedonic relevance
   E. biological symmetry

19. Dopamine, norepinephrine, and acetylcholine are all

   A. hormones excreted by the endocrine glands
   B. secretions of the exocrine glands
   C. drugs used in the therapeutic treatment of memory disorders
   D. enzymes involved with the degradation of interneuron signals
   E. neurotransmitters that excite or inhibit a neural signal across a synapse

20. The cognitive theory of depression states that depression results from

   A. anger directed toward the self and significant others
   B. an excess of certain neurotransmitters in the brain
   C. failure in adult love relationships
   D. maladaptive interpretations of life events
   E. oral fixations from disturbed mother-infant relationships

21. All of the following infant behaviors are usually considered by developmental psychologists to be reflexes EXCEPT

    A. rooting
    B. reaching
    C. sucking
    D. grasping
    E. crying

22. The MOST common form of color blindness is related to deficiencies in the

    A. blue-yellow system
    B. red-green system
    C. process of visual summation
    D. bipolar cells
    E. secretion of rhodopsin

23. A person is asked to listen to a series of tones presented in pairs, and asked to say whether the tones in each pair are the same or different in pitch.
    In this situation, the experimenter is MOST likely measuring the individual's

    A. sound localization ability
    B. dichotic listening ability
    C. difference threshold
    D. echoic memory
    E. attention span

24. A survey shows that children who have encyclopedias in their homes earn better grades in school than children whose homes lack encyclopedias. The researcher concludes that having encyclopedias at home improves grades.
    This conclusion is erroneous PRIMARILY because the researcher has incorrectly

    A. failed to allow for experimenter bias
    B. identified the independent variable
    C. identified the dependent variable
    D. inferred correlation from causation
    E. inferred causation from correlation

25. The release of those with mental disorders from mental hospitals for the purpose of treating them in their home communities is called

    A. deinstitutionalization
    B. milieu therapy
    C. primary prevention
    D. secondary prevention
    E. noncrisis intervention

KEY (CORRECT ANSWERS)

1. E	11. B
2. E	12. E
3. A	13. A
4. B	14. B
5. C	15. C
6. E	16. A
7. C	17. D
8. B	18. A
9. D	19. E
10. B	20. D

21. A
22. B
23. C
24. E
25. A

TEST 2

DIRECTIONS: Each question or incomplete statement is followed by several suggested answers or completions. Select the one that BEST answers the question or completes the statement. *PRINT THE LETTER OF THE CORRECT ANSWER IN THE SPACE AT THE RIGHT.*

1. The painful experience associated with termination of the use of an addictive substance is known as

    A. discontinuance
    B. tolerance
    C. withdrawal
    D. forced independence
    E. transduction

    1.____

2. When parents refuse to accept several psychologists' diagnosis of a child's mental illness, they are using which of the following defense mechanisms?

    A. Denial
    B. Displacement
    C. Projection
    D. Rationalization
    E. Regression

    2.____

3. After several trials during which a dog is given a certain kind of food at the same time that a specific tone is sounded, there is evidence of conditioning if the dog salivates when _____ presented _____.

    A. the tone is; only
    B. the food is; only
    C. the food and tone are; together
    D. a different tone is; with the food
    E. a different kind of food is; without a tone

    3.____

4. A complex pattern of organized, unlearned behavior that is species-specific is called a(n)

    A. drive
    B. need
    C. motive
    D. emotion
    E. instinct

    4.____

5. Of the following, the firing of neurons would be CORRECTLY described as a(n)

    A. protoplasmic transfer of ions
    B. finely graded response
    C. all-or-none response
    D. osmotic process
    E. symbiotic function

    5.____

6. Distrust of others is symptomatic of

    A. mania
    B. dementia
    C. catatonia
    D. paranoia
    E. hebephrenia

    6.____

7. Sigmund Freud believed that dream analysis was a useful device for

    A. decreasing repression
    B. sublimating the id
    C. strengthening the superego
    D. displacing instinctual forces
    E. gaining insight into unconscious motives

    7.____

8. When rehearsal of incoming information is prevented, which of the following will MOST likely occur?

   A. The information will remain indefinitely in short-term memory.
   B. There will be no transfer of the information to long-term memory.
   C. The sensory register will stop processing the information.
   D. Retrieval of the information from long-term memory will be easier.
   E. Information already in long-term memory will be integrated with the incoming information.

9. Which of the following behavior-therapy techniques is normally used to reduce fear of heights?

   A. Time-out
   B. Punishment
   C. Discrimination learning
   D. Token economy
   E. Systematic desensitization

10. Painkilling substances produced by the brain are known as

    A. cortisols   B. endorphins   C. glucocorticoids
    D. pheromones   E. hormones

11. Receptors that are especially important for helping a person maintain balance are located in the

    A. gyrus cinguli   B. inner ear   C. tendons
    D. ossicles   E. ligaments

12. In terms of the effect on the central nervous system, alcohol is MOST accurately classified as which of the following types of drug?

    A. Depressant   B. Narcotic   C. Psychoactive
    D. Stimulant   E. Hallucinogen

13. Research findings in the area of interpersonal attraction indicate that individuals are MOST likely to be attracted to others who are

    A. critical of them
    B. similar to them in attitudes and values
    C. like their parents
    D. willing to do favors for them
    E. indulgent of their failings

14. On a fishing trip, Ed realizes that he has mistakenly packed the sewing box instead of the tackle box. He wants to fish but returns home because he does not have any line or hooks.
    Ed's failure to realize that sewing thread can be used as fishing line and that a bent needle can be used as a hook is an example of

    A. poor problem representation
    B. cognitive accommodation
    C. backward masking

D. functional fixedness
E. proactive interference

15. Of the following, the response MOST likely acquired through classical conditioning would be the

    A. startled response of a baby the first time the baby hears thunder
    B. child's fear of dogs after he has been bitten by a dog
    C. cry of pain expressed by a man whose hand has been cut on a piece of broken glass
    D. uncontrollable blinking of a woman who has just gotten dust in her eye
    E. salivation of a dog that is halfway through a bowl of its favorite food

16. If a man who is a heavy smoker is given an electric shock every time he takes a puff on a cigarette, which of the following behavior-modification techniques is being used?

    A. Systematic desensitization
    B. Modeling
    C. Aversive conditioning
    D. Homogeneous reinforcement
    E. Interlocking reinforcement

17. The failure of bystanders to give victims of automobile accidents needed assistance is sometimes explained as an instance of

    A. group polarization
    B. deindividuation
    C. situational attribution
    D. diffusion of responsibility
    E. mere exposure effect

Questions 18-19.

DIRECTIONS: Questions 18 and 19 are to be answered on the basis of the situation described below.

In an experiment designed to determine whether watching violent scenes on television increases the frequency of aggressive behavior in children, one group of subjects saw a nonviolent cartoon and another group saw a violent cartoon. In the play period that followed the viewing of the cartoons, researchers observed the two groups of children together and counted instances of aggressive behavior.

18. The control group in the experiment is the group that

    A. the researchers thought would be most aggressive
    B. performed the larger number of aggressive acts
    C. performed the smaller number of aggressive acts
    D. watched the violent cartoon
    E. watched the nonviolent cartoon

19. The dependent variable in the experiment is the

    A. amount of aggressive behavior exhibited by the children
    B. amount of time that each child spent interacting with the other children

C. group in which each child was originally placed
D. violent cartoon
E. nonviolent cartoon

20. Which of the following is MOST characteristic of individuals with chronic schizophrenia?

    A. Extreme mood swings
    B. Disordered thinking
    C. Profound sadness
    D. Unaccountable loss of body function
    E. Loss of memory

21. Activation of the sympathetic branch of the autonomic nervous system results in a(n) _____ in _____.

    A. increase; salivation
    B. increase; digestion
    C. increase; respiratory rate
    D. decrease; heart rate
    E. decrease; pupil dilation

22. The terms *modeling* and *imitation* are MOST closely associated with which of the following?

    A. Classical conditioning
    B. Gestalt theory
    C. Hypothesis testing
    D. Operant conditioning
    E. Social learning theory

23. In a famous series of experiments conducted by Harry Harlow, infant monkeys were separated from their mothers at birth. The infants were then given two surrogate mothers (a terrycloth *mother* and a wire *mother*), each of which alternately had a nursing bottle that provided food to the infants.
    The experimental results showed that in frightening situations, the infant monkeys

    A. were more likely to become aggressive toward the wire mother than toward the terrycloth mother
    B. failed to seek out either of the mothers because of their lack of experience in seeking contact comfort
    C. preferred the wire mother, even when the terrycloth mother had the nursing bottle
    D. preferred the terrycloth mother, even when the wire mother had the nursing bottle
    E. would run and cling to whichever mother had the nursing bottle

24. According to Sigmund Freud, a child's early experience in coping with external demands leads to the development of the

    A. unconscious
    B. preconscious
    C. Oedipus complex
    D. id
    E. ego

25. According to Albert Bandura, people who believe that their efforts will be successful and that they are in control of events have a high level of

    A. insight
    B. self-efficacy
    C. social responsibility
    D. reciprocal determinism
    E. self-monitoring skill

KEY (CORRECT ANSWERS)

1.	C	11.	B
2.	A	12.	A
3.	A	13.	B
4.	E	14.	D
5.	C	15.	B
6.	D	16.	C
7.	E	17.	D
8.	B	18.	E
9.	E	19.	A
10.	B	20.	B

21. C
22. E
23. D
24. E
25. B

TEST 3

DIRECTIONS: Each question or incomplete statement is followed by several suggested answers or completions. Select the one that BEST answers the question or completes the statement. *PRINT THE LETTER OF THE CORRECT ANSWER IN THE SPACE AT THE RIGHT.*

1. Which of the following has been MOST effective in the treatment of schizophrenia? 1.____

   A. Administration of L-dopa
   B. Prefrontal lobotomy
   C. Psychoanalytic therapy
   D. Drug therapy that blocks neurotransmitter sites
   E. Drug therapy that increases the activity of limbic system neurons

2. Which of the following allows the examination of living brain tissue visually without performing surgery? 2.____

   A. Computerized axial tomography
   B. Stereotaxic examination
   C. Retrograde degeneration
   D. Biofeedback
   E. Ablation

3. The change in the curvature of the lens that enables the eye to focus on objects at various distances is called 3.____

   A. accommodation   B. adaptation   C. conduction
   D. convergence   E. consonance

4. The hypothesis that intelligence is in part inherited is BEST supported by the fact that the IQ correlation for 4.____

   A. pairs of twins reared together is greater than the correlation for pairs of twins reared apart
   B. pairs of identical twins is greater than for pairs of fraternal twins
   C. pairs of fraternal twins is greater than the correlation for other pairs of siblings
   D. adopted children and their adoptive parents is greater than zero
   E. adopted children and their adoptive parents is greater than the correlation for the same children and their biological parents

5. The technique of strengthening behavior by reinforcing successive approximations is called 5.____

   A. positive reinforcement   B. negative reinforcement
   C. distributed practice   D. modeling
   E. shaping

6. According to Jean Piaget, which is the EARLIEST stage at which a child is capable of using simple logic to think about objects and events? 6.____

   A. Sensorimotor   B. Preoperational
   C. Symbolic   D. Concrete operational
   E. Formal operational

7. Bipolar disorders are MOST effectively treated with a combination of tricyclic antidepressants and

   A. acetaminophen
   B. antianxiety drugs
   C. beta-blockers
   D. amphetamines
   E. lithium carbonate

8. The tendency of most people to identify a three-sided figure as a triangle, even when one of its sides is incomplete, is the result of a perceptual process known as

   A. closure
   B. proximity
   C. similarity
   D. feature analysis
   E. shape constancy

9. According to Carl Rogers, the role of the therapist in person-centered psychotherapy is to

   A. accept the client unconditionally so that the client's own desire for mental health and positive growth will flourish
   B. express warmth and empathy and suppress negative feelings that arise in the relationship with the client
   C. use a didactic approach to teach the client to correct maladaptive behavior
   D. establish behavior-change programs to alter the problematic behavior that is often learned in early childhood
   E. define ideal characteristics of mental health for the client and to encourage the client to incorporate these elements in his or her personality

10. One criticism of Sigmund Freud's psychosexual theory of development is that it

    A. emphasizes developmental changes in the oral and anal stages
    B. views adult disorders as adjustments to the environment
    C. views fear of loss as a motivating drive
    D. is based on empirically unverifiable constructs
    E. is based on ethnographic studies

11. For MOST people, which of the following is an activity based in the right hemisphere of the brain?

    A. Muscular control of the right hand
    B. Simple spatial reasoning
    C. Arithmetic reasoning
    D. Language comprehension
    E. Speech

12. Which of the following are the stages in Hans Selye's general adaptation syndrome?

    A. Appraisal, stress response, coping
    B. Shock, anger, self-control
    C. Anxiety, fighting, adapting
    D. Alarm, resistance, exhaustion
    E. Attack, flight, defense

13. Of the following situations, the defense mechanism of reaction formation is BEST exemplified when a(n)

    A. college student speaks sharply to her roommate after quarreling with her professor about her grades
    B. woman who is unaware of her anger toward her friend expresses affection for that friend
    C. runner forgets the name of the opponent who just defeated her in an event for which she held the record
    D. man who dislikes his supervisor believes that his supervisor dislikes him
    E. elderly man lights up a cigarette just after learning that he has been cured of a respiratory ailment

14. The reticular activating system

    A. is the major system in the brain for controlling emotions
    B. functions primarily in the control of motor responses
    C. regulates levels of arousal
    D. regulates body temperature
    E. controls the uptake of pituitary hormones

15. Which of the following types of test is designed to measure an individual's knowledge of a subject?

    A. Achievement   B. Attitude
    C. Aptitude   D. Projective
    E. Interest inventory

16. A word or part of a word that is in itself meaningful, but that cannot be broken into smaller meaningful units, is called a

    A. grapheme   B. morpheme   C. phoneme
    D. performative   E. holophrase

17. Which of the following studies has had the MOST profound impact on ethical issues in psychological research?

    A. Stanley Milgram's study of obedience
    B. Solomon Asch's study of conformity
    C. Daryl Bem's study of self-perception
    D. William McGuire's study of self-concept
    E. Leon Festinger's study of cognitive dissonance

18. Behaviorally oriented therapists seek to modify a client's behavior by

    A. repressing the client's deviant thoughts
    B. relating past events to the client's current behavior
    C. removing the underlying causes of the client's behavioral problems
    D. explaining the significance of the client's dreams
    E. changing the contingencies of reinforcement for the client

19. If Carmelita stares at a red spot for one minute and then shifts her gaze to a white piece of paper, she is likely to experience an afterimage that is

    A. green   B. red   C. blue   D. violet   E. black

20. The place in the retina where the optic nerve exits to the brain is called the

    A. lens
    B. sclera
    C. fovea
    D. blind spot
    E. aqueous humor

21. Responses extinguish fastest when they are learned through which type of reinforcement schedule?

    A. Continuous
    B. Negative
    C. Variable-interval
    D. Variable-ratio
    E. Fixed-interval

22. According to Benjamin Whorf's linguistic relativity hypothesis, which of the following is TRUE?

    A. Individuals have a natural predisposition to learn language.
    B. Individuals learn positive instances of concepts faster than they learn negative instances.
    C. Children learn their first language from their relatives and their peer group.
    D. Different languages predispose those individuals who speak them to think about the world in different ways.
    E. Children learn quantifying words such as *more* and *further* sooner than they do absolutes such as *every* and *all*.

23. In their discussions of the process of development, the advocates of nature in the nature-nurture controversy emphasize which of the following?

    A. Socialization
    B. Cognition
    C. Maturation
    D. Experience
    E. Information processing

24. Which of the following is an example of metacognition?

    A. Memorizing 100 words in a foreign language
    B. Recognizing the faces of people after meeting them once
    C. Solving a complex problem in a slow, deliberate way
    D. Understanding the role of various parts of the brain in memory
    E. Knowing the effectiveness of different strategies for learning statistical formulas

25. The debate over whether development occurs gradually, without discernible shifts, or through a series of distinct stages is termed _____ vs. _____.

    A. nature; nurture
    B. developmental; cognitive
    C. cross-sectional; longitudinal
    D. continuity; discontinuity
    E. maturation; learning

KEY (CORRECT ANSWERS)

1.	D	11.	B
2.	A	12.	D
3.	A	13.	B
4.	B	14.	C
5.	E	15.	A
6.	D	16.	B
7.	E	17.	A
8.	A	18.	E
9.	A	19.	A
10.	D	20.	D

21. A
22. D
23. C
24. E
25. D

TEST 4

DIRECTIONS: Each question or incomplete statement is followed by several suggested answers or completions. Select the one that BEST answers the question or completes the statement. *PRINT THE LETTER OF THE CORRECT ANSWER IN THE SPACE AT THE RIGHT.*

1. Lawrence Kohlberg's theory of moral reasoning is BEST described by which of the following? 1.____

    A. Personal conscience is innate and all human beings develop it at the same rate.
    B. By adulthood, all people judge moral issues in terms of self-chosen principles.
    C. Ethical principles are defined by ideals of reciprocity and human equality in individualistic societies, but by ideals of law and order in collectivistic societies.
    D. Children grow up with morals similar to those of their parents.
    E. Children progress from a morality based on punishment and reward to one defined by convention, and ultimately to one defined by abstract ethical principles.

2. The intelligence quotient (IQ) has traditionally been based on the relationship between an individual's mental age and his or her 2.____

    A. stage of cognitive development
    B. level of physiological development
    C. reading ability
    D. chronological age
    E. quantitative aptitude

3. In Ivan Pavlov's experiments in classical conditioning, the dog's salivation was a(n) 3.____

    A. unconditioned stimulus *only*
    B. unconditioned response *only*
    C. conditioned response *only*
    D. unconditioned and a conditioned stimulus
    E. unconditioned and a conditioned response

4. Which of the following is a characteristic common to all individuals with a narcissistic personality disorder? 4.____

    A. A domineering attitude toward others
    B. An unwarranted sense of self-importance
    C. Restricted ability to express warmth and affection
    D. Inability to form social relationships
    E. Oversensitivity to rejection or possible humiliation

5. Hypnosis has been found useful in the treatment of 5.____

    A. pain   B. autism   C. dementia
    D. paranoia   E. schizophrenia

6. In a normal distribution of test scores, the percentage of scores that fall at or below the mean score is 6.____

    A. 17.5   B. 25   C. 50   D. 66.6   E. 95

7. Persistent repetitive thoughts that cannot be controlled are known as

   A. compulsions   B. obsessions   C. phobias
   D. delusions   E. sublimations

8. Of the following statements, it is TRUE that behaviorism

   A. was formulated to account for cognitive development
   B. is rooted in Sigmund Freud's view of the importance of early experiences
   C. focuses on the development of thought processes and knowledge
   D. holds that development is largely a product of learning
   E. emphasizes the dominance of heredity over environment

9. Individuals diagnosed as having personality disorders

   A. are typically afraid to leave their homes
   B. are consistently psychotic in their cognition and affect
   C. may function reasonably well in society
   D. experience symptoms characterized by sudden onset and short duration
   E. develop their problems as a result of drug abuse

10. The mean will be higher than the median in any distribution that

    A. is symmetrical
    B. is not normal
    C. is positively skewed
    D. represents measures for a random sample
    E. represents measures for a biased sample

11. Which of the following is usually cited as a characteristic of autistic children?

    A. Minor developmental delays in academic achievement
    B. Above-average performance on tests of creativity
    C. Severely impaired interpersonal communication
    D. Tendency to seek younger playmates
    E. Paranoia comparable with that experienced in schizophrenia

12. The goal of rational-emotive therapy is to help clients

    A. focus on the significance of childhood events for current feelings of self-worth
    B. correct self-defeating thoughts about their lives
    C. avoid putting themselves in risky situations
    D. practice relaxation techniques and autohypnosis to reduce anxiety
    E. use introspection to alleviate their feelings of self-doubt

13. A person with sight in only one eye lacks which of the following visual cues for seeing in depth?

    A. Retinal disparity   B. Linear perspective
    C. Motion parallax   D. Relative size
    E. Texture gradient

14. Multiple personality disorder is a type of

    A. dissociative disorder
    B. schizophrenia
    C. dementia praecox
    D. bipolar disorder
    E. manic-depressive psychosis

15. The intensity at which a sound becomes audible for a given individual is known as the individual's

    A. contrast sensitivity
    B. absolute threshold
    C. response threshold
    D. critical frequency
    E. just noticeable difference

16. A teacher asks students to think of as many uses for a brick as possible. By listing 50 uses, most of which the class finds new and unusual, Susan is displaying

    A. computational learning
    B. paired-associate learning
    C. hypothetical thinking
    D. divergent thinking
    E. convergent thinking

17. The PRIMARY effect of the myelin sheath is to

    A. increase the velocity of conduction of the action potential along the axon
    B. increase the velocity of conduction of the action potential across the synapse
    C. facilitate the incoming stimulus signals at sensory receptors
    D. reduce the amount of unused neurotransmitter in the synaptic cleft
    E. protect the terminal buttons of the neuron from destruction by enzymes

18. Which of the following was TRUE of Solomon Asch's experiments on conformity?

    A. People conformed if they knew and respected the authority figure present.
    B. An increase from 7 to 12 confederates increased conformity by experimental subjects.
    C. Experimental subjects conformed less frequently when their judgments were made known to the group.
    D. About 99% of the judgments made by the experimental subjects were wrong.
    E. If the confederates' judgments were not unanimous, the degree of conformity by experimental subjects decreased.

19. Which of the following concepts was advanced by social psychologists to help explain why people who are part of a crowd sometimes commit aggressive, antisocial acts that they would not commit if they were alone?

    A. Groupthink
    B. Cognitive dissonance
    C. Social facilitation
    D. Deindividuation
    E. Catharsis

20. A somatoform disorder is BEST described as an illness that

    A. results from inadequate parenting in childhood
    B. occurs when defense mechanisms are used inappropriately
    C. is psychological in nature with no physical symptoms
    D. is physical in nature with no psychological symptoms
    E. is physical in nature and caused by psychological factors

21. It is widely known in Jerry's social circle that he is the most stubborn and inflexible member of the group. Yet Jerry complains that all his friends are opinionated and rigid. Jerry's complaints are MOST clearly a sign of

    A. displacement
    B. repression
    C. projection
    D. reaction formation
    E. rationalization

22. Which of the following is a genetic disorder that results in a deficiency of a liver enzyme which, if not treated soon after birth, may eventually lead to profound mental retardation?

    A. Down syndrome
    B. Tay-Sachs disease
    C. Fetal alcohol syndrome
    D. Toxoplasmosis
    E. Phenylketonuria (PKU)

23. Electroconvulsive therapy has been MOST successful in the treatment of

    A. phobias
    B. schizophrenia
    C. psychogenic amnesia
    D. multiple personality
    E. clinical depression

24. Of the following, MOST useful in understanding an employer's interpretation of an employee's poor performance would be _____ theory.

    A. Cannon's
    B. the reinforcement
    C. the attribution
    D. the arousal
    E. the cognitive dissonance

25. Of the following, a MAJOR change in perspective in the field of developmental psychology over the past twenty-five years is a

    A. shift from an emphasis on childhood and adolescence to an interest in development over the life span
    B. shift from a cognitive to a psychoanalytic interpretation of developmental phenomena
    C. shift in research focus from cognitive to personality development
    D. decrease in interest in the physiological factors affecting growth and development
    E. decrease in interest in the study of the cognitive components of intellect

KEY (CORRECT ANSWERS)

1.	E	11.	C
2.	D	12.	B
3.	E	13.	A
4.	B	14.	A
5.	A	15.	B
6.	C	16.	D
7.	B	17.	A
8.	D	18.	E
9.	C	19.	D
10.	C	20.	E

21. C
22. E
23. E
24. C
25. A

EXAMINATION SECTION
TEST 1

DIRECTIONS: Each question or incomplete statement is followed by several suggested answers or completions. Select the one that BEST answers the question or completes the statement. *PRINT THE LETTER OF THE CORRECT ANSWER IN THE SPACE AT THE RIGHT.*

1. Which early approach in psychology fostered the development of modern-day applied psychology?

    A. Structuralism
    B. Behaviorism
    C. Functionalism
    D. Pragmatism

    1.____

2. Psychology's answer to the question of whether we are *born* or *made* tends to be

    A. we are *born*
    B. we are *made*
    C. we are both *born* and *made*
    D. neither

    2.____

3. With which of the following would a behaviorist agree?

    A. Conscious experiences can be studied in an objective, precise way.
    B. In order to understand behavior, one must understand the motives behind the behavior.
    C. Behavior can only be explained in terms of phenomenology, that is, an individual's interpretation of experience.
    D. Psychology should be the science of behavior that can be observed by others.

    3.____

4. Which of the following would NOT be expected of an experimental psychologist?
    To

    A. study the effects of reward on learning
    B. look at the relationship between sleep deprivation and task performance
    C. conduct psychotherapy
    D. determine the forces that motivate behavior

    4.____

5. For which of the following is Wilhelm Wundt primarily known?
    The

    A. establishment of the first formal laboratory for research in psychology
    B. distinction between mind and body as two separate entities
    C. discovery of how signals are conducted along nerves in the body
    D. development of the first formal program for training in psychotherapy

    5.____

6. Nature is to nurture as heredity is to

    A. the environment
    B. instincts
    C. genetics
    D. maturation

    6.____

7. *Conscious experiences and perceptions are more than the sum of their parts.* This statement is the basic premise of

   A. introspectionism
   B. structuralism
   C. psychoanalysis
   D. Gestalt psychology

8. G. Stanley Hall is noteworthy in the history of psychology because he

   A. established the first American research laboratory in psychology
   B. launched America's first psychological journal
   C. was the driving force behind the establishment of the American Psychological Association
   D. all of the above

9. A psychologist whose major interest is in how behavior changes as a function of age would specialize in the study of

   A. personality
   B. development
   C. psychometrics
   D. cognition

10. The two disciplines from which psychology emerged were

    A. sociology and philosophy
    B. philosophy and physiology
    C. physiology and theology
    D. physiology and sociology

11. Another name for the behavioral approach in psychology is

    A. stimulus-response psychology
    B. structuralism
    C. applied psychology
    D. Gestalt psychology

12. Janet trained her dog to sit on command by following this behavior with a reward of a dog biscuit and praise. Janet used the principles of

    A. behaviorism
    B. humanism
    C. cognitive psychology
    D. functionalism

13. Empiricism means that knowledge should be acquired through

    A. logical reasoning
    B. common sense
    C. historical tradition
    D. direct observation

14. According to Sigmund Freud, an individual's personality is largely determined by

    A. self-actualizing tendencies
    B. forces in the environment
    C. strivings for superiority
    D. forces in the unconscious

15. Humanists believe that people's behavior is governed by

    A. their self-concepts
    B. unconscious sexual urges
    C. the outcomes of their responses
    D. biochemical processes

16. The main contribution of physiology to the eventual emergence of psychology as a discipline was its   16.____

   A. emphasis on pure reasoning as the path to knowledge
   B. focus on body chemistry as the primary determinant of behavior
   C. emphasis on the scientific method as the primary means of collection information about behavior
   D. treatment of the mind and the body as two distinctly different entities

17. Which psychologist took the stand that organisms tend to repeat responses that lead to positive outcomes and tend not to repeat responses that lead to neutral or negative outcomes?   17.____

   A. Sigmund Freud   B. B.F. Skinner
   C. Carl Rogers   D. Abraham Maslow

18. Which early approach in psychology concentrated on breaking down conscious experience into its basic elements?   18.____

   A. Structuralism   B. Behaviorism
   C. Functionalism   D. Humanism

19. Which of the following demonstrates that psychology has evolved within a sociohistorical context?   19.____
    The

   A. fact that Freud's theory of unconscious sexual conflicts developed during an era of repressed sexuality
   B. demand for psychological services during and after World War II
   C. rise of behaviorism in a pragmatic United States
   D. all of the above

20. B.F. Skinner's contention that behavior is fully determined by one's environment implies that   20.____

   A. we cannot really be held responsible for our actions
   B. punishment is the most effective method for controlling offensive behavior
   C. behavior is a function of genetic predispositions that are only minimally influenced by experience
   D. our thoughts and feelings are the result of reinforcement

21. It would be possible to have more than one _____ in a single data set.   21.____

   A. mean   B. median
   C. mode   D. none of the above

22. A hypothesis is a   22.____

   A. random guess as to what might happen in an experiment
   B. tentative statement about the relationship between two or more variables
   C. conclusion drawn from an experiment
   D. all of the above

23. Which of the following statements is FALSE?

    A. Psychologists sometimes expose animals to treatments that would be unacceptable with human subjects.
    B. There are absolutely no ethical restrictions on what can be done to animals in the name of science
    C. Only a small percentage of psychological studies involve animals.
    D. None of the above

24. The FINAL step in a scientific investigation is to

    A. conduct the study
    B. analyze the data
    C. decide whether or not the hypothesis was supported
    D. report the findings

25. A correlation coefficient of zero describes a _____ relationship between two variables.

    A. positive   B. negative   C. perfect   D. lack of

KEY (CORRECT ANSWERS)

1. C
2. C
3. D
4. C
5. A

6. A
7. D
8. D
9. B
10. B

11. A
12. A
13. D
14. D
15. A

16. C
17. B
18. A
19. D
20. A

21. C
22. B
23. B
24. D
25. D

TEST 2

DIRECTIONS: Each question or incomplete statement is followed by several suggested answers or completions. Select the one that BEST answers the question or completes the statement. *PRINT THE LETTER OF THE CORRECT ANSWER IN THE SPACE AT THE RIGHT.*

1. A researcher wants to see if a protein-enriched diet will enhance the maze-running performance of rats. One group of rats is fed the high-protein diet for the duration of the study; the other group continues to receive ordinary rat chow. In this experiment, the diet fed to the two groups of rats is the _____ variable.

    A. correlated   B. control   C. dependent   D. independent

2. In a study of personality and depression, Professor Norton finds a correlation of -.59 between optimism and depression and a correlation of .32 between introversion and depression. What can Professor Norton safely conclude?
    I. Optimism is inversely related to depression.
    II. Optimism is more strongly related to depression than is introversion.
    III. High optimism scores tend to be associated with low depression scores.
    IV. Low optimism causes high depression.
   The CORRECT answer is:

    A. I only   B. II only   C. I, II   D. I, II, III   E. I, II, III, IV

3. A psychologist monitors a group of nursery school children, recording each instance of altruistic behavior as it occurs. The psychologist is using

    A. the experimental method   B. naturalistic observation
    C. case studies   D. the survey method

4. The first step in a scientific investigation is to

    A. choose the subjects   B. formulate a testable hypothesis
    C. choose a research method   D. operationally define the variables

5. A researcher has children watch 30 minutes of violent television, and then counts the number of times they hit each other in a one-hour play period afterward as a measure of aggression. The researcher concludes that television violence causes aggression. However, this conclusion is invalid because

    A. there was no control group
    B. the study is strictly correlational
    C. aggression wasn't operationally defined
    D. it is unethical to force children to watch violent television

6. Researchers must describe the actions that will be taken to measure or control each variable in their studies.
   In other words, they must

    A. provide operational definitions of their variables
    B. decide if their studies will be experimental or correlational
    C. use statistics to summarize their findings
    D. decide how many subjects should participate in their studies

7. Which of the following correlation coefficients would indicate the STRONGEST relationship between two variables?

   A. .58   B. .19   C. -.97   D. -.05

8. The experiment is a research method in which the investigator

   A. systematically observes two variables to see whether there is an association between them
   B. observes behavior as it occurs in its natural environment
   C. conducts an in-depth investigation of an individual subject
   D. manipulates a variable under carefully controlled conditions and observes whether there are changes in a second variable as a result

9. In the double-blind procedure,

   A. subjects are unaware of which treatment condition they are in
   B. the experimenter doesn't know which subjects are in the experimental or control groups
   C. no one keeps track of who is in which group
   D. both A and B

10. Random assignment of subjects occurs when

    A. subjects are allowed to choose which group or condition in the study they would like to be in
    B. a different method is used to assign each subject to a group or condition in the study
    C. all subjects have an equal chance of being assigned to any group or condition in the study
    D. all topics have an equal chance of being assigned to a particular experimenter

11. By definition, the population

    A. is that group of people to whom the conclusion of the study will apply
    B. is a subset of the sample
    C. consists of those individuals who actually participate in the study
    D. both A and B

12. Subjects' self-reports often indicate that they are healthier, happier, and less prejudiced than other types of evidence would suggest. The MOST likely explanation is

    A. experimenter bias
    B. faulty memory
    C. the social desirability bias
    D. a tendency to agree with almost every statement

13. Any measurable conditions, events, characteristics, or behaviors that are controlled or observed in a study are called

    A. hypotheses   B. correlations
    C. variables   D. confounds

14. The standard deviation is a measure of

    A. central tendency
    B. the amount of variability in a data set
    C. the degree of relationship between two variables
    D. the difference between the largest and smallest scores in a data set

15. In an experiment, the variable that is ultimately measured is called the _____ variable.

    A. dependent
    B. independent
    C. observed
    D. response

16. Suppose that high alcohol consumption among college students is associated with low grade point averages. Based on this information, we can conclude that

    A. high alcohol consumption causes students to get lower grades
    B. getting low grades causes students to drink more alcohol
    C. stress causes students both to get lower grades and to consume more alcohol
    D. none of the above

17. Experimenter bias occurs when

    A. experimenters' beliefs in their own hypotheses affect either the subjects' behavior or their observations of the subjects
    B. experimenters explicitly instruct the subjects to behave in a way that will be consistent with the hypothesis
    C. experimenters desire to make a favorable impression on their subjects
    D. experimenters conduct their studies in a completely objective manner

18. The correlation coefficient is a measure of

    A. central tendency
    B. the amount of variability in a data set
    C. the degree of relationship between two variables
    D. the difference between the largest and smallest scores in a data set

19. The independent variable is a hypothesized _____; the dependent variable is a hypothesized _____.

    A. cause; cause
    B. cause; effect
    C. effect; effect
    D. effect; cause

20. Suppose that students who work more hours at their jobs tend to have lower grade point averages, and that they also tend to get less sleep. If we were to correlate the two variables of grade point average and number of hours at work, we would find _____ relationship.

    A. no
    B. a positive
    C. a negative

21. When psychologists say that their results are statistically significant, they mean that the results

    A. have important practical applications
    B. have important implications for scientific theory
    C. are unlikely to be due to the fluctuations of chance
    D. all of the above

22. A confounding of variables occurs when

    A. two or more variables are linked together in a way that makes it difficult to sort out their specific effects
    B. the sample is not representative of the population
    C. subjects are influenced by the social desirability bias
    D. subjects experience some change from a nonexistent or ineffective treatment due to their expectations

23. By definition, a sample

    A. is that group of people to whom the conclusion of the study will apply
    B. is a subset of the population
    C. consists of those individuals who actually participate in the study
    D. both B and C

24. In descriptive/correlational research, the investigator

    A. systematically observes two variables to see whether there is an association between them
    B. manipulates a variable under carefully controlled conditions and observes whether there are changes in a second variable as a result
    C. exposes subjects to two closely related treatment conditions
    D. manipulates two or more independent variables simultaneously

25. Replication involves

    A. having each subject participate in the experiment several times to check the accuracy of the results
    B. manipulating several independent variables at once
    C. having each subject participate in both the experimental and control groups
    D. the repetition of a study to see whether the earlier results are duplicated

KEY (CORRECT ANSWERS)

1. D
2. D
3. B
4. B
5. A

6. A
7. C
8. D
9. D
10. C

11. A
12. C
13. C
14. B
15. A

16. D
17. A
18. C
19. B
20. C

21. C
22. A
23. D
24. A
25. D

TEST 3

DIRECTIONS: Each question or incomplete statement is followed by several suggested answers or completions. Select the one that BEST answers the question or completes the statement. *PRINT THE LETTER OF THE CORRECT ANSWER IN THE SPACE AT THE RIGHT.*

1. Internal functions such as heartbeat, breathing, and stomach contractions are controlled by the _____ nervous system.   1._____

   A. central   B. autonomic   C. somatic   D. endocrine

2. When a dominant gene is paired with a recessive gene, the gene pair is said to be   2._____

   A. homozygous
   B. phenotypic
   C. heterozygous
   D. polygenic

3. Damage to the cerebellum is MOST likely to result in   3._____

   A. problems with coordination of movement
   B. impairment of short-term memory
   C. difficulties in judging distance
   D. eating irregularities

4. A marathon runner may well experience a phenomenon known as *runner's high* because the pain of a long run may trigger the release of _____ in the brain.   4._____

   A. morphine
   B. endorphins
   C. placebos
   D. naloxone

5. The master gland of the endocrine system is the   5._____

   A. thyroid gland
   B. adrenal gland
   C. pancreas
   D. pituitary gland

6. The basic parts of a neuron are   6._____

   A. vesicles, terminal buttons, synapse
   B. cell body, axon, dendrites
   C. myelin, nodes, axon terminals
   D. hindbrain, midbrain, forebrain

7. A person might end up in a coma if the following area of the brain is damaged: 7._____

   A. Reticular formation
   B. Medulla
   C. Hypothalamus
   D. Pons

8. _____ function in the endocrine system much like _____ in the nervous system.   8._____

   A. Hormones; dendrites
   B. Hormones; neurotransmitters
   C. Endorphins; sensory neurons
   D. Neurotransmitters; hormones

9. Which of the following structures is not part of the hindbrain?   9._____

   A. Cerebellum
   B. Thalamus
   C. Medulla
   D. Pons

10. An inadequate supply of _____ in the brain has been implicated as a factor in the memory loss seen with Alzheimer's disease.

    A. dopamine
    B. acetylcholine
    C. serotonin
    D. norepinephrine

11. When one member of a gene pair is more influential, such that its trait is expressed over the trait of the other gene, it is said to be

    A. expressive
    B. genotypic
    C. phenotypic
    D. dominant

12. The _____ is the junction between two neurons.

    A. synapse
    B. terminal button
    C. postsynaptic membrane
    D. node

13. Research results indicate that lefthanders are over-represented in groups suffering from all but which of the following?

    A. Alcoholism
    B. Schizophrenia
    C. Mental retardation
    D. Multiple personality disorder

14. A neural impulse is initiated when a neuron's charge momentarily becomes less negative, or even positive.
    This event is called

    A. an action potential
    B. a resting potential
    C. impulse facilitation
    D. neuromodulation

15. In people whose corpus callosums have not been severed, verbal stimuli are identified more quickly and more accurately when

    A. sent to the right hemisphere first
    B. sent to the left hemisphere first
    C. presented to the left visual field
    D. presented auditorally rather than visually

16. The blood-brain barrier is a semipermeable membrane-like mechanism that

    A. keeps neurotransmitters from entering the bloodstream
    B. stops some chemicals from passing from the bloodstream to the brain
    C. prevents ions in the blood from entering the brain
    D. regulates the flow of blood to the brain and spinal cord

17. A split-brain person has a severed

    A. cerebral cortex
    B. cerebellum
    C. medulla
    D. corpus callosum

18. An impulse moves from one neuron to another through the action of

    A. neurotransmitters
    B. hormones
    C. action potentials
    D. neuromodulators

19. The _____ is the largest and most complex part of the human brain. 19.____

    A. medulla   B. cerebrum
    C. cerebellum   D. limbic system

20. The main reason for the characterization of the left hemisphere as the *dominant* hemisphere was 20.____

    A. the evidence that the left hemisphere usually processes language
    B. the evidence that the left hemisphere usually processes complex information
    C. the fact that the majority of people are righthanded
    D. that split-brain patients use only their left hemisphere for processing information

Questions 21-25.

DIRECTIONS: Questions 21 through 25 are to be answered on the basis of the brain chart shown below.

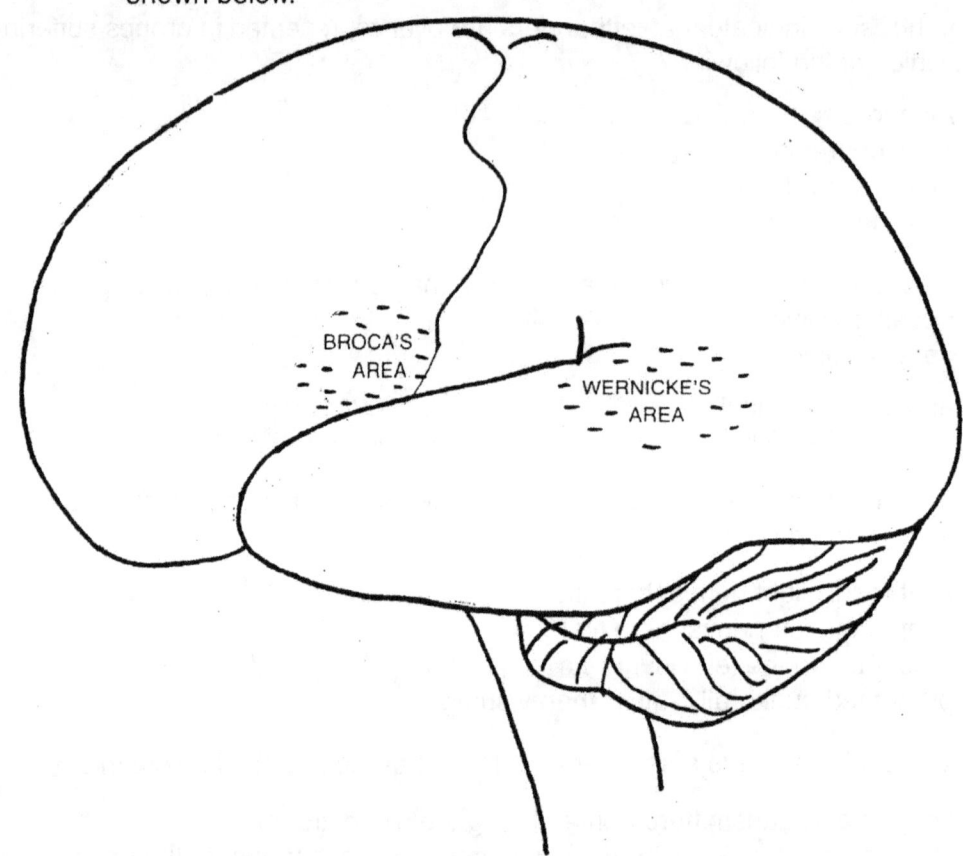

21. Identify and name the area that is responsible for handling visual information. 21.____

22. Identify the area responsible for higher mental processes, motor movement, planning, and impulse control. 22.____

23. Identify and name the area that is responsible for processing tactile information. 23.____

24. Identify and name the area that is responsible for processing of auditory information. 24.____

25. Circle the area that if lesioned will produce difficulties in the production of speech. 25.____

KEY (CORRECT ANSWERS)

1. B
2. C
3. A
4. B
5. D

6. B
7. A
8. B
9. B
10. B

11. A
12. A
13. D
14. A
15. B

16. B
17. D
18. A
19. B
20. A

21. Occipital lobe
22. Frontal lobe
23. Parietal lobe
24. Temporal lobe

Glossary of Psychometric Terms

TABLE OF CONTENTS

	Page
Ability Tests ... Bimodal	1
Central Tendency ... Correlation	2
Criterion ... Distribution	3
Equivalent Form ... Frequency Distribution	4
Grade Equivalent ... Interval Scale	5
Level of Significance ... Nominal Scale	6
Normal Curve ... Practice Effect	7
Pretest ... Ranking	8
Rating ... Scaling	9
Scaling ... Statistical Procedures	10
Statistic(s) ... Variance	11

Glossary (of Psychometric Terms)

ABILITY TESTS
Tests that purport to measure an individual's over-all facility in doing given things. Often a distinction is attempted between that facility which results from heredity and that which results from learning. In such cases, *ability* tests are usually applied to the "native" aspect and *achievement* tests to the learned aspect.
E-IQ tests, Dominance test.

ACHIEVEMENT TESTS
Tests that purport to measure an individual performance or competence relative to a given subject, usually a subject taught in the schools. Achievement tests are concerned with learned outcomes (generally knowledge and/or understanding) rather than "native" capacity or ability to learn the subject.
EX-Metropolitan Achievement Tests, MacGinitie.

AGE EQUIVALENTS
A method of expressing scores on standardized tests. The raw score typical of pupils of different ages is determined and then any pupil's raw score may be converted to the age to which it pertains. Usually given in years and months.
EX-Mental age = 12.6; reading age = 10.4.

APPLIED RESEARCH
Aims to solve an immediate practical problem. It is research performed in relation to actual problems and under conditions in which they are found in practice.
EX-Is *oral presentation or written presentation* more effective in *improving students' performance on tests? Is reading comprehension improved* by using the *individualized approach* as opposed to the *traditional reading group approach?*

BAR GRAPH
Any graphic presentation that uses bars of various length to symbolize differences in quantity, size, amount, etc.

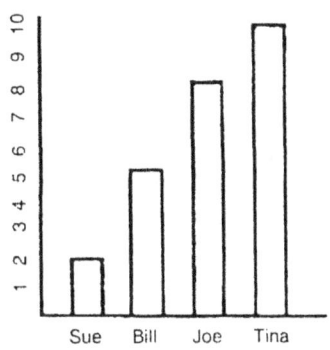

BASIC RESEARCH
Has as its aim obtaining data that can be used to formulate, expand, or evaluate theory. Its essential aim is to expand the frontiers of knowledge without regard to practical application, though the results may be used to solve practical problems.
EX-Is there a relationship between disruptive behavior and reading achievement? Is there a relationship between oral language skills and written language skills?

BIMODAL
A distribution of measures, particularly test scores, with two foci of central tendency rather than one. A superficial indication of bimoesdality is the presence of two modes separated by scores or score intervals whose frequency is appreciably less than that of the modes. Bimodality in a distribution can be suggestive of several attributes of the group or of the test or other measuring procedure in use. It often indicates that the group which is bimodal involves two subgroups having important mean differences as to age, mentality, reading ability, nationality, etc.
Ex-

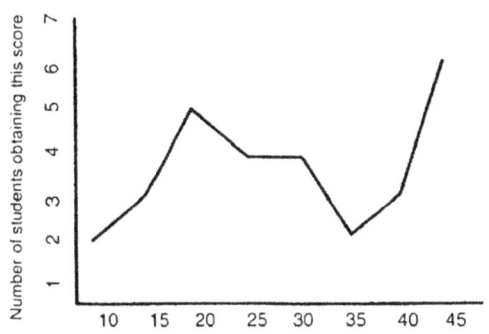

CENTRAL TENDENCY
In a distribution of scores or other measures, the point or interval at which a plurality or majority of scores tends to cluster. Unless there is such a clustering, the distribution has no central tendency.
EX-All distributions have a central tendency

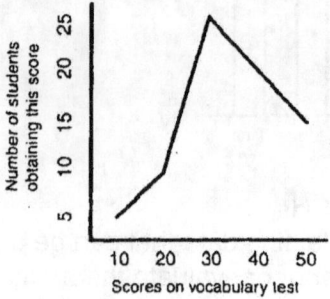

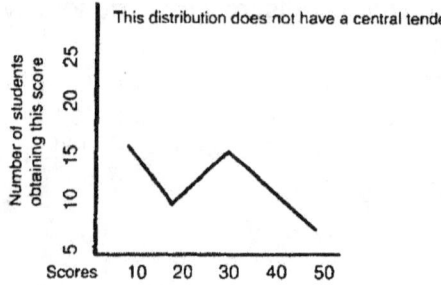

This distribution does not have a central tendency

CHECK LISTS
A device used in observation to direct attention to factors to be observed and sometimes to provide space for recording ratings or comments relative to them.
EX-
1. Can read accurately at a rate of 15 words/minute.
2. Can discriminate between two similarly spelled words.
3. Can follow orally given direction.

C.A. (CHRONOLOGICAL AGE)
A child's age expressed in years and months. Used in reckoning the intelligence quotient and any other index involving a comparison between skill or knowledge and age.
EX-Billy is five years and three months old. His C.A. = 5.3.

CLASSIFICATION
One of four basic forms of measurement (types of measurement symbols). Involves the establishment of categories (classification), the designation of symbols for the categories, and then the assignment of the symbols to phenomena according to the category to which they belong. This is sometimes referred to as the Nominal Level of measurement.
EX-Blood typing, draft classifications; A, B, C, D, F, as course marks.

COEFFICIENT OF CORRELATION (r)
A measure of the degree with which the variation of one variable is associated with variation of another variable.
EX-

	Intelligence	Grades	Conclusion
Joe	118 (2)	3.5 gpa	
Sue	103 (4)	2.5 gpa	If you have high in
Fred	110 (3)	2.0 gpa	telligence you'll
Linda	130 (1)	4.0 gpa	have high grades

CONCEPT
An abstraction from observed events; it is a word that represents the similarities or common aspects of objects or events that are otherwise quite different from one another. The purpose of a concept is to simplify thinking by including a number of events under one general heading.
EX-Words such as chair, dog, tree, liquor and thousands of others in our language represent common aspects of otherwise diverse things.

CONSTRUCTS
Higher level abstractions that cannot be easily illustrated by pointing to specific objects or events.
EX-Problem-solving ability, motivation, justice or intelligence.

CORRELATION
The statistical technique used for measuring the degree of relationship between two variables is called *correlation*. Correlation shows us the extent to which values in one variable are linked or related to values in another variable. An important use of such measurement is in prediction. When correlational analysis indicates some degree of relationship between two variables, we can use the information

about one of them to make predictions about the other. EX-Having found that intelligence and achievement are correlated, one can make predictions about the future achievement of school children from the results of a test of intelligence given at the beginning of the school year. The accuracy of such prediction is a function of the degree of relationship; that is, the extent of the correlation. The higher the correlation, the more accurate the predictions.

CRITERION
Anything with which a measuring procedure is compared in determining its validity. Specifically a measuring procedure for a given phenomenon for which exemplary validity is claimed or assumed and with which other similar procedures are asked to have high positive correlations.
EX-To show your reading program's effectiveness, you decide all children must advance one year in ability to read. The improvement goal of one year is your criterion.

CUMULATIVE FREQUENCY
A column in a conventional tabulation of scores or other measures that shows the frequency of scores up to and including any given interval.
EX-

No. of students receiving score	Score	Cumulative frequency
1	98	9
2	95	8
3	80	6
2	78	3
1	75	1

DERVIED SCORE
A test score that has been converted to an index of rank, scale position, or classification, as distinct from a raw score, which is the number of correct responses or the immediate numerical weight given the test. Percentile rank, standard scores, mental age.
EX-A child gets 9 spelling words right out of 10; he got a 90%. He did better than all the rest of the class. His derived score is A.

DEPENDENT VARIABLES
Variables that are a consequence of or dependent upon antecedent variables. In research studies, the dependent variable is the phenomenon that is the object of study and investigation. It is the one that must always be assessed.
EX-This is sometimes called assigned variable.

DESCRIPTION
An informal type of measurement expression used to indicate the status of phenomena in which ordinary language is used. The information is not quantified. This is also called the Nominal level of measurement.
EX-Scale rank and classification symbols associated with appraisal of citizenship, study habits, social adjustment.

DESCRIPTIVE RESEARCH
Describes and interprets *what is*. It is concerned with conditions or relationships that exist; practices that prevail; beliefs, points of view, or attitudes that are held; processes that are going on; effects that are being felt; or trends that are developing.
EX-There are several subcategories of descriptive research:
a. Case studies
b. Surveys
c. Developmental studies
d. Follow-up studies
e. Documentary analysis
f. Trend studies
g. Correlational studies

DEVIATION
Departure from a given condition. In particular, the numerical difference between a test score or other measure of an individual and given point of reference, usually the mean of a group of test scores or other measures.
EX-The class average on a test = 85, Jill received a 35. This is a large deviation.

DISTRIBUTION
A table or graph showing the scores or other measures found for a group, so arranged that the number who have a given score or who fall within a given range of scores is apparent.
EX-

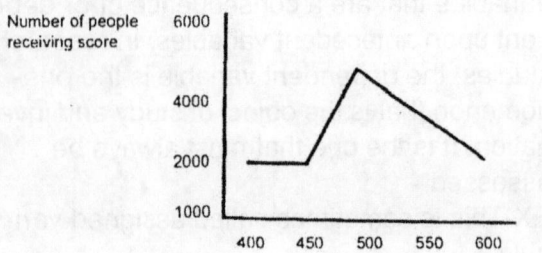

EQUIVALENT FORM
Either of two forms of a measuring instrument, particularly a standardized test which is parallel in content, difficulty, and norms, but different as to terms.
EX-Stanford-Binet Forms L and M.

EVALUATION
The process of assigning symbols to phenomena. These symbols
signify the worth of the phenomena relative to some scheme of
value.
EX-Grading student's paragraphs A, B, C, D or F.

EXPERIMENTAL DESIGN
The conceptual framework within which the experiment is conducted. It serves two functions. It provides opportunity for the comparisons required by the hypotheses of the experiment and it enables the experimenter through his statistical analysis of the data to make a meaningful interpretation of the results of the study.
EX-
One group → pretest → treatment → post-test
Exp.group → pretest → treatment I → post-test
Control group → treatment II

EXPERIMENTAL RESEARCH
A scientific investigation in which an investigator manipulates and controls one or more independent variables and observes the dependent variable or variables for variation concomitant to the manipulation of the independent variables. Its major purpose is to determine "what may be."
EX-Will subjects receiving individualized instruction achieve more than the students receiving traditional reading group instruction?

EX POST FACTO RESEARCH
Similar to experimental research except investigator cannot directly manipulate independent variables.
EX-Did my students achieve less than a comparable class because they didn't have a regular teacher?

EXTERNAL CRITERION
One needs an external criterion that is known to be a measure of the variable involved and can be used to compare one's predictions. Success in college, as reflected by grade point average is a clearly defined external criterion for validating those tests that are constructed for the selection of college applicants.
EX-Number of library books read outside of class assignments is an *external criterion* of reading enjoyment.

FREQUENCY
Refers in statistics to the number of times a score is repeated or to the number of scores appearing in a given interval.
EX-Joe and Sally got 85% on the spelling test, Fred, Donna, Shirley and Bob got 80%. Frequency for 85 = 2. Frequency for 80 = 4.

FREQUENCY DISTRIBUTION
A systematic arrangement of individual measures from highest to lowest. The use of this technique merely involves making a list of the individual measures in a column, with the highest measure at the top, the next highest, second from the top, continuing down until the lowest measure is recorded at the bottom of the column.
EX-

# of words correct	# of people rec'd score frequency
10	2
7	6
5	5
3	2
1	1

GRADE EQUIVALENT
The grade for which the ability is typical.
EX-Kathy is achieving at the 4th grade level, 3rd month on the Metropolitan Achievement tests. Her grade equivalent is 4.3.

HISTORICAL RESEARCH
A procedure supplementary to observation. A process by which the historian seeks to test the truthfulness of the reports of observations made by others. Its major purpose is to tell "what was."
EX-Tracing the evaluation of the open classroom.

HYPOTHESIS
A tentative proposition suggested as a solution to a problem or as an explanation of some phenomenon. It presents in simple form a statement of the researcher's expectations relative to a relationship between variables with the problem. It is then tested in a research study.
EX-Students who attend a remedial reading clinic five hours a week will improve their scores on the Metropolitan Primary Achievement Tests significantly more than students who attend the clinic for only three hours a week.

INDEPENDENT VARIABLES
Variables that are antecedent to the dependent variable are called independent variables. This is the factor that is measurably separate and distinct from the dependent variable but may relate to the dependent variable. Many factors that may function as independent variables are discriminate aspects of the environment, such as, social class, home environment, and classroom conditions. In addition, characteristics of the individual himself such *as* age, sex, intelligence and motivation-may be independent variables that can be related to the dependent variable.
EX-A child's height (dependent variable) would be dependent to a certain extent upon his age (independent variable). These terms are often used even in the absence of empirical or theoretical reasons for considering one to be the antecedent and the other to be the consequence. They are used to indicate the direction of predictionfrom individuals' positions on the independent variable to their positions on the dependent variable. This is sometimes called the active variable. Examples of Dependent and Independent variables:

1. *Reading achievement* (D.V.) is affected by *Self-concept* (I.V.).
2. *Word knowledge* (D.V.) is dependent on *Social economic status* (I.V.).
3. *Reading achievement* (D.V.) is dependent on *Reading enjoyment* (I.V.).

INFERENTIAL STATISTICS
The process of going from the part to the whole. A population comprises all the possible cases (persons, objects or events) that constitute a known whole. A sample is a portion of a population.
EX-A representative sample of 1000 six year old children obtain a mean raw score of 48 on the WISC. It is then inferred that the "average" 6 year old will obtain a score of 48 of the WISC.

INFERRED DIMENSION
A property or quality of a phenomenon not itself observable but imput or *inferred* to a phenomenon.
EX-A child's knowledge is measured by an I.Q. test.

INTERCORRELATION
A term applied to each of the correlations among a group of tests. Usually displayed in tables showing the correlation of each test with each of the other test. They are then used to show the extent of interrelationships among a certain group of tests.
EX-If a child scores high on the reading comprehension tests in Gates-MacGinite test, then he will probably score high on the vocabulary test.

INTERVAL SCALE
Not only indicates the relative position of individuals but also provides additional information about these positions because this type of scale uses predetermined equal intervals.

Such scales do not necessarily have a true zero point. Arbitrary zero points may be used, but such points are by no means absolute. Consider intelligence tests, for example. In these tests there are zero points and it is conceivable that one's score could be zero, but zero scores in these tests do not mean zero intelligence. For this reason it is not possible to compare an intelligence test score of 75 with a score of 150 and say the latter score is twice as high as the former.
EX-Number of correct spelling words on an exam. Score on the Stanford-Binet test.

LEVEL OF SIGNIFICANCE
A statistical term used to indicate the amount of confidence in whether or not the difference between two means, two percentages or other comparable measures is statistically significant (not due to chance). Also referred to as significance of difference and statistical difference.
EX-If Suzie got a 93% on a spelling test and Bill got a 90%, is Suzie a significantly better speller, or is her better score simply due to chance?

MEASUREMENT
The assignment of a symbol, often a number, so as to characterize the status of a phenomenon relative to some dimension, usually by indicating its scale position, its rank, or its classification per this dimension.
EX-Joe got 15 out of 20 spelling words correct, or 75% of them correct. This is a measurement of correct replies. If the score he received is the fourth highest test score, it is a measurement of his rank compared to others.

MEAN
The most widely used measure of central tendency is the mean, which is popularly known as the average or *arithmetic average*. It is the sum of all the values in a distribution divided by the number of cases. In terms of a formula it is:
$X = EX/IN$ where: X = the mean
E = the sum of
X = each of the values in the distribution
N = number of cases
EX-The average or mean Reading test score -

Jo- 8
Sally - 3
Mike - 6
Tom - 7
24/4 = 6 = ave.

MEDIAN
The score or point that divides a distribution of scores into two equal groups with half of the scores falling above and half below. Used as a representative score or a measure of central tendency.
EX-Scores: 4 12 18 21 26. 18 is the center score, it is the median.

MODE
The score or measure that occurs most frequently in a distribution.
EX - 3 students got 90 on their exam.
6 students got 85 on their exam.
1 student got 84 on his/her exam.
8 students got 80 on their exam.

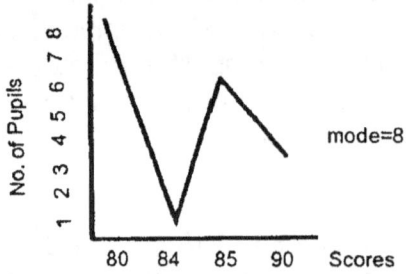

NOMINAL SCALE
The simplest type of scale and provides the lowest level of quantification of the objects to be measured. A nominal scale simply sorts objects, or classes of objects, into mutually exclusive categories. Our data will only tell us how many of the subjects belong to each groupA or how many students of a class are boys and how many are girls. Dividing individuals into such categories as smokers and non-smokers; Democrats, Republicans, and independents; elementary, junior high, and secondary; tall and short; and so on, are all examples of nominal scales.
EX-When we label the experimental units in a study as groups A, B, C, and D, or when we divide the students of a class into boys and

girls, we are using a nominal scale in each of these examples.

NORMAL CURVE
A symmetrical distribution of measures with the same number of cases at specified distances below the mean as above the mean. Its mean is the point below which exactly 50% of the cases are located. The median and the mode in such a distribution are identical values and coincide with the mean. In a normal curve, most of the cases concentrate near the mean.
EX-

NORMS
Statistics based upon a standardization group or a group that is purported to be representative of a much larger population. These norms are thus assumed to be representative of large groups.
EX-All fifth-grade children or all twelve-year-olds, grade, age percentile, and standard score norms are the most common forms.

OBSERVATION
The most widely used and usually most crude method of behavioral measurements. Involves direct perception of the dimensions of the phenomenon being measured. With appropriate attentional, perceptual, and recording aids, observation can be a highly reliable procedure.
EX-Frequency count-Phillip got out of his seat without permission six times in the fifty minute reading period. Interval count-Mary was not attending to the lesson for 40% of the thirty second intervals recorded.

OPERATIONAL DEFINITION
Ascribes meaning to a concept or construct by specifying the operations that must be performed in order to measure the concept. This type of definition is essential in research, since data must be collected in terms of observable events. When one defines a concept or construct operationally, he chooses discriminable events as indicators of the abstract concept and devises operations to obtain data relevant to the concepts. An operational definition thus refers to the operations by which an investigator may measure a concept. These are essential to research because they permit investigators to measure abstract concepts and constructs and permit a scientist to move from the level of constructs and theory to the level of observation, upon which science is based.
EX-Operationalized definition of achievement-scores obtained on the Stanford Diagnostic Achievement Test. Operationalized definition of reading enjoyment number of books read outside of class, not for assignments.

ORDINAL SCALE
The use of the ordinal scale permits the sorting of objects or classes of objects on the basis of their standing relative to each other. This scale not only categorizes but also ranks the objects on the basis of some criterion. A teacher who ranks his students on the basis of their intelligence, achievement, class participation, discipline, creativity, or any other characteristic is making use of an ordinal scale.
EX-Rank in class, percentile rank, percentiles.

POPULATION
Used in an abstract sense in measurement and statistics to indicate any given group of things, the total group in question not just part of it.
EX-All the pupils in the sixth grade in your school district is the population from which your sample (the children in your sixth grade class) is taken.

PRACTICE EFFECT
It is known that a performance of any task affects a reperformance of that task, usually in the direction of improvement. *Practice effect* is the term for the significance of such reperformance when the same test is administered to the same individual more than once.
EX-When pupils do better on a quiz the second time it is given in a week, is this because they know the material better or because they have had practice with the question.

PRETEST
Any measuring instrument (usually an achievement test) administered prior to a period of instruction, an experiment, or other circumstance of interest. As a rule pretests are used to establish the initial status of pupils so that the amount of their learning may be judged from the results of a later retest.
EX-Students are given the Metropolitan Primary Achievement test in September and again in May. The tests in September would be a pretest.

PROBABILITY
As applied to behavioral measurement, the concept that any measure or statistic is somewhat subject to chance variation. Hence it deviates from some theoretically "true" measure. Such deviation is commonly called error and its probable extent can be determined and stated mathematically. *See Level of Significance.*
EX-There is .05 or 5% chance that these scores were obtained by chance.

PRODUCT ANALYSIS
A basic procedure of educational evaluation in which the things that pupils produce in the course of instruction are appraised in appropriate ways and given scores or ratings.
EX-Compositions, outlines.

PRODUCT MOMENT FORMULA
A widely used formula for the correlation coefficient. Let Zx be the standard score for variable y. If the pairs of Zx's and Zy's for each individual are multiplied, then added for all individuals and divided by the number of cases, the result is the product moment formula for the correlation coefficient. The correlation coefficient is the mean of the set of products of standard scores for the two variables.

EX- $r = \sum \frac{(Zx\,Zy)}{n}$

Zx = Z - scores for all x
Zy = Z - scores for all y
n = number of subjects

PROFILE
An analytic graphic presentation of a pupil's scores on a test battery, scores on parts of a given test, marks in several school subjects, ratings on several personality variables, etc.
EX-

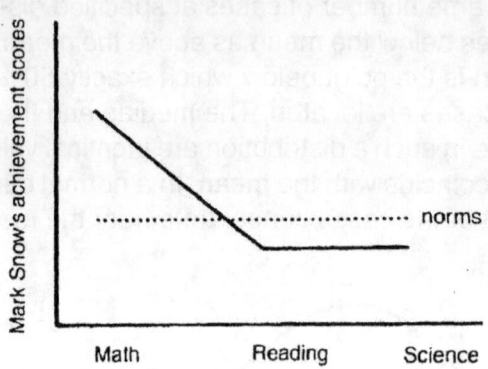

RANDOM SAMPLING
The basic characteristic of random sampling is that all members of the population have an equal and independent chance of being included in the sample. That is, for every pair of elements x and y, x's chance of being selected equals y's chance, and the selection of x in no way affects y's probability of selection.
EX-Mary, Joe and Sally are in Ms. Brown's class. She decides to choose 2 of them to do an experiment. She puts all of their names in a hat. They all have an equal chance to be chosen and if one is chosen this does not affect the chances of the others being chosen.

RANGE
The difference between the highest and lowest scores in a given distribution of scores.
EX-If the highest score in a distribution as 74 and the lowest as 30, the range would be: R = 74 - 30 = 44.

RANKING
The process of ordering the constituents of a group in terms of
some dimension. Rank numbers indicate the relative position of
the constituents.
EX-Scores on a reading achievement test

S	6.3	6.1	6.0	6.0	6.0	5.5	5.1
R	1	2	4	4	4	6	7.5

RATING
A direct appraisal of a dimension in terms of some descriptive scale or verbal classification scheme.
EX-Children are rated by their teacher for their disruptive behavior: 1 = very disruptive; 2 = average; 3 = quiet.

RATIO SCALE
The highest level of measurement is provdied by a ratio scale. In addition to having equal intervals, a ratio scale measures from a meaningful zero. Most physical measures have a meaningful zero. The scale used in education measurements are seldom of this level of measurement.
EX-Using a ratio scale we can say that John is 48 inches tall, Ralph is 45 inches tall, and Paul is 44 inches tall; but using an interval scale we are only able to say that John is 3 inches taller than Ralph, whp is one inch taller than Paul. Not only can we say that the difference between 60 and 90 pounds is the same as the difference between 90 pounds and 120 pounds, but we can say that 120 pounds is twice as heavy as 60 pounds. We can do this because zero weight is an actual possibility.

RAW SCORE
The first quantitative untreated result obtained in scoring a test.
EX-Bill got 98% on vocabulary test
   Jill got 83% on vocabulary test.
   Tony got 78% on vocabulary test.

READING GRADE
A type of "norm" score derived from standardized tests that states a pupil's ability to read in terms of grade equivalents. Reading grade means the school grade whose average performance is most like that of the pupil in question. By interpolation, the reading grade be fractional. As with reading age, reading grade refers only to a given standardized test.
EX-Ann received a 6.3 on the Gates-MacGinities Test. She is performing at sixth grade, three month level of achievement.

RELIABILITY
The extent to which a measuring device is constant in measuring whatever it measures.
EX-Will Greg receive approximately the same score on the Reading Achievement test if he takes it a second time two weeks after he took it the first time?

RESEARCH PROBLEM
A question concerning the relationships existing between sets of events (variables) in education. Research is conducted in order to find answers to these questions. One of the most fruitful sources for the beginning researcher is his experience as an educational practitioner. Decisions must be made daily about the probable effects of educational experience on pupil behavior.
EX-What is the effectiveness of using verbal instructions compared to written ones?

RETEST (also called a Post-test)
A test readministered at the end of a period of instruction or other activity, the result of which is to be compared with an earlier administration of a test.
EX-A list of spelling words are given at the beginning of the week to determine which words a child needs to learn. After working on the words all week, a test is given Friday to find if the pupils learn the words. The test on Friday would be considered a retest or post-test.

RHO (Q)
The rank-difference measure of correlation. Individuals are assigned ranks with respect to each of two variables, and for each individual the difference (d) in rank is determined. These differences are squared and summed for all cases and substitution is made in the following formula.

EX- $Q(rho) = \dfrac{1 - 6E d^2}{N(N^2 - 1)}$

SAMPLE
A sample is a portion of a population.
EX-The children in Ms. Smith's class is a sample of the population of sixth grade students in that district. Reading Group A is Ms. Smith's class is a sample of her sixth grade class.

SCALING
Measurement in terms of defined and precise units that represent given amounts or degrees

of some dimension. Scale numbers indicate the number of units and hence the amount or degree of the dimension. Scale numbers refer to a fixed point of reference, usually a zero.
EX-Rate your agreement with this statement on a scale of 1 to 5.

SCALING
Measurement in terms of defined and precise units that represent given amounts or degrees of some dimension. Scale numbers indicate the number of units and hence the amount or degree of the dimension. Scale numbers refer to a fixed point of reference, usually a zero.
EX-Rate your agreement with this statement on a scale of 1 to 5.
1 = strongly agree
2 = agree
3 = undecided
4 = disagree
5 = strongly disagree

SCORING
A process of assigning a score (usually a number or letter symbol) to a test or pupil product. For a test, this is often done by comparing a paper with the key, marking the questions answered correctly and adding up the total.
EX-Bill got 9 words right. Score = 9.
   Judy got 15 words right. Score = 15.
   Ruth got 12 words right. Score = 12.

SELF-EVALUATION
Any of many concepts and procedures concerned with an individual observing and judging his own performance, achievement, or adjustment.
EX-Coopersmith Self-Esteem Inventory.

STANDARD DEVIATION
An index of variation in a group of mesures. It represents the square root of the mean of the squared deviations of the individual measures.

EX- $SD = \sqrt{\dfrac{\Sigma d^2}{N-1}}$

d^2 = difference between score and mean
n = number of subjects

STANDARD SCORE (z score)
A general term referring to any of a number of scores that indicate how many standard deviations a measurement is above or below the mean. It is found by determining the difference between the raw score (X) and the mean (X) and dividing by the standard deviation (S).

Ex- $Z = \dfrac{X - \overline{X}}{S}$

X = Bills score
X = Class average
X = Standard deviation: (equation needed).

STANDARDIZED TESTS
Tests, usually published, which have been preadministered to a population of known characteristics and yield scores in terms of this population. This population is selected so as to be a representative sample of the total population for which the test is designed.
EX-Stanford-Binet Intelligence Test, Metropolitan Primary Achievement Test, Ginn Reading Achievement Test.

STANINE
Any one of nine intervals on a scale of standard scores. The "stanine" (abbreviation for standard-nine) scale spans the normal curve in nine intervals of size equal to one half of a standard score. The stanine intervals have values from 1 to 9 and the middle interval, 5, extends from standard score - 1/4 to + 1/4.
EX-

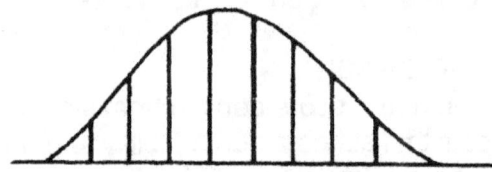

STATISTICAL PROCEDURES
Basic methods of handling quantitative information in such a way as to make that information meaningful. These procedures have two principal advantages for the researcher. First, they enable him/ her to describe and summarize his observations. Such techniques are called *descriptive statistics*. Second, they help him/her determine how reliably (s)he can infer that phenomena observed in a limited group, *a sample,* will also occur in the unobserved

larger population of concern, from which the sample was drawn. In other words, how well (s)he can employ inductive reasoning to infer that what (s)he observes in the part will be observed in the whole. For problems of this nature (s)he will need to employ *inferential statistics.*

EX-Finding the mean score-*descriptive statistics.* Finding if there is significant differences-inferential *statistics.*

STATISTIC(S)
Any derived quantity obtained from a set of raw scores or measures.
EX-N, mean, standard deviation, median, mode, quartile deviation, correlation coefficient.

TESTS
Any of a great number of procedures in which individuals respond to a common stimulation in comparable ways and which yield a measure of the individuals with respect to one or more dimensions.
EX-Achievement tests, Personality tests, Spelling tests, Performance tests, Ability tests.

VALIDATION
The process of establishing on the basis of empirical data the validity of a test, usually a standardized one, by comparing its results with one or more criteria. Typically involves, as a minimum item analysis, correlation of results with other test scores, analysis of distributions of scores, and determination of reliability.
EX-See test manual or Mental Measurement Yearbook by Buros to find out about a test validation.

VALIDITY
The extent to which an instrument measures what it is supposed to measure.
EX-A test measures a pupil's reading comprehension not size of vocabulary or general knowledge.

VARIABLE
A concept that can take on different values.
EX-It can vary within an individual from one time to another, between individuals at the same time, between the averages for groups, and so on. Social class, sex, motivation, intelligence quotient, and spelling test scores are other examples of variables. Educational researchers are interested in determining how such variables are related to each other.

VARIANCE
The mean of the squared deviation scores.

EX- $S^2 = \sum \dfrac{(X-\overline{X})^2}{N}$

$X - \overline{X}$ = difference between score and mean
N = number of subjects

GLOSSARY OF BASIC PSYCHIATRIC TERMS

TABLE OF CONTENTS

	Page
Accident Prone ... Anxiety	1
Anxiety Reaction (Anxiety Neurosis) ... Catatonic State	2
Character Disorder ... Conversion	3
Conversion Reaction ... Depression	4
Disorientation ... Environment	5
Epilepsy ... Free Association	6
Frustration ... Hypnosis (Hypnotic Trance)	7
Hypochondriasis ... Insight	8
Instinct ... Looseness of Association	9
Maladjustment ... Mind	10
Motivation ... Object	11
Obsession ... Paranoid State	12
Pathogenesis ... Projective Tests	13
Psyche ... Psychosomatic	14
Psychosurgery ... Reversal	15
Sadism ... Stress	16
Subject ... Turning Against the Self	17
Unconscious ... Waxy Flexibility	18

GLOSSARY OF BASIC PSYCHIATRIC TERMS

A

ACCIDENT PRONE
Special susceptibility to accidents due to psychological causes.

ADDICTION
A descriptive name for a type of psychiatric illness (character disorder) characterized by excessive psychological and/or physiologic dependence upon the intake of some substance, as, for example, alcohol or an opiate.

ADJUSTMENT
The series of technics or processes by which the individual strives to meet the continuous changes that take place within himself and in his environment. Synonym: adaptation. (Some authorities consider adjustment to refer particularly to psychological activity and adaptation to physiologic activity.)

AFFECT
Generalized feeling tone. (Usually considered to be more persistent than emotion and less so than mood.)

Affective, pertaining to affect.

Affective psychosis, a psychosis characterized by an extreme alteration in mood in the direction of mania or of depression.

AGGRESSION (Aggressive Drive)
A term used in various ways; in the usq.ge of psychiatry, an instinct-like force, much influenced by early experience, motivating the individual to destructive activity.

AIM
Intention or purpose; in psychiatric literature the term is used chiefly in the discussion of instincts; the *aim* of an instinctual drive may be defined as an action on the part of the individual that involves the *object* of the drive and results in gratification. Thus, the aim of the instinctual drive, hunger, is eating.

AMBIVALENCE
The experiencing of contradictory strivings or emotions toward an object or situation. In extreme form, characteristic of *schizophrenia.*

ANAL CHARACTER (PERSONALITY)
(1) In psychoanalysis a pattern of behavior in an adult that originates in the anal eroticism of infancy and is characterized by such traits as excessive orderliness, miserliness, and obstinacy.
(2) A type of character (personality) disorder in which many of the individual's conflicts and defenses remain those appropriate to the muscle-training period, usually characterized by such traits as parsimony, rigidity, and pedantry.

ANAL PERIOD
One of the developmental stages; the muscle-training period.

ANTHROPOLOGY
The science of man or mankind in the widest sense; the history of human society; the developmental aspects of man as a species.

ANXIETY
(1) Apprehension, the source of which is largely unknown or unrecognized. It is different from fear, which is the emotional response to a consciously recognized and usually external danger.
(2) A state of tension and distress akin to fear, but produced by the threatened loss of inner control rather than by an external danger.

Anxiety attack, a phenomenon characterized by intense feelings of anxiety plus such physiologic manifestations as increased pulse and respiratory rates and increased perspiration.
ANXIETY REACTION (ANXIETY NEUROSIS)
A *psychoneurosis* characterized by the more or less continuous presence of anxiety in excess of normal and occasional clear-cut *anxiety attacks.*
ATTITUDE
One's physical and emotional position and manner with respect to another person, thing, or situation.

Attitude therapy, a method of treatment utilizing the assumption by the personnel of attitudes calculated to exert a favorable effect upon the patient.
AUTISM
Self-preoccupation with loss of interest in and appreciation of other persons and socially accepted behavior. *Autistic thinking,* thought processes determined by inner needs and relatively uninfluenced by environmental considerations, a characteristic of *schizophrenia*.
AUTISTIC CHILD
In child psychiatry, a child who responds chiefly to inner thoughts who does not relate to his environment, and whose overall functioning is immature and often appears retarded.

B

BASIC DRIVE
In human psychology, one of a group of hereditarily transmitted motivating forces, deriving ultimately from biochemical changes within the organism; used synonymously with instinct.
BEHAVIOR (HUMAN)
All the activity of a human being that is capable of observation by another person.
BEHAVIOR DISORDER
See Personality Disorder.
BLOCKING
(1) Difficulty in recollection, or interruption of a train of thought or speech, caused by unconscious emotional factors.
(2) An involuntary, functional interference with a person's thinking, memory or communication. (Usually the term is employed with reference to a psychotherapeutic situation.)

C

CASTRATION
Literally, the removal or the destruction of the gonads (ovaries or testes). In psychoanalytic terminology, the loss of the penis.
CASTRATION ANXIETY
Anxiety due to danger (fantasied) of loss of the genitals or injuries to them. May be precipitated by everyday events that have symbolic significance and appear to be threatening, such as loss of job, loss of a tooth, or an experience of riciule or humiliation.
CATALEPSY
A condition usually characterized by trance-like states. May occur in organic or psychological disorders or under hypnosis.
CATATONIC STATE (Catatonia)
(1) A state characterized by immobility with, muscular rigidity or inflexibility and at times by excitability. Virtually always a symptom of schizophrenia.
(2) One of the four classic schizophrenic subgroups (syndromes), usually beginning at a

relatively early age and characterized by a rapid onset and interference with normal motor function.

CHARACTER DISORDER
See Personality Disorder.

COMPENSATION
(1) A defense mechanism, operating unconsciously, by which the individual attempts to make up for (i.e., to compensate for) real or fancied deficiencies.
(2) A conscious process in which the individual strives to make up for real or imagined defects in such areas as physique, performance, skills, or psychological attributes.

COMPLEX
(1) A group of associated ideas that have a common emotional tie. These are largely unconscious and significantly influence attitudes and associations. Examples are:

Inferiority Complex - Feelings of inferiority stemming from real or imagined physical or social inadequacies that may cause anxiety or other adverse reactions. The individual may overcompensate by excessive ambition or by the development of special skills, often in the very field in which he was originally handicapped.

Oedipus Complex - Attachment of the child for the parent of the opposite sex, accompanied by envious and aggressive feelings toward the parent of the same sex. These feelings are largely repressed (i.e., made unconscious) because of the fear of displeasure or punishment by the parent of the same sex. In its original use, the term applied only to the male child.

(2) In psychoanalytic terminology, a group of associated ideas and feelings that, though unconscious, influence the subject's conscious attitudes and behavior.

COMPULSION
(1) An insistent, repetitive, and unwanted urge to perform an act that is contrary to the person's ordinary conscious wishes or standards. Failure to perform the compulsive act results in overt anxiety.
(2) An act that is carried out, in some degree, against the subject's conscious wishes, either to avoid the anxiety that would otherwise appear, or to dispel a disturbing *obsession*.
compulsive, pertaining to a compulsion.

COMPULSIVE PERSONALITY
A type of personality disorder; more specifically, a type of neurotic personality. *See* Anal Character (Personality).

CONFLICT
A struggle between two or more opposing forces. *Intrapersonal* (*intrapsychic; conflict,* a struggle between forces within a single personality. *Interpersonal conflict,* a struggle between two or more individuals.

CONGENITAL
Present from birth; mayor may not be hereditary.

CONSCIENCE
Equivalent to the conscious portion of the superego; in strict psychoanalytic terminology, the "ego ideal."

CONSCIOUS
Aware or sensible; "mentally awake."

CONVERSION
Sensory or motor dysfunctions by which the subject gives symbolic expression to a conflict (of which he is not conscious).

CONVERSION REACTION
A psychoneurosis, formerly called "conversion hysteria," characterized by conversions.
CULTURE
The characteristic attainments of a people.
CYCLOTHYMIA
A tendency or a proneness to repeated, exaggerated, largely irrational alterations in mood, usually between euphoria and depression.
Cyclothymic, pertaining to cyclothymia.
Cyclothymia personality, a type of psychotic personality disorder, often the precursor of manic-depressive psychosis.

D

DEATH INSTINCT (Thanatos)
In Freudian theory, the unconscious drive toward dissolution and death. Coexists with and is in opposition to the life instinct (Eros).
DEFENSE MECHANISM
(1) A specific process, operating unconsciously, that is employed to seek relief from emotional conflict and freedom from anxiety.
(2) A psychological technic performed by the ego but carried out below the subject's threshold of awareness, designed to ward off anxiety or unpleasant tensions.
DELIRIUM
An altered level of consciousness (awareness), often acute and in most instances reversible, manifested by disorientation and confusion and induced by an interference with the metabolic processes of the neurons of the brain. *Delirium tremens,* an agitated delirious state occurring as a complication of chronic alcoholism.
DELUSION
A fixed idea, arising out of the subject's inner needs and contrary to the observed facts as these are interpreted by normal persons under the same circumstances; a symptom of psychosis.
DEMENTIA
A chronic, typically irreversible deterioration of intellectual capacities, due to organic disease of the brain that has produced structural changes (the actual death of neurons).
Dementia paralytica, formerly "paresis," a chronic syphilitic inflammation of the brain and its membranous coverings resulting, if untreated, in progressive dementia and paralysis and ultimately in death.
Dementia praecox, an old (obsolescent) (and misleading) term for schizophrenia.
DENIAL
A *defense mechanism* in which the ego refuses to allow awareness of some aspect of reality.
DEPRESSION
(1) Psychiatrically, a morbid sadness, dejection, or melancholy; to be differentiated from grief, which is realistic and proportionate to what has been lost. A depression may be a symptom of any psychiatric disorder or may constitute its principal manifestation.
(2) A pathologic state brought on by feelings of loss and/or guilt and characterized by sadness and a lowering of self-esteem.
Neurotic depressive reaction, a state of depression of neurotic intensity in which *reality-testing* is largely unimpaired and in which physiologic disturbances, if present, are usually mild.
Psychotic depressive reaction, a state of depression of psychotic intensity in which reality-testing is severely impaired and in which physiologic disturbances *(vegetative signs)* are usually conspicuous.

Reactive depression, a state of depression -- intensity not specified -- for which the precipitating stress can be clearly discerned and seen to be of some magnitude.

DISORIENTATION

Confusion of the subject with respect to such information as the correct time and place, a knowledge of his personal identity and an understanding of his situation; typically seen in *delirium* and *dementia*.

DISPLACEMENT

A general term for a group of psychological phenomena (technics) in which certain strivings or feelings are (unconsciously) transferred from one object, activity, or situation to another (which acquires a similar meaning). The defense technic of sublimation is one example of a successful displacement.

DISSOCIATION

A breaking of psychic connections, of associations.

DISSOCIATIVE REACTION

Formerly called "hysterical amnesia." A psychoneurosis in which a group of thoughts, feelings and memories becomes separated from the rest of the personality.

DRIVE

See Basic Drive.

DYNAMIC (PSYCHODYNAMIC)

Pertaining to the forces operating within the personality and determining the behavior, particularly unconscious forces. Dynamic psychiatry, a psychiatry concerned with the understanding of such motivating forces.

E

EGO

(1) In psychoanalytic theory, one of the three major divisions of human personality, the others being the id and superego. The ego, commonly identified with consciousness of self, is the mental agent mediating among three contending forces: the external demands of social pressure or reality; the primitive instinctual demands arising from the id imbedded as it is in the deepest level of the unconscious; and the claims of the superego, born of parental and social prohibitions and functioning as an internal censor or "conscience."

(2) One of the three agencies or aspects of the mind, the ego is the aspect that is in contact with the environment through the sensory apparatus, that appraises environmental and inner changes and that directs behavior through its control of the motor apparatus.

ELECTROCONVULSIVE THERAPY (E.C.T., ELECTROSHOCK THERAPY)

A method of treatment of psychiatric disorders by passing an electric current through the brain, producing an artificial seizure.

ELECTROENCEPHALOGRAPH

An instrument, based on the string galvanometer, for measuring very small changes in potential derived from the electrical activity of the neurons of the brain. *Electroencephalogram,* the record obtained with the electroencephalograph, a "brain-wave tracing."

EMPATHY

(1) An objective awareness of the feelings, emotions, and behavior of another person. To be distinguished from sympathy, which is usually nonobjective and noncritical.

(2) A deep recognition of the significance of another person's behavior, which retains a certain objectivity and yet involves intellectual, emotional and motivational experiences corresponding to those of the other person.

ENVIRONMENT

All that surrounds the individual, including living and non-living, material and immaterial elements.

EPILEPSY

A disorder characterized by periodic seizures, and sometimes accompanied by a loss of consciousness. May be caused by organic or emotional disturbances.

Major epilepsy (grand mal) - Characterized by gross convulsive seizures, with loss of consciousness.

Minor epilepsy (petit mal) - Minor nonconvulsive epileptic seizures; may be limited to only momentary lapses of consciousness.

ETHOLOGY

The scientific study of the instincts. *Ethologist,* one who makes a scientific study of the instincts.

ETIOLOGY

Pertaining to causation; in medicine and nursing, pertaining to the causation of disease.

EUPHORIA

(1) An exaggerated feeling of physical and emotional well-being inconsonant with reality.

(2) An exaggerated (unrealistic) sense of well-being.

EXHIBITIONISM

Erotic pleasure in exposing the body to the view of others; in adults, a form of perversion when it is the principal form of erotic expression.

EXTROVERSION

A state in which attention and energies are largely directed outward from the self, as opposed to interest primarily directed toward the self, as in introversion.

F

FACULTY

A power or a function, especially a mental one.

FAMILY TRIANGLE

The situation, involving the child and the parents, in which the child experiences the wish to displace the parent of the same sex and possess the parent of the opposite sex. Family-triangle period, a developmental phase characterized by maximum intensity of these strivings. Synonymous with *Oedipal period*.

FANTASY (PHANTASY)

An image -- conscious or unconscious -- formed by recombinations of memories and interpretations of them.

FEAR

An experience, having both psychological and physiologic components, stimulated by the awareness of impending danger in the environment.

FIXATION

The persistence into later life of interests and behavior patterns appropriate to an earlier developmental phase.

FLATNESS OF AFFECT

A lack of normal emotional responsiveness, especially characteristic of *schizophrenia*.

FLIGHT OF IDEAS

A morbid type of thought sequence manifested through speech, characterized by its rapidity and by numerous and sudden shifts in topics, but that tends to be comprehensible to the normal observer. Typical of mania.

FREE ASSOCIATION

(1) In psychoanalytic therapy, spontaneous, uncensored verbalization by the patient of whatever comes to mind.

(2) A technic, used in *psychoanalysis,* in which the patient reports verbally his thoughts, emotions and sensations in whatever order they occur, making no effort at deliberate organization, censorship, or control.

FRUSTRATION

A blocking or nongratification of needs.

FUGUE

A major state of personality dissociation characterized by amnesia and actual physical flight from the immediate environment.

FUNCTIONAL

Pertaining solely or primarily to function. *Functional psychosis,* a psychosis occurring on the basis of disturbed mental functioning in the absence of structural brain damage.

G

GARRULOUSNESS

Excessive talkativeness, especially about trivial things.

GENITAL PHASE (OF DEVELOPMENT)

In psychoanalytic terminology, a synonym for emotional maturity.

GROUP

Any two or more persons who are set off from others, either temporarily or permanently, by a special type of association (relationship), as, for example, an important common interest.

Group therapy, a form of *psychotherapy* taking place among a group of patients under the guidance of a therapist.

H

HALLUCINATION

A sensory experience, occurring (in the absence of adequate reality-testing) on the basis of the subject's inner needs and independently of stimulation from the environment.

HALLUCINOGEN

A chemical substance capable of inducing hallucinations.

HEBEPHRENIA

One of the classic schizophrenic subgroups, the one having the most ominous prognosis. *Hebephrenic schizophrenia* is a synonym.

HEREDITARY

Genetically transmitted from parent to offspring.

HETEROSEXUAL

Pertaining to the opposite sex.

HOMEOSTASIS

A tendency to uniformity and stability in the normal body states of the organism (Walter B. Cannon).

HOMOSEXUAL

(adj.) Pertaining to an erotic interest in members of one's own sex. (noun) One having an erotic interest in members of his own sex.

(1) Sexual attraction or relationship between members of the same sex.

Latent homosexuality - A condition characterized by unconscious homosexual desires.

Overt homosexuality - Homosexuality that is consciously recognized or practiced.

(2) *Homosexuality,* a condition characterized by the subject's having an erotic interest in members of his own sex, a form of *personality disorder.*

HYPNOSIS (HYPNOTIC TRANCE)

(1) A state of increased receptivity to suggestion and direction, initially induced by the

influence of another person. The degree may vary from mild suggestibility to a trance state so profound as to be used in surgical operations.

(2) An artificially induced state, akin to sleep, in which the subject enters into so close a relationship with the hypnotist that the suggestions of the latter become virtually indistinguishable from the activity of his own ego.

HYPOCHONDRIASIS

(1) Overconcern with the state of physical or emotional health, accompanied by various bodily complaints without demonstrable organic pathology.

(2) A severe type of *psychoneurosis,* characterized by a morbid preoccupation with one's body and a partial withdrawal of interest from the environment. *Hypochondriac,* one afflicted with hypochondriasis.

HYSTERIA

A *psychoneurosis;* the older term for the conditions now designated as *conversion reaction* and *dissociative reaction.*

HYSTERICAL PERSONALITY

(1) A personality type characterized by shifting emotional feelings, susceptibility to suggestion, impulsive behavior, attention seeking, immaturity, and self-absorption; not necessarily disabling.

(2) A form of *personality disorder (neurotic personality)* characterized by conflicts and defenses similar to those found in persons with hysteria.
Hysteric, one afflicted with hysteria.

I

ID

The one of the three agencies or aspects of the mind that contains the psychic representations of the instinctual drives.

IDEATION

The process of forming ideas.

IDENTIFICATION

The adoption -- unconsciously -- of some of the characteristics of another person. Strictly speaking, the term refers to the result of the defense mechanism of *introjection.* (Sometimes identification and introjection are used loosely as synonyms.)

ILLUSION

A false perceptual experience occurring in response to an environmental stimulus; usually a symptom of serious mental illness.

INCEST

Culturally prohibited sexual relations between members of a family, usually persons closely related by blood, as father and daughter, mother and son, or brother and sister. INHIBITION

(1) Interference with or restriction of activities; the result of an unconscious defense against forbidden instinctual drives.

(2) The restraining or the stopping of a process; in psychiatry, the term usually refers to an inner force that opposes the gratification of a basic drive.

INSANITY

Now a term of legal or medicolegal significance only, referring to a mental disorder of sufficient gravity to bring the subject under special legal restrictions and immunities.

INSIGHT

(1) Self-understanding. A major goal of psychotherapy. The extent of the individual's understanding of the origin, nature, and mechanisms of his attitudes and behavior.

(2) In the broad psychiatric sense, the patient's knowledge that he suffers from an emo-

tional illness; in the narrow psychiatric sense, the patient's knowledge of the specific, hitherto unconscious, meaning of his symptom(s) or of some other aspect of illness.

INSTINCT

A term of many meanings; in dynamic psychiatric usage it is usually considered as synonymous with *basic drive.*

INSULIN COMA THERAPY

A method of treatment of psychoses through the induction of a series of comas by means of insulin injections.

INTERNALIZE

To place within (the mind). Said of a conflict or a state of tension that, in its original form, existed between an individual and some aspect of his environment, but that has come to exist within the mind (i.e., between one aspect of the personality and another). Thus *anxiety* is often found to be an *internalized fear.*

INTERPERSONAL

Existing between two or more individuals; often contrasted with intrapersonal.

INTERPRETATION

A scientific guess, made by a psychotherapist about a patient, explaining some aspect of the latter's thoughts, feelings or behavior.

INTRAPERSONAL (INTRAPSYCHIC)

Existing within a mind or a personality; often contrasted with *interpersonal.*

INTROJECTION

One of the *defense mechanisms;* the psychological process whereby a quality or an attribute of another person is taken into and made a part of the subject's personality (unconsciously). Often used loosely as synonymous with *identification.*

INVOLUTION (INVOLUTIONAL PERIOD)

A period in late middle age in which retrogressive physiologic changes take place, causing a loss of the capacity for reproduction. *Involutional psychosis,* a psychosis for which a major precipitating factor has been the advent of involution.

ISOLATION

One of the *defense mechanisms;* the psychological process whereby the actual facts of an experience are allowed to remain in consciousness, but the linkage between these facts and the related emotions or impulses is broken.

L

LATENCY (LATENCY PERIOD)

One of the phases of human development, occurring between the *family-triangle period* and *puberty* (approximately, ages 6 to 11 or 12 years), characterized by a relative instinctual quiescence coupled with a rapid intellectual development.

LEVELS OF AWARENESS (LEVELS OF CONSCIOUSNESS)

An expression referring to the fact that mental activity takes place with varying degrees of the subject's awareness: an individual may be entirely unaware, dimly aware, or fully aware of a given bit of mental activity.

LIBIDO

An inclusive term for the sexual-social drives.

LOBOTOMY (PREFRONTAL)

A psychosurgical procedure in which certain tracts of the brain are severed, thus stopping the interaction between the prefrontal areas (of the cerebral cortex) and the rest of the brain. Sometimes used as a therapeutic measure in severe psychoses.

LOOSENESS OF ASSOCIATION

A symptom of serious mental illness, usually of *schizophrenia,* in which the logical connections between a patient's successive thoughts are absent or are not discernible to the observer.

M

MALADJUSTMENT
A state of disequilibrium between the individual and his environment, in which his needs are not being gratified.

MALINGER
To feign an illness.
Malingerer, one who feigns an illness.

MANIA
(1) A suffix denoting a pathological preoccupation with some desire, idea, or activity; a morbid compulsion. Some frequently encountered manias are: *dipsomania,* compulsion to drink alcoholic beverages; *egomania,* pathological preoccupation with self; *kleptomania,* compulsion to steal; *megalomania,* pathological preoccupation with delusions of power or wealth; *monomania,* pathological preoccupation with one subject; *necromania,* pathological preoccupation with the dead; pyromania, morbid compulsion to set fires.
(2) A morbid state of extreme euphoria and excitement with loss of reality-testing; one of the phases of *manic-depressive psychosis.*
Manic (adj.), pertaining to mania; (noun), one who suffers from mania.

MANIC-DEPRESSIVE REACTION
A group of psychiatric disorders marked by conspicuous mood swings, ranging from normal to elation or to depression, or alternating. Officially regarded as a psychosis but may also exist in milder form.
Depressed phase - Characterized by depression of mood with retardation and inhibition of thinking and physical activity.
Manic phase - Characterized by depression of mood with retardation of thought, speech, and bodily motion, and by elation or grandiosity of mood, and irritability.

MASOCHISM
(1) Pleasure derived from undergoing physical or psychological pain inflicted by oneself or by others. It may be consciously sought or unconsciously arranged or invited. Present to some degree in all human relations and to greater degrees in all psychiatric disorders. It is the converse of sadism, in which pain is inflicted on another, and the two tend to coexist in the same individual.
(2) Finding gratification in pain; in the narrow sense, one of the perversions.

MASTURBATION
Erotic stimulation of one's external genitalia.

MATURITY
The state of being fully adult; psychologically characterized particularly by the ability to love others in a relatively non-selfish way.

MECHANISM (MENTAL, DEFENSE)
See Defense Mechanism.

MILIEU
The total environment, emotional as well as physical.
Milieu therapy, treatment by means of controlled modifications of the patient's environment.

MIND
The body in action as a unit. *Mental,* pertaining to mind as thus defined. *Mental illness,* accurately speaking, any illness of the mind, regardless of severity; often incorrectly restricted to severe psychiatric conditions.

MOTIVATION
A psychological state that incites to action.

MOURNING
The process that follows upon the loss of a love object, through which the subject gradually frees himself from the disequilibrium caused by the loss.

MULTIPLE PERSONALITY
A morbid condition, related to *dissociative reaction,* in which the normal organization of the personality is split up into distinct portions, all having a fairly complex organization of their own. (If there are only two such portions, the term dual personality is used.)

MUSCLE-TRAINING PERIOD
One of the developmental stages, lasting from the end of *infancy* to the beginning of the *family-triangle period* (about age 1½ to age 3), during which the child receives training in sphincter control and other motor activities. Synonymous with *anal period.*

MYELIN
The fatlike substance that forms a sheath around the medullated nerve fibers. *Myelinization,* the process of acquiring a myelin sheath.

N

NARCISSISM (NARCISM)
(1) Self-love, as opposed to object-love (love of another person). Some degree of narcissism is considered healthy and normal, but an excess interferes with relations with others.
(2) Self-love; extreme narcissism is the emotional position found in the newborn infant and in certain psychoses. The term is derived from the Greek legend of Narcissus, a youth who fell in love with his own image.
Narcissistic, loving oneself excessively in a childish or an infantile fashion.

NARCOSYNTHESIS
A form of psychiatric treatment in which contact is established with the patient while he is under the influence of a hypnotic drug.

NEGATIVISM
A tendency to resist suggestions or requests, often accompanied by a response that is, in some sense, the opposite of the one sought. *Negativistic,* expressing negativism.

NEOLOGISM
A newly coined word, or the act of coining such a word; a phenomenon seen in *schizophrenia* and in some cases of *organic brain disease.*

NEURASTHENIA
One of the psychoneuroses, related to *anxiety reaction,* characterized by chronic feelings of fatigue and tension and often by disturbances in the sexual function and minor disturbances in the digestive function.

NEUROPHYSIOLOGY
The physiology of the nervous sytem. *Neurophysiologist,* a specialist in neurophysiology.

NEUROSIS
See psychoneurosis.

O

OBJECT
A term with several meanings. In the broadest sense, it is used in contrast with the term *subject* and means anything in the environment, including another person. In a narrower sense, *object* refers to "a satisfying something" in the environment that is capable of offering instinctual gratification. Thus, *love object* refers to a person toward whom the subject experiences libidinal strivings.

OBSESSION
(1) Persistent, unwanted idea or impulse that cannot be eliminated by logic or reasoning.
(2) A thought, recognized by the subject as more or less irrational, that persistently recurs, despite the subject's conscious wish to avoid or ignore it.
obsessive, pertaining to or afflicted with obsessions.

OBSESSIVE-COMPULSIVE NEUROSIS
One of the psychoneuroses, characterized by *obsessions* and *compulsions* and an underlying personality type whose conflicts involve problems of the muscle-training period.

OEDIPUS
A character in Greek legend, who unwittingly killed his father and married his mother and was subsequently punished by the gods by being blinded. *Oedipus complex,* a term referring to the erotic attachment of the (normal as well as neurotic) small child to the parent of the opposite sex, repressed largely because of the fear of bodily mutilation ("castration") by the presumedly jealous parent of the same sex. *Oedipal period,* same as *family-triangle period.*

ORAL PERIOD
The first postuterine developmental period, roughly synonymous with infancy, in which the individual's central experiences are those involved in the act of sucking.

ORAL PERSONALITY
One of the *personality disorders,* characterized by the persistence in adult life of problems and defenses appropriate to the *oral period* of development.

ORGANIC
Based on structural alterations, gross or microscopic. *Organic psychosis,* a psychosis the etiology of which involves structural damage. (The term also includes *toxic psychosis,* in which the physical alterations are at a submicroscopic -- i.e., chemical -- level.)

ORGANISM
A general term for any living creature, including man.

OVERCOMPENSATION
A conscious or unconscious process in which a real or fancied physical or psychological deficit inspires exaggerated correction.

OVERT
Discernible; "out in the open."

P

PANIC (PANIC REACTION)
A morbid state characterized by extreme fear and/or anxiety, causing a temporary disorganization of the personality.

PARANOIA
Traditionally considered to be one of the three major functional (nonorganic) psychoses, but now generally thought to be one variety of paranoid schizophrenia. A pathologic state, characterized by extreme suspiciousness and highly organized delusions of persecution, occurring in the presence of a clear sensorium and relatively appropriate affective responses.

Paranoid, pertaining to paranoia or paranoid schizophrenia.

Paranoid reaction, an acute, often self-limited state, resembling paranoia; the term is inclusive of paranoid syndromes arising on the basis of organic disease.

PARANOID SCHIZOPHRENIA
One of the four major schizophrenic subgroups, characterized by the usual features of *schizophrenia* plus delusions of persecution and/or grandeur (often loosely organized), auditory hallucinations in keeping with the delusions, and a marked, generalized suspiciousness.

PARANOID STATE
Characterized by delusions of persecution. A paranoid state may be of short duration or

chronic.

PATHOGENESIS

The mode of development of disease states.

PERCEPTION

A psychological experience in which sensory stimuli are integrated to form an image (the significance of which is influenced by past experiences).

PERSONALITY

The whole group of adjustment technics and equipment that are characteristic for a given individual in meeting the various situations of life.

PERSONALITY DISORDER

In the limited (diagnostic) sense, a type of psychiatric illness in which the patient's inner difficulties are revealed, not by specific symptoms but by an unhealthy pattern of living. Thus used, roughly synonymous with *character disorder* and *behavior disorder*. In a broader sense, "disorder of the personality" is often used as equivalent to "mental illness" or "emotional illness:'

PERVERSION (SEXUAL PERVERSION)

A form of personality disorder, characterized by an alteration from the normal of the *aim* and/or the *object* of libidinal strivings. Examples: *sadism, masochism, voyeurism.*

PHANTASY

See fantasy.

PHOBIA

(1) An obsessive, unrealistic fear of an external object or situation. Some of the common phobias are *acrophobia,* fear of heights; *agoraphobia,* fear of open places; claustrophobia, fear of closed spaces; *mysophobia,* fear of dirt and germs; *xenophobia, fear of strangers.*

(2) The dread of an object, an act or a situation that is not realistically dangerous, but that has come to represent a danger.

Phobic, pertaining to phobias.

PHOBIC REACTION

One of the psychoneuroses, formerly called *anxiety hysteria,* characterized by the presence of phobias.

PRECONSCIOUS

One of the three levels of *awareness,* the quality attaching to an idea, a sensation or an emotion of which the subject is not spontaneously aware but can become aware with effort.

PREMORBID PERSONALITY

The status of an individual's personality (conflicts, defenses, strengths, weaknesses) before the onset of clinical illness.

PRIMARY GAIN

The adjustment (adaptational) value of a neurotic symptom per se.

PROJECTION

One of the *defense mechanisms,* a technic whereby feelings, wishes or attitudes, originating within the subject, are attributed by him to persons or other objects in his environment.

PROJECTIVE TESTS

(1) Psychological tests used as a diagnostic tool. Among the most common projective tests is the Rorschach (inkblot) test.

(2) A relatively unstructured, although standardized, psychological test in which the subject is called upon to respond with a minimum of intellectual restrictions, thereby revealing characteristic drives, defenses and attitudes. (Examples are the Rorschach and the Thematic Apperception Tests.)

PSYCHE
Actually synonymous with *mind;* frequently used in expressions suggesting a mind-body duality, as, for example, "psychosomatic," "psychophysiologic," and "psychic versus organic factors:'

PSYCHIATRY
That branch of medicine that deals with the causes, the diagnosis, the treatment and the prevention of mental disorders.

Psychiatrist, a physician specializing in psychiatry.

Psychiatric nurse, a nurse specializing in the care of patients having mental disorders.

Psychiatric team, a group of professional and semiprofessional persons working together under the direction of a psychiatrist in the treatment of psychiatric, patients. (Usually the membership of such a team includes psychiatrist, psychiatric nurse, clinical psychologist, psychiatric social worker, occupational therapist, and psychiatric aide.)

PSYCHOANALYSIS
(1) A theory of human development and behavior, a method of research, and a system of psychotherapy, originally described by Sigmund Freud (1856-1939). Through analysis of free associations and interpretation of dreams, emotions and behavior are traced to the influence of repressed instinctual drives in the unconscious. Psychoanalytic treatment seeks to eliminate or diminish the undesirable effects of unconscious conflicts by making the patient aware of their existence, origin, and inappropriate expression.

(2) The term designates 1. a *method* of (a) psychotherapy and (b) psychological research, and 2. a body of *facts and theories* of human psychology. Both the method and the body of knowledge represent the work of Sigmund Freud and his followers. *Psychoanalyst,* a professional person, usually a physician, who has received specialized formal training in the theory and the practice of psychoanalysis.

PSYCHONEUROSIS (NEUROSIS)
(1) One of the two major categories of emotional illness, the other being the psychoses. It is usually less severe than a psychosis, with minimal loss of contact with reality.

(2) A mild to moderately severe illness of the personality (mind), in which the ego function of reality-testing is not gravely impaired, and in which the maladjustment to life is of a relatively limited nature.

Psychoneurotic, pertaining to or characteristic of a psychoneurosis.

PSYCHOPATHIC PERSONALITY
An older term for one of the varieties of *personality disorder,* roughly synonymous with the current (official) category of "sociopathic personality disturbance," a form of illness characterized by emotional immaturity, the use of short-term values and behavior that is asocial or antisocial.

PSYCHOSIS
(1) A major mental disorder of organic and/or emotional origin in which there is a departure from normal patterns of thinking, feeling, and acting. Commonly characterized by loss of contact with reality, distortion of perception, regressive behavior and attitudes, diminished control of elementary impulses and desires, and delusions and hallucinations. Chronic and generalized personality deterioration may occur. A majority of patients in public mental hospitals are psychotic.

(2) A very serious illness of the personality (mind), involving a major impairment of ego function, particularly with respect to reality-testing, and revealed by signs of a grave maladjustment to life.

Psychotic, pertaining to or afflicted with psychosis.

PSYCHOSOMATIC
Adjective to denote the constant and inseparable interdependence of the psyche (mind) and

the soma (body). Most commonly used to refer to illnesses in which the manifestations are primarily physical with at least a partial emotional cause.

PSYCHOSURGERY

A form of neurosurgery in which specific tracts or other limited portions of the brain are severed or destroyed with the intention of producing favorable effects upon the patient's psychological status.

PSYCHOTHERAPY

(1) The term for any type of mental treatment that is based primarily upon verbal or non-verbal communication with the patient in distinction to the use of drugs, surgery, or physical measures such as electric or insulin shock.

(2) A term with many shades of meaning. In the broadest sense it is equivalent to "psychological treatment measures;" in a narrower sense *psychotherapy* refers to a direct relationship between one or more patients and a professional person, the therapist, in which the latter endeavors "to provide new life experiences which can influence the patient in the direction of health" (Levine).

PSYCHOTIC PERSONALITY

A variety of personality disorder, synonymous with the current official term "personality pattern disturbance," in which, despite the absence of the usual clinical symptoms of psychosis, the individual's fundamental conflicts and defenses are those of a *psychotic*.

R

RATIONALIZATION

The process of constructing plausible reasons for one's responses (usually to avoid awareness of neurotic motives).

REACTION FORMATION

One of the *defense mechanisms,* a technic whereby an original attitude or set of feelings is replaced in consciousness by the opposite attitude or feelings.

REALITY-TESTING

The process of determining objective (usually external) reality, a function of the ego.

RECONSTITUTE

To form again. The term is used of a personality that, having become more or less disorganized through illness, resumes its previous defense measures and type of adjustment.

REGRESSION

(1) The partial or symbolic return to more infantile patterns of reacting.

(2) One of the *defense mechanisms;* a process in which the personality retraces developmental steps, moving backward to earlier interests, defenses, and modes of gratification.

REPRESSION

(1) A defense mechanisms, operating unconsciously, that banishes unacceptable ideas, emotions, or impulses from consciousness or that keeps out of consciousness what has never been conscious.

(2) One of the *defense mechanisms,* a technic whereby thoughts, emotions and/or sensations are thrust out of consciousness.

REVERSAL

One of the *defense mechanisms,* a technic whereby an instinctual impulse is seemingly turned into its opposite, as, for example, when *sadism* is replaced by *masochism.*

S

SADISM

A form of perversion characterized by the experiencing of erotic pleasure in inflicting pain on another person. Often used more broadly as meaning the enjoyment of cruelty. *(See Masochism.)*

SCHIZOID

Schizophrenic-like. *Schizoid personality,* a form of *personality disorder* (subgroup of *psychotic personality*) characterized by withdrawn, self-centered, often eccentric behavior.

SCHIZOPHRENIA

(1) A severe emotional disorder of psychotic depth, characteristically marked by a retreat from reality with delusion formation, hallucinations, emotional disharmony, and regressive behavior. Formerly called dementia praecox. Its prognosis has improved in recent years.

(2) One of the major *functional psychoses;* more accurately, a group of interrelated symptom syndromes, having in common a number of features, including *associative looseness, autistic thinking, ambivalence* and inappropriateness of *affect.* The classic subgroups are: *catatonic, paranoid, simple* and *hebephrenic* schizophrenia; other varieties are: *schizoaffective, undifferentiated, childhood* and *latent* schizophrenia. *Schizophrenic,* pertaining to or afflicted with schizophrenia.

SECONDARY GAIN

The adjustment value or gratification that occurs as a result of the way in which a patient's environment responds to his illness (not an integral part of the symptoms per se).

SELF-CONCEPT

A person's image of himself, usually his conscious image.

SENILE

Pertaining to (extreme) old age, particularly to the deterioration in adjustment capacity occurring in old age.

Senile psychosis, an organic psychosis resulting from the brain damage accompanying advanced age.

SHOCK TREATMENT

A form of psychiatric treatment in which electric current, insulin, or carbon dioxide is administered to the patient and results in a convulsive reaction to alter favorably the course of mental illness.

SIMPLE SCHIZOPHRENIA

One of the four classic *schizophrenia* subgroups, characterized by slow, insidious onset and chronic course, with the illness being shown by emotional coldness, withdrawal and eccentricity, rather than by more striking symptoms.

SOMATOPSYCHIC

A term of recent coinage, intended to indicate psychological effects of somatic pathology.

SPLIT PERSONALITY

A term calling attention to the schizophrenic's inappropriate-ness of affect; the "split" is thus between emotions and ideation.

STRESS

Any circumstance that taxes the adjustment capacity of the individual.

SUBJECT

The person under discussion or study, as, for example, a patient or a person upon whom an experiment is performed.

SUBLIMATION

(1) A defense mechanism, operating unconsciously, by which instinctual but consciously unacceptable drives are diverted into personally and socially acceptable channels.

(2) One of the *defense mechanisms,* the only one that is never pathogenic; a technic whereby the original aim or *object* of a basic drive is altered in a manner that allows the release of tension and, at the same time, is socially acceptable.

SUPEREGO

One of the three major aspects or agencies of the mind; similar to the term "conscience" but more inclusive since it involves both conscious and unconscious components. (*See* Ego.)

SUPPRESSION

A technic of adjustment -- differing from the *defense mechanisms* in that it is fully conscious and very rarely pathogenic -- whereby the ego denies expression to a thought or an impulse. (It is often contrasted with *repression,* which is automatic, unconsciously effected and frequently pathogenic.)

SYMBOLISM

The use of one mental image to represent another.

T

TOXIC

Pertaining to, or due to the action of, a poison.

Toxic *psychosis,* a psychosis brought about by the action of a poisonous substance or, more broadly, a psychosis brought about by any chemical interference with normal metabolic processes (grouped with the *organic psychoses*).

TRANSFERENCE

The attributing by the subject, to a figure in his current environment, of characteristics first encountered in some figure of his early life, and the experiencing of desires, fears, and other attitudes toward the current figure that originated in the relationship with the past figure. The term is most commonly used with respect to feelings of a patient toward his therapist.

Counter-transference, transference feelings of a therapist toward his patient.

TRAUMA

Harm or injury; sometimes, the circumstances productive of harm or injury. In psychiatry, the term is inclusive of purely emotional as well as physical injury.

Traumatic, harmful, pertaining to trauma.

TRAUMATIC NEUROSIS (WAR NEUROSIS)

An acute morbid reaction related to *psychoneurosis* but occurring only in response to overwhelming trauma or stress. The condition is characterized by a temporary, partial disorganization of the personality, followed by such symptoms as anxiety, restlessness, irritability, impaired concentration, evidence of autonomic dysfunction and repetitive nightmares in which the traumatic experience is "relived."

TURNING AGAINST THE SELF

One of the *defense mechanisms,* a technic in which an unacceptable drive (usually aggressive) is diverted from its original object and (unconsciously) made to operate against the self, in whole or in part.

U

UNCONSCIOUS
  (1) That part of the mind the content of which is only rarely subject to awareness. It is the repository for knowledge that has never been conscious or that may have been conscious briefly and was then repressed.
  (2) In psychiatry, one of the three *levels* of *awareness;* thoughts, sensations, and emotions at this level cannot enter the subject's awareness through any voluntary effort on his part, but they continue to exert effects upon his behavior.

UNDOING
One of the *defense mechanisms,* a technic in which a specific action is performed that is (unconsciously) considered by the subject to be in some sense the opposite of a previous unacceptable action (or wish), and thus to neutralize ("undo") the original action.

V

VEGETATIVE SIGNS (OF DEPRESSION)
A traditionally grouped set of findings, including anorexia, weight loss, constipation, amenorrhea, insomnia and "morning-evening variation in mood," that, when found in combination, are indicative of severe depression.

VOYEURISM
A form of *personality disorder* (more specifically, of *perversion*), in which the subject receives his principal erotic gratification in clandestine peeping.

W

WAXY FLEXIBILITY
A phenomenon, associated with *catatonic schizophrenia,* in which the body, particularly the extremities, will remain for long periods of time in any positions selected by the examiner.

www.ingramcontent.com/pod-product-compliance
Lightning Source LLC
Chambersburg PA
CBHW082036300426
44117CB00015B/2507